D1451601

About Island Press

Island Press is the only nonprofit organization in the United States whose principal purpose is the publication of books on environmental issues and natural resource management. We provide solutions-oriented information to professionals, public officials, business and community leaders, and concerned citizens who are shaping responses to environmental problems.

In 2005, Island Press celebrates its twenty-first anniversary as the leading provider of timely and practical books that take a multidisciplinary approach to critical environmental concerns. Our growing list of titles reflects our commitment to bringing the best of an expanding body of literature to the environmental community throughout North America and the world.

Support for Island Press is provided by the Agua Fund, The Geraldine R. Dodge Foundation, Doris Duke Charitable Foundation, Ford Foundation, The George Gund Foundation, The William and Flora Hewlett Foundation, Kendeda Sustainability Fund of the Tides Foundation, The Henry Luce Foundation, The John D. and Catherine T. MacArthur Foundation, The Andrew W. Mellon Foundation, The Curtis and Edith Munson Foundation, The New-Land Foundation, The New York Community Trust, Oak Foundation, The Overbrook Foundation, The David and Lucile Packard Foundation, The Winslow Foundation, and other generous donors.

The opinions expressed in this book are those of the author(s) and do not necessarily reflect the views of these foundations.

Intown Living

Intown Living

A DIFFERENT AMERICAN DREAM

ANN BREEN AND DICK RIGBY

 **ISLAND**PRESS

Washington • Covelo • London

ISLAND PRESS is a trademark of the Center for Resource Economics.

Island Press
1718 Connecticut Ave, N.W., Suite 300
Washington, D.C. 20009

Library of Congress Cataloging-in-Publication data.

Breen, Ann.

Intown living : a different American dream / Ann Breen and Dick Rigby.
— 1st Island Press ed. paperback ed. 2004.

   p. cm.

Originally published: Westport, Conn. : Praeger, 2004.
Includes bibliographical references and index.

ISBN 1-59726-002-9 (pbk. : alk. paper)

1. City and town life—United States—Case studies. 2. City and town life —
Canada — Case studies. 3. Urban renewal—United States. 4. Central business
districts — United States. 5. Housing development — United States.
6. City planning—United States. I. Rigby, Dick. II. Title.

  HT123.B735 2005

  307.76'0973—dc22

                                                                    2004028901

Contents

Preface

We have long believed that if the city could once again be seen as an attractive place to live—if we as a nation could repopulate our center cities where needed infrastructure is already in place—it would help curb sprawl and stem the loss of valuable open space at the edges of our metropolitan areas and produce a healthier, more energetic, and better connected population.

About our title, *Intown Living: A Different American Dream*. Originally we were going to concentrate strictly on downtowns. But definitions of downtown vary and are sometimes difficult to pin down. Further, some cities take a very expansive view of "downtown" to the point of being misleading. In our first case study, Atlanta, we discovered the Midtown neighborhood there had more of the urban characteristics we sought than the core downtown as of 2003. And when we next visited Houston and Dallas and found that they too had near-downtown neighborhoods where Intown Living was flourishing more than in their traditional downtowns, despite pretty heroic efforts, we changed the title to reflect this fact.

The idea for this book occurred during back-to-back community consulting assignments in Dallas and Houston in the late 1990s. In each of these quintessentially suburban, sprawling metropolises noted for deadly downtowns, we found to our surprise and delight a nascent center city residential population. Not huge in numbers, but clearly not just a few cranks and bohemians. In fact, more than a few pillars of the establishment were included.

We began in the late 1990s to consciously track articles and research on the Intown Living phenomenon in cities where this was new, or if not new, expanding significantly. We decided not to look at New York, Boston, and San Francisco, for example, which have had major intown populations for years—which accounts in part for their popularity. By looking primarily at cities without a tradition of Intown Living, or where it was growing apace, we came to sense that there was something of importance going on, a detectable and potentially significant countertrend to our overwhelmingly suburban housing pattern. At the same time, we resolved not to kid ourselves, that the nation remains firmly un-urban.

A word about the consulting work we were doing as it bears directly on the approach we're taking in this book. The community consulting work we perform is as co-directors of The Waterfront Center, a nonprofit entity we established in 1981 to deal with urban waterfront planning, development, and culture.

Ann brought training in urban and regional planning, and Dick has a background that includes journalism and politics and an interest in urban matters. The approach we learned to take as consultants in tackling a city's urban waterfront was to get out and see it on foot and to talk to as many and as diverse a group of citizens as possible—to try to grasp as much as we could about the spirit of the place, its self-image, the artistic scene, the nature of its leadership, something of its recent history, and its economic picture, as well as the usual physical planning dimensions. We're believers in the maxim that the only way to understand a place is to explore it in person, on foot.

For us, two ideas became axiomatic in our community work. First, projects should be planned to reflect the individuality of the place. We and our colleagues have gone so far as to issue an "Urban Waterfront Manifesto" warning against the formulaic urban development approach with installations such as "urban entertainment centers" full of chain stores and bars. Second, whatever was to be accomplished with the waterfront should be done in concert with and in mutual support of the nearly always adjoining central downtown district.

So it was in Houston, with its Buffalo Bayou (which famously flooded in June 2001), and in Dallas, whose Trinity River flooded in the 1920s and was relocated behind walls in an Army Corps of Engineers project, that we worked to gain an understanding of what was happening in their downtowns.

We found traditional offices converted to condominiums in mid-downtown Dallas, being sold as "lofts," and factory conversions to housing occurring in the center of Houston. These were places where no one except vagrants (or prisoners) had resided in recent memory.

We likewise found these residential developments taking place amid a great deal of activity in the downtowns in general, with a light rail system up and running in Dallas, beautification efforts evident, plus thriving cultural entities. And also in Houston, a new baseball stadium downtown, a new rail line along Main Street, and a historic park restoration, plus a fledgling restaurant and club scene.

It was in Houston that we gained a particular insight that stayed with us and has been reconfirmed in our research. We were told that the business leadership there came to see that it had to revive its downtown or risk losing out in recruiting the bright young talent needed for today's companies. The experience was that when they took candidates on tours of the handsome suburban areas of Houston, they balked. Where, they wanted to know, were the action, the clubs, the street life?

And so the Houston business establishment, which had very little to show by way of response (opera houses don't quite make it), woke up to the need to bring vitality to its center. They merely had to look down the superhighway to Austin, which is successfully luring young professionals with, among other things, a major local music scene and artists. It did not take great imagination to see that luring a residential population to downtown was a key to enlivening the area.

In documenting the growth of Intown Living, we combine our on-the-ground case study approach, trying to understand the different dynamics of each city, with local and national research and analysis. We looked for commonalities that we cite in our findings. In taking a basically journalistic approach, we rely a good deal on newspapers and periodicals—the first rough drafts of history in *Washington Post* editor Ben Bradlee's famous characterization.

In each case city, we obtained as good and current population numbers and demographics as was possible for the neighborhoods selected. After this we interviewed residents, trying to match interviewees with the population profile, as well as business and civic leaders, developers, and Realtors. Our interviews were conducted anonymously, with people we quote given a general description (professor, developer, etc.). Woven into this are quotes by name taken from publications.

In keeping with our "see-it-first-hand" approach, we base our conclusions and recommendations primarily on our case research. We sense that this results in somewhat different insights and emphases from what we've read in the literature. Our principal finding about which groups were propelling the Intown Living phenomenon was not what we expected to find. We use strictly secondary sources for our Gazetteer, however, which adds capsule information about Intown Living in cities other than our eight cases.

The case cities are: Atlanta, Dallas, Houston, Memphis, Minneapolis, New Orleans, Portland, Oregon, and Vancouver, British Columbia. We trust that the selection includes a mixture of places where most readers are surprised to find Intown Living to be occurring, as well as places that have been especially skillful in using historic preservation, urban policies, and financial incentives to induce people to live in the cities. We could readily have selected eight other cities, such as San Diego, Seattle, Chicago, Washington, D.C., Providence, Philadelphia, Toronto, and Cleveland. See the Gazetteer for a sample of cities experiencing Intown Living.

Three caveats: Cities are dynamic places, and trends evident today can be altered tomorrow. We're reminded of this when we read such works as Myron Orfield's *Metro Politics*.[1] Although the revised edition was written in 1997, its focus is on 1990 census data. Thus he is describing a concentration of ghetto populations and transitional poverty neighborhoods that were growing in size in the 1970s and 1980s in center cities. Ghettos are where over 40 percent of the population lives below the poverty line. The 1990s changed this, and research published by the Brookings Institution in 2003 shows a thinning of below–poverty line populations in core cities and a spread into older suburbs, for instance. In other words, a respected researcher like Orfield was simply overtaken by events in what is a rapidly fluctuating market, namely America's downtowns. We are thus going to resist suggesting that what we describe in our eight case cities in 2003 is necessarily predictive or permanent. A recession, sharp increases in crime, renewed terrorist attacks or a spike in mortgage interest rates could easily alter what we describe.

Second, we use census data with some reluctance. Basically, what else is there? The figures produced by downtown business organizations are generally not reliable. But census data is not that reliable, either. A source in one city said he had worked on the census in 1990 and was certain that it was off by 20 percent. The U.S. Census Bureau acknowledges it undercounted the original 1990 census by eight million and that it double-counted four million others, a net difference of four million or a little more than the population inside the Los Angeles city limits.[2] A major limitation is that census tracts often do not square with neighborhood boundaries. In Atlanta's Midtown, they lined up nicely; in Minneapolis, there is not a one-on-one match of tracts to neighborhoods.

Third, there's an element of boosterism in all of our eight cities, as with places everywhere. We're always amused at how cities come up with their lists of firsts, the largest, longest, or biggest whatever. Thus Memphis tells us its 4.8–mile riverwalk on the Mississippi is "unmatched in the nation," while other cities have been building extensive trails along the Mississippi and other waterfronts for more than thirty years. Knowing this, we've tried to filter out the parochial and the gossamer and to look behind the glowing pictures downtown business groups and the local governments tend to present. But city pride is a powerful—and necessary—force, and we no doubt have some of it reflected in the pages that follow.

Acknowledgments

We are grateful to the hundred-plus people we interviewed in the course of our field research. As we promised anonymity we cannot list them, but you know who you are, and many of you will see your insights reflected here. We appreciate the courtesy and openness with which we were received, as with the developer whom we called unannounced and who told us to come on over and spent the next hour-and-a-half with us in a fascinating discussion.

There are two groups that don't usually come in for high praise that we were especially struck with in our travels: real estate developers and city bureaucrats. Perhaps developers working with the challenges of historic buildings and inner-city properties are a different breed from the stereotype, but we found them by and large to be forthright, insightful, sincerely interested in their work and their cities, and often funny.

Likewise, while we encountered a few stereotypical city bureaucrats very cautious and uninformative in their approach, we were also treated to enthusiastic people with widespread knowledge who were candid with us (the anonymity helped here) and who were respected forces in their cities. We had a business leader in one city refer to a city department head as one of the "jewels" of the city. In another place, multiple people told us we *had* to see a certain city official. We did and immediately understood why she was so highly recommended.

In each of our case cities we had one or two key people guiding us to interview candidates and/or materials. Numerous others in each place helped, but we want to keep the list manageable.

Atlanta: Lou McBryan (Dick's son-in-law) and Will Herbig.

Dallas: Gail Thomas.

Houston: Toni Beauchamp and Bob Eury.

Memphis: Benny Lendermon.

Minneapolis: Steve Durrant and Kit Richardson.

New Orleans: Patty Gay and Allen Eskew.

Portland: Zari Santner.

Vancouver: Larry Beasley.

We want to acknowledge our staff at The Waterfront Center, Martine Hergenreder and Steve Rogers, who ably kept the ship afloat to allow us to concentrate on our research and writing. We are grateful to our "merry mappers," as they are known to us, Diane Charyk Norris and Charles Norris, who skillfully drew the maps that accompany our case city chapters. We thank our cheerful and indefatigable researcher/proofreader Roberta A. Donovan. It is she who took to the Internet and libraries to gather the huge pile of articles and research papers that we have amassed in the last three years.

1

Introduction

> The essence of the city is the communion of citizens at every level and under every circumstance. The variety and multitude of opinions, talents, drives, and culture that such diversity implies: it is this marvelous mixture—the fusion of diversities into a whole . . . which is the unique aspect of the city.
>
> —*Arthur Erickson,*
> The City as Dwelling: Walking, Sitting, Shaping

If and when America becomes serious about curbing wasteful sprawl development, the nation will *have* to rebuild our cities and promote Intown Living. In our view we have more anti-sprawl rhetoric today than meaningful action.

We believe the country will have to refocus on our cities, towns, and traditional suburbs because the basic alternative to handling a growing population (up officially 13.2 percent in the past decade) is continued plowing up open spaces for new subdivisions. This is not an original thought of ours; leaders in historic preservation and the environmental movements have been saying this for years, even decades.

Patricia Gay, executive director of the Preservation Resource Center in New Orleans, has been one of the strongest advocates of the need to repopulate cities with middle-class residents in particular. Urban policies "almost never take action to increase the middle class, because of the risk of displacement," even though "displacement occurs when neighborhoods are not stable and when buildings deteriorate to an uninhabited state.

Displacement occurs when residents of any income level are forced to move out because of crime," she writes. She notes that public subsidies fuel sprawl, while urban programs create enclaves for the poor. "We have confined our urban revitalization efforts and considerable resources in poverty programs. We have ignored the need for diversity and jobs generated by an urban middle class."[1]

Richard Moe, president of the National Trust for Historic Preservation, puts it bluntly:

Efforts to manage sprawl often focus on protecting open space and farmland, but that is only half of the equation. The other half is encouraging reinvestment in existing communities. It comes down to this: If we can't make older neighborhoods more attractive and viable as alternatives to spread-out new subdivisions and strip malls, we're never going to be able to put the brakes on uncontrolled sprawl.[2]

These sentiments are echoed by Steve Belmont in a recent book, *Cities in Full*:

The most effective way to curb sprawl is to implement a program of urban neighborhood renewal on a massive scale, and to shift investment in transportation infrastructure from suburbs to cities. Focus middle-class housing subsidies and incentives on cities as well . . . America's leadership will begin to heal the social and environmental maladies of the metropolis when they realize smart growth begins with metropolitan recentralization.[3]

None of this is new. William Whyte's critique about "smog-filled deserts" (read: subdivisions) contained in *The Exploding Metropolis* dates to 1958. An early analysis came from Real Estate Research Corporation in 1974, "The Costs of Sprawl."[4] Likewise, the environmental movement has targeted sprawl for years. The Sierra Club has mounted a major campaign on the issue. The Bank of America weighed in with a similar analysis in 1995. Recently environmentalists, particularly the Trust for Public Land, have come to realize that rebuilding cities is essential to curbing sprawl. The Trust for Public Land and the National Trust for Historic Preservation have led the charge in the public campaign to rebuild and repopulate our cities.

We believe further that we *ought* to repopulate central cities (as well as older suburbs and towns) for economic, social, health, environmental, and psychological reasons:

- The economic rationale for Intown Living is twofold. First, using land with already-built infrastructure makes sense, basically recycling what we already have invested in rather than expensively consuming and servicing new territory. Second, we must nurture the burgeoning "information age" economy. Urban centers of vitality are necessary engines for this sector because many of the people powering today's commerce want to be with each other in hip urban settings for face-to-face exchanges.

- The social agenda is to help reunite a society now split between haves and have-nots, often along racial lines. Intown Living by and large is more inclusive, more tolerant, and considerably more diverse than its subdivision counterparts.
- The current campaign to curtail obesity has brought to the fore how basically unhealthy the suburban, car-dominated lifestyle is.
- Environmentally, we want to curb the excessive gasoline consumption, unhealthy air quality, and farmland destruction that subdivision sprawl entails.
- The psychological aspect is that many people today lead insulated and isolated lives. This suits some just fine, but it leaves others feeling empty. For them, Intown Living offers opportunities for more contact. Robert D. Putnam writes in *Bowling Alone: The Collapse and Revival of American Community,* "Without at first noticing, we have been pulled apart from one another and from our communities over the last third of the century."[5]

SICK CITIES

Let us recall how sick American cities became in the 1970s because it is important background for appreciating the rebound that was experienced in the 1990s and continues today.

From a Rand Corporation study written in the late 1970s we have this searing description:

The quality of urban life has deteriorated. Interracial tensions periodically erupt in mob violence. Roving gangs of adolescents terrorize peaceable citizens. Muggings, burglaries, rape and vandalism are commonplace. Drug abuse is widespread. Public schools are patrolled by guards, but classrooms are nonetheless vandalized, students robbed and teachers beaten . . . Unoccupied buildings are stripped and burned. Neighborhood retailers close their shops after a series of armed robberies or a night of looting. Public streets are littered and potholed. The sites of demolished buildings are piled high with rat-infested rubbish.[6]

Working against those of us who believe in making cities inviting, safe, and lively is the fact that America has a long and strong tradition of antiurban intellectualism, beginning with Thomas Jefferson and running through Henry Adams and Henry James to Frank Lloyd Wright and Lewis Mumford. This is documented in Morton and Lucia White's classic, *The Intellectual Versus the City.*

While cities were struggling for decades, local governments and downtown executives doggedly labored to try to turn things around with varying techniques and results. We can point to the waterfront regeneration in many North American cities over the last thirty years as a welcome sign of hope. In cities as varied as Portland, Maine, Wilmington, North Carolina, Tempe, Arizona, and Missoula, Montana, not to mention the well-known Baltimore and Boston, new commercial, cultural, recreational, and residential opportunities have opened up.

Also, downtown malls or festival marketplaces such as Station Square in Pittsburgh and Faneuil Hall in Boston were making big headlines thirty or so years ago, and the press eagerly told the stories. A 1984 *Time* magazine cover featured James Rouse with the headline "Cities are Fun!" This, along with publicity about the South of Houston section of Manhattan— the SoHo syndrome in the phrase of authors Roberta Brandes Gratz and Norman Mintz—has helped change city imagery at a time when people were receptive. Loft living became *very* trendy. Argue Gratz and Mintz:

The SoHo syndrome has done more to retain the middle class and stimulate new economic innovations than any planning or government-funded program . . . In almost every downtown, we have either visited or received reports that young, active, entrepreneurial, retired, adventuresome people, alone and in pairs, are resettling old districts that have survived, like SoHo and TriBeCa.[7]

Working as well in our favor is the success of the TV shows, such as *Seinfeld, Friends, Sex in the City,* and even *Cheers,* which popularized city lifestyles in general. We heard several spontaneous references to the *Seinfeld* show in our case city interviews when we asked people what made Intown Living inviting.

URBANITY

Our term for what's being sought by people moving into city neighborhoods is *urbanity*. The ingredients that comprise urbanity can and do occur in small towns, medium-sized cities, and traditional suburbs. (As we mention chapter 2, there's a huge difference between a traditional suburb and today's subdivisions.)

Urbanity occurs in the neighborhoods we discuss in our cases, and in other places such as the "Latte Towns" in the memorable moniker of David Brooks in *BOBOS* in Paradise (*Being Bourgeois Bohemians): The New Upper Class and How They Got There.*[8]

We think there are five characteristics of urbanity which are present to one degree or another in our case study neighborhoods and in other urban-type places as well:

- Walkability
- Density
- Diversity
- Hipness
- Public Transit

Let's take them up in order.

WALKABILITY

In a city or small town walking is the norm, the everyday, the way of life. Urban walking is much more than going to the store for milk and eggs or to work.

We, like so many, go back to Jane Jacobs and her pioneering work of 1961, *The Death and Life of Great American Cities,* for insights. She posits: "A city sidewalk by itself is nothing. It is an abstraction. It means something only in conjunction with the buildings and other uses that border it . . . If a city's streets look interesting, the city looks interesting; if they look dull, the city looks dull."[9] Urban walkability is about the "daily ballet" on the good city sidewalk, in her famous phrase.[10] Allan Jacobs gets at this aspect in his book, *Great Streets:*

There is magic to great streets. We are attracted to the best of them not because we have to go there but because we want to be there. The best are as joyful as they are utilitarian . . . They are symbols of a community and its history; they represent public memory. They are places for escape and romance, places to act and to dream; to remember things that may never have happened and to look forward to things that, maybe, never will.[11]

The urban sidewalk, as one of our interviewees noted, is where the community is observed, where you see neighbors, check out visitors, and watch children or shopkeepers. The urban front porch.

Urban walkability is how daily business is conducted. As a clever advertising campaign by the Center City Commission in Memphis puts it: "Remember Walking? Everybody does it downtown."

Use of the car is often the exception, not the rule. We learned in Vancouver that 39, yes, 39 percent of people walk to work!

Many a New Yorker owns no car in our most urban center. We encountered numbers of instances in our research where people had gone from two cars to one. Real walkable urban neighborhoods are full of not just the necessities, but also the amenities that make a viable neighborhood. Cafes, bars, and restaurants are part of the mix. There are clubs in some areas, movie theaters, other entertainment venues, galleries, and interesting shops as well. There are also parks or other communal gathering spots where there's no commerce necessarily.

In some of the neighborhoods we discuss in our case examples where a residential population is new, there's a lament that the grocery store hasn't arrived yet. Or, as we relate from Vancouver, when it did open, the streets came to life and a vibrant center for the community was born. A developer in Memphis told us it took him a while to figure out that people asking for a grocery really were after a sense of community and a sense of permanence in a new development.

Beyond the practical functions and the romance are other factors, such as the presence of trees, groundcovers and flowers to make the walking experience pleasant, especially on hot days, and offering a sense of seasonality. Well-tended and wide-enough sidewalks plus short blocks create a sense that a person is getting somewhere. The downtowns of Portland, Oregon and Minneapolis are in sharp contrast in these regards. Vancouver distinguishes itself as an eminently walkable place, helped by the fact that its core downtown is relatively compact, surrounded almost completely by water, and that it has vibrant street-level commerce.

DENSITY

Dense development goes hand-in-hand with walkability. It means the presence of a sufficient resident population near to commercial centers and public transit. Public transit in turn lets residents range far afield without having to resort to a car. One standard we heard was that it takes 2,500 residential units to support a full-line grocery.

Steve Belmont in *Cities in Full* uses a density benchmark of 7,500 people per square mile and finds that only ten of America's fifty largest cities achieve it, including, surprisingly perhaps, Los Angeles. Of our case study cities, Minneapolis ranks twelfth with 6,970 people per square mile in a city with many suburban-feeling neighborhoods, but also high-rise apartments. Well down the list are Portland, Oregon, with many low-rise apartments and condominiums, under 5,000 per, followed by Houston, Atlanta, New Orleans, and Memphis. New York by contrast has over 25,000 people per square mile.[12]

American aversion to high density harks back to the end of the nineteenth century, when our industrial cities housed the crowded tenements, such as the Lower East Side of New York. The prevailing view was that cities bred crime, disease, and low morals, and that they were noisy, dirty, unsanitary, and generally fearsome. The analysis was that everybody was too close together, serving to heighten interest on the part of the middle class in the suburbs, where they would be separated from the lower orders. The squalor was real and was well documented by such writers as Jacob Riis.

"The festering metropolis" was a standard phrase of the turn of the century, compounded when European immigrants began piling into American cities. The American Dream of the freestanding, low-density suburban house, far removed from urban turmoil, has more than a little class, religious and, later, racial prejudice about it.

Low density defines subdivision development. It also contributes to subdivisions being pedestrian unfriendly and car-dependent. Many of these areas throughout the nation, for instance, don't even have sidewalks. What people seeking an urban neighborhood require is that there be a certain amount of density to enable sufficient and differing land uses to be clustered together to make it interesting and changeable.

Jane Jacobs wrote eloquently about the importance of density. Planners of her day (and today for that matter) confused density with overcrowding, a fallacy she skewered in the following passage, after noting that overcrowding exists in low-density places and that the most dense areas are the liveliest:

Everyone is aware that tremendous numbers of people concentrate in city downtowns and that, if they did not, there would be no downtown to amount to anything—certainly not one with much downtown diversity.

But this relationship between concentration and diversity is very little considered when it comes to city districts where residence is a chief use. Yet dwellings form a large part of most city districts. The people who live in a district also form a large share, usually, of the people who use the streets, the parks and enterprises of the place. Without help from the concentration of the people who live there, there can be little convenience or diversity where people live, and where they require it.[13]

In density also are the "eyes on the street" in the often-used phrase of Jane Jacobs, meaning simply that there's safety in numbers.

And as authors Gratz and Mintz state as they wind up their work about downtowns: "The critical antidote to sprawl is density, concentration, and the rebuilding of centers. In essence, forging reconnections."[14]

DIVERSITY

Jane Jacobs in the passage cited earlier linked density and diversity. Indeed they go together.

Cities are a mélange of different neighborhoods, each with their own character, architecture, and people. The mix of ages, cultures, incomes, uses, and lifestyles gives cities their buzz. In New Orleans' historic warehouse area, for instance, a new hotel is next to a warehouse where forklift trucks still haul materials. Down the street are apartment conversions, galleries, and first-rate museums, creating surprises and pedestrian interest. Here, too, one finds a store below and living unit above, a corner bar as a hangout for locals, restaurants both top-end and neighborhood style. In Minneapolis's Mill District, new and old structures stand side by side, fronting riverside parks with stunning river views that add to the appeal.

It's axiomatic that historic areas are intriguing to walk around, and it is usually easy to do so by virtue of their being compact. Having different housing types, low- and high-rise mixed together, even when they are all brand-new as in Vancouver, makes an area appear interesting.

Diversity of incomes, we came to find, usually has to be induced. The gentrifying neighborhoods of the type we researched appeal to a prosperous clientele who eventually run up prices and force out lower-income residents. Cities such as Portland and Vancouver mandate fixed percentages of subsidized housing for the express purpose of insuring a mixture of populations. When subsidies are supplied to developers, it is a relatively easy thing to make and enforce this policy. In Memphis an experiment is under way in the Uptown neighborhood where middle-income housing is being introduced into an area dominated by public housing in the past, a public policy to deliberately create a diversity of population (and presumably races).

Our case cities are populated by and large by young professionals with a sizeable gay proportion. Tolerance for different lifestyles figures large in Richard Florida's Creative Class analysis that we'll take up in the next chapter. And most districts we looked at had some post–55-year-olds, thus adding to an area's diversity.

Then there's the contrast. One of the allures of the subdivision for those seeking it is its comforting uniformity and the homogeneity of the single-family neighborhood. These areas by definition and design deliberately lack density because what is desired is the patch of private territory and spacing between houses. Many subdivisions are populated by virtually the same age group, whose children are likewise identical in ages. This lack of diversity may be one of the key reasons many young professionals eschew the subdivison lifestyle and choose to go where the action is: in the city or an older suburb.

HIPNESS

Obviously very subjective and less quantifiable, the hipness of an area was found to be a major factor in the neighborhoods we explored. As much as hip means being up on the latest ideas and styles, it can be ephemeral, as were the art galleries that helped establish SoHo as the "in" neighborhood of New York for a while and then were priced out and relocated to Chelsea or Brooklyn, to be upstaged by the Meat Packing District and the East Village. Areas can be hip or hot in one era in a city's history, as the downtown Market Square area of Houston was in the 1960s. But then it emptied out for a variety of reasons, including the building of the Galleria mixed-use project that stole attention from downtown.

On the other hand, Georgetown in Washington, D.C., Greenwich Village in New York, the French Quarter in New Orleans, Beacon Hill in Boston, Nob Hill in San Francisco, or Michigan Avenue in Chicago have enduring staying power. Their vitality can wax and wane, but they remain. One hopes that today's hip areas, should they fall out of fashion, endure as vital neighborhoods.

We heard various phrases for what we are talking about. The recruit in Houston who was being shown the beautiful River Oak section of houses wanted to know instead where the nighttime "action" was. In Memphis it was "wanting to be part of the excitement" that exists downtown between Beale Street and the bars and restaurants of Peabody Place and elsewhere. In Minneapolis, preceding the population influx in the North Loop warehouse area there was a nearby nighttime scene of clubs and restaurants, safe enough for suburbanites.

Other words that apply to some case neighborhoods are edgy, funky, different—these in particular were used for the South Main area of Memphis, but they also apply to the Pearl District of Portland, the small Crescent District of Midtown Atlanta, and the warehouse section of Yaletown in Vancouver.

Art galleries are often barometers of hipness. In Memphis, New Orleans, and Portland, monthly gallery openings are major social scenes that draw thousands. A Saturday gallery walk is being discussed in Atlanta's Midtown. Weekend gallery openings occur in New Orleans. The presence of artists living in a neighborhood is another bellwether. Atlanta's Midtown attracted many in its earlier, less expensive days, and residents we interviewed reflected that the area was now less eclectic as prices have risen, but for Atlanta, Midtown is still a very happening area. Artists move in first, then pioneering residents, then commerce, and then higher rents driving out the artists—a familiar pattern occurring in cities everywhere.

A cover feature article in the May 15, 1995 issue of *Newsweek* entitled "Bye-Bye, Suburban Dream" spoke of several residential projects in Memphis being the "centers of coolness" there, by which they meant attracting a young crowd, as indeed they are.

Are Vancouver's burgeoning residential areas on the waterfront exhibiting vitality and hipness? We say yes, even in a newly developed area (ten years old), by virtue of the density and diversity built in, its attractiveness to a young and often gay population, themselves quite progressive, giving the neighborhood its buzz—helped along by the occasional coffee bar. Speaking of which, it is almost a rule that the arrival of a Starbucks shop is seen as an indicator that a neighborhood has "arrived." In Midtown Atlanta, those we interviewed referred to the arrival of Starbucks there as a cause for a party. Later came the upscale Whole Foods store, truly signifying arrival.

You know hipness when you see it, as distinct from being able to pin down precisely what it constitutes. We believe it is an important feature that is drawing people into newly developing urban residential neighborhoods.

PUBLIC TRANSIT

By this we mean rail as opposed to buses. Portland has a well-used bus network, but it is an exception to the rule. Buses are often shunned by the middle class, "loser cruisers" in Steve Belmont's phrase. He goes on to state flatly that "Rail transit is an ingredient without which cities cannot achieve and sustain commercial and residential densities sufficiently high to support vitality."[15]

We agree and note the presence of rail in all of our eight case cities. Rail serves Atlanta's Midtown (MARTA); Dallas's Uptown has its McKinney Avenue trolley and the city has DART; Houston's midtown and downtown connect to the Museum District with METRORail; Memphis has two lines, one along Main Street, the other tying the riverfront to Main and South Main; Minneapolis will have a downtown-to-airport-to-mall line; in New Orleans, the St. Charles trolley runs through the Lafayette Square District; in Portland, a streetcar links the Pearl District to downtown and the MAX rail line, plus the 23rd Street neighborhood; and in Vancouver, the Skytrain runs near the North False Creek area connecting to suburbs to the east. People living intown use it for commuting to jobs outside downtown.

The irony of the new popularity of streetcars is that American cities had wonderful systems into the 1940s and '50s. Cities had multiple lines tying together their neighborhoods and the downtown with amazing efficiency, as in Los Angeles. After World War II these systems were dumped in favor of the auto in yet another classic blunder harming American cities (along with urban renewal and federally underwritten urban expressways). For example, Memphis is justly proud of its historic streetcars running along Main Street in a system reintroduced in the mid-1990s. The irony is that back in the 1920s Memphis had 127 miles of tracks for streetcars that carried 161,000 riders a day, the equivalent of two-thirds of the city's population. And 80 percent of the streetcars ran down Main Street, making it the hot spot of the city.[16]

Rail service is an asset to any residential neighborhood. When Houston's ten-mile Main Street line begins operating in 2004, we anticipate that the already booming Midtown area immediately south of the CBD will further take off, becoming more dense as higher apartments are built, reflecting the increase in land prices. It will be a boon for anyone living there and working downtown, in the Museum District or in the Medical District.

In several of our case cities, the transit link is a symbol for the subject neighborhood. The business association Uptown Dallas uses the McKinney Avenue trolley as its logo. Portland's streetcar likewise distinguishes the Pearl District.

Streetcars of another day helped create what we have been terming traditional suburbs, characterized by compact development built around the central transit stop. These streetcar suburbs are today some of the country's finest residential neighborhoods with handy commercial areas, and they have many of the characteristics we call urbanity.

The destruction of these systems is a scandal, related tellingly by Gratz and Mintz in *Cities Back from the Edge* and by Helen Leavitt in *Superhighway-Superhoax*. They among others report how General Motors led a consortium to buy up streetcar companies (they were private then), secretly forming National City Lines. Court documents revealed in 1947 that this front bought streetcar lines strictly to dismantle them, replacing them with buses, in nearly fifty cities. They also make the point that the streetcar was essentially pedestrian-oriented and built to a pedestrian scale as opposed to the highway and high-speed roadway.[17]

2

Background

Cities are resilient; they hold more lasting value than can be destroyed in a few decades, more lasting value than is found in the thin smear of suburban development intended to replace urban life.
—*John Norquist,* The Wealth of Cities

SUBURBS, SUBDIVISIONS . . . SPRAWL

Let's discuss the dominant suburbs, where fully half the population lives. The first thing to say is that they are not uniform and it is a mistake, we feel, to talk about a city/suburban dichotomy. Some older, compact suburbs have strong urban centers, often have a system of sidewalks amid their single-family, green-lawned homes, and possess much of the urbanity we outlined in chapter 1. Bethesda, Maryland and Winnetka, Illinois come to mind. At the same time, some cities, like our case example of Minneapolis, have large areas of predominately single-family housing stock, quite suburban in density and appearance.

Let's also quickly make distinctions between "suburbs" and "subdivisions." The post–World War II sprawl of subdivisions into the farmlands and open spaces surrounding every city large and small as builders scrambled to meet a pent-up housing demand differed fundamentally from previous suburban development. Levittown's 17,000 look-alike homes built on Long Island potato farms is the symbol and prototype of the new approach. It was the first time a sophisticated, industrial-type approach was taken to home construction, and it soon spread throughout the industry. Levitt houses were in fact cheaper to buy than a city apartment was to rent in those days (early 1950s).

What characterizes this kind of settlement is, among other things, the lack of a town center, few, if any, sidewalks, near total car dependency, and a uniformity of building type. Subdivisions are very alive and well today and with the same essential characteristics, although some have design changes (such as putting the garage behind instead of beside the house). *Subdivision* is the term we will use for the type of development we point to when talking about sprawl. Efforts by developers today to install some sort of "community center" amid subdivision sprawl is affirmation that the market is seeking a sense of community to one degree or another. The truth, however, remains: Everyone still must operate out of the automobile, so it is debatable whether you can genuinely urbanize a subdivision.

In contrast is the older, traditional suburb, many built around commuter rail stations. Brookline and Wellesley outside Boston, Chestnut Hill and Bryn Mawr of Philadelphia, Takoma Park and Silver Spring, Maryland, near Washington, D.C., Evanston and Highland Park north of Chicago, Santa Monica (a California version) outside Los Angeles, and Highland Park (Texas-style) in greater Dallas. The Galleria area on the western side of Houston is another, newer expression. In these places there is a real commercial center—in one of the more overworked expressions of the time, "a sense of place."

The key demographic today, however, is that there is a relatively smaller percentage of the population fitting the subdivision profile, namely the nuclear family. Mom, Dad, and one or two kids is only 23 percent of our population now. For them, the subdivision continues to make perfectly good sense. There is safety offered, generally good schools and green lawns and usually cheaper housing costs because of relatively cheap land. If the price to live here is driving around constantly, so be it.

The other three-quarters of the population is by definition something else: single, unmarried couples, married couples with no children, divorced with or without children, reconstituted families with children, and older couples and empty nesters. There were more families without children under 18 (38.1 million) than with (37.5 million) in the 2000 census. And families are shrinking—the average family size now is 3.17. In other words, the market for people attracted to a nonsubdivision location is growing, giving us the opportunity to expand the populations of cities, traditional suburbs, and towns.

THE MESS WE'RE IN

How did we get into the mess of sprawl subdivisions chewing up the landscapes surrounding Phoenix, Denver, our own Washington, D.C. and the rest? We are not going to repeat here the many good synopses available of the modern history of the American city.[1]

It's an oft-told story of turn-of-the-century city expansion and then overcrowding, the spread of traditional suburbs, particularly along transit lines. Then came the decline in the 1960s and 1970s (later for some) featuring massive white/middle class flight and the concentration of the poor in urban centers, the devastation brought about by well-meaning but wrongheaded business/political leadership selecting federal urban renewal and expressway programs as the cure for urban ills, which accounts even today for some of the desolate areas of our downtowns. Race obviously was a factor in the middle-class exodus, but we note that professional blacks are moving into suburbs outside Atlanta (it's called "bright flight" there). And when pressed about staying in the city to help less fortunate blacks or other poor people, they reply in so many words, "We're just doing what the whites did as they prospered, and we want the same things for our kids, good schools, no crime, healthy air, lawns, and barbecues."

Bruce Katz, director of the Center on Urban and Metropolitan Policy at the Brookings Institution in Washington, D.C., has a good outline of what is happening. He says the country is decentralizing overall, even as some city centers strengthen. According to Katz, America's cities and metropolitan areas are experiencing similar patterns of growth and development—explosive sprawl where farmland once reigned, matched by decline or slower growth in the central cities and older suburbs. He documents that growth in the suburbs is double that of central cities, 18 percent versus 9.1 percent from 1990 to 2000. Further, he points out, it's the fringe areas outside a city such as Atlanta where growth is fastest. Employment centers have followed, and in places like Chicago and Detroit, fully 60 percent of the workforce is located more than 10 miles from the city center.[2] The consequences of this pattern are obvious: traffic congestion, environmental problems, and social issues such as a disconnect between jobs and where poor people live.

We would add another terrible consequence that relatively few mention. It's the pervading ugliness of the sprawl development pattern. Not the cul-de-sac homes themselves which, with their lawns and shrubs, are by and large handsome enough. It's the miles of disjointed commercial strips that serve these neighborhoods that are mind-bogglingly ugly, with glaring signs, each bigger than the next, competing for the motorists' attention. With acres of macadam everywhere, usually in front of stores, which can be strung out for miles. Where cheapness of construction prevails, as in, "this place may not be here long." Where chain restaurants and stores dominate. And when there's a big box-enclosed mall instead of strip commerce, it is again surrounded by deadly blacktop. A notable exception to the inattention to this aspect of sprawl is James Howard Kunstler's colorful first book, *The Geography of Nowhere: The Rise and Decline of America's Man-Made Landscape*. In it he writes that what's been built in the last fifty years is for the most part "depressing, brutal, ugly, unhealthy and spiritually degrading."[3] Amen.

Another characteristic is the disconnectedness of the elements of sprawl—the housing, malls, office parks, schools. Everything is scattered along the umbilical that is the highway. The elements of daily life not only are not walkable, they may be miles away and separated from each other.

Americans are so inured to this sprawl pattern they don't see it anymore. To us the ripping up of our landscape to create the brutally ugly highwayscape of sprawl is an epic tragedy. In the classic phrase of Peter Blake, written forty years ago, we are: "God's Own Junkyard."[4]

We discuss traffic in a separate section, but we mention here an immediate, obvious consequence of subdivision sprawl: The Texas Transportation Institute estimates that the annual bill for traffic congestion in the U.S. in 1999 was $78 billion, caused by people being stuck in traffic burning fuel and losing work or home time. Many spend more on travel than on housing, so far-flung have settlements become. This contributes to environmental degradation, such as creating air pollution (Atlanta and Houston have been put on the black list by the Environmental Protection Agency and denied highway funds because of bad air), contributing to water pollution with runoff from the increased amounts of macadam laid over the land, and diminishing the green open spaces of metropolitan areas and their role in making air breathable and agriculture sustainable.

CAUSES

Analysts all unite in blaming the federal government's mortgage insurance, transportation, and water/sewer grant programs for underwriting sprawl. The Federal Housing Administration and Veterans Administration after World War II underwrote only new houses, meaning that the rehabilitation of an older city property could not benefit from the same financing. There's no disputing the fact that highways (90 percent underwritten by the federal government for major roads, 50 percent otherwise, coming from the unending tap of the highway revolving fund of a gasoline tax) help stimulate sprawling subdivisions, or else how would they get built and how would people get to and from them? Another culprit is local zoning that mandates separation of uses—low-density houses here, industrial parks there, commercial along these roads, a school plunked here and there, and so forth. Houses and commerce shall not mix is the watchword.

But what isn't discussed usually is why is this so. The suburb/subdivision will always be with us. Its imagery and ethos are deeply imbedded in the American psyche, reinforced in years past by the imagery of magazines, movies, and then television. Plus, it meets pragmatic objectives today for a sizable segment of the populace.

A full-page ad in the July 8, 2003, *Washington Post* put it this way:

YOU'RE LOOKING AT THE MOST POWERFUL ECONOMIC FORCE
IN THE COUNTRY; THE AMERICAN DREAM (Caps in original.)

Pictured is a lawnmower, a truck, and a new two-story subdivision-style house. The ad, by FannieMae, reports that the agency, which underwrites mortgages, has put over 50 million families into homes. FannieMae says it expects 30 million new American homes by 2010. "And when they dream of owning a home, we'll be there." So this ethic continues to run strong. Anthony Downs, writing in "New Visions for Metropolitan America" in 1994, said the dream has five components: owning a detached, single-family home on a large lot; owning a car; working in a low-rise building in an attractive setting surrounded by free parking; living in a small community with a strong local government; and being free of signs of poverty.

The answer, it seems to us, is that sprawl is what at least half of the voting public wants. The American Dream may be choking, but it is still alive, and it creates the necessary political support to underwrite the highway and water/sewer programs very much in use today. The development community often says, defensively, that it is merely supplying what the customer wants when it builds its next subdivision on a former farm. Well, they are essentially right for a sizable portion of the population. This is important to understand because if, as we advocate in our last chapter, we are going to reorient ourselves as a nation to become more urban and to curtail the underwriting of sprawl, we have a challenge.

What's wrong about the current policies is that *all* of us help to subsidize the suburban sprawl—city dweller, farmer, and small town resident alike. It's *our* taxes that pay to subsidize the roads and infrastructure that enable new development. Also, city residents in their more efficient, denser configuration pay the same flat rate for utilities as subdivision dwellers. This underwrites the costs of supplying pipelines and wiring to more far-flung, spread-out areas.

While sprawl is simple to comprehend, the overall development pattern outside central cities is getting increasingly complex. Many an inner suburb is taking on the characteristics of the city it grew from, namely congestion, crime, the addition of new immigrant populations, and a steady buildup. And many a suburban town has grown to city size in population, while still lacking real urbanity, like Glendale, Arizona, a suburb of Phoenix, which became the one hundredth largest city in the country with a population of 182,219 in 1996 (it hit 219,000 in 2000). Plano, Texas, north of Dallas, had a population of 192,280 then and was already the nation's eighty-eighth largest (it's now past 222,000). An analysis of mid-century census estimates found that sixty-six of 219 cities with over 100,000 people were suburban, mostly in the South and West.[5]

The fastest-growing places from 2000 to 2002 were counties in the Southwest, the census reported in 2003. Researchers at the FannieMae Foundation term these areas "Boomburgs" and call them the ultimate symbol of post–World War II sprawl. Robert Fishman, in his classic *Bourgeois Utopias,* called them "Technoburgs" and distinguished them from traditional suburbs with their ties to a central city.[6] Whatever their names, they are "cities" in the sense that they have over 100,000 people, but they are essentially large subdivisions without a central business core.

Robert Lang and Patrick Simmons found fifty-three "Boomburgs" in the 2000 census, concentrated in California. They range in size from Mesa, Arizona, with 400,000 to Westminster, Colorado, with 100,940. Further, these are not job centers but strictly suburban residential communities, often governed by homeowners' associations, another growing trend of the times. Using 1950 as a starting point when a fledgling "Boomburg" passed the 2,500-person threshold, Lang and Simmons came up with astonishing growth rates in certain places. Like Irving, outside Dallas, which has grown by 7,211 percent! It went from 2,621 people to 191,615 in the past five decades. Similar stories come from Henderson, Nevada, and Chandler, Arizona, which had growth rates over 4,000 percent in the 1950-to-2000 period.[7] Take prosperous Scottsdale, Arizona. In 1950 it had barely 2,000 people. By the mid-1990s it had grown to three times the physical size of San Francisco and had 165,000 people.[8] By 2000 it was over 200,000, an astonishing increase in fifty years.

Decentralization is happening in mid-America as well. A study published in 2002 about Missouri found that the state's population was dispersing, that the smaller cities were growing, and unincorporated areas likewise were experiencing growth in a highly decentralized pattern. "Growth in the Heartland" found that expansion in Columbia, Springfield, Joplin, and St. Joseph was double that of St. Louis and Kansas City. In the vast area of unincorporated farmland, the study found growth of 12.3 percent in the 1990s, 50 percent faster than elsewhere. Rural counties that were losing people before grew in the 1990s, with eight of ten adding people and nine of ten adding jobs.[9]

Part of this decentralization is racially motivated, researchers report. William Frey, a demographer at the University of Michigan, found that the forty fastest-growing rural counties were overwhelmingly white. Said Calvin Beale of the U.S. Department of Agriculture,

It's fairly clear to me that a certain amount of the movement into rural areas can fairly be described as white flight. I have rarely heard anyone mention race in the context of talking about this. They talk about getting away from urban crime, drugs, congestion and school problems. But it also means getting away from areas that have significant percentages of blacks, Hispanics and Asians.

The studies noted that many of the inner rings of suburbs from which people are leaving now were experiencing the problems traditionally associated with the inner city.[10] A 2003 study we'll discuss showed, in fact, that the concentrated clusters of poverty in the inner city dispersed dramatically between 1990 and 2000 as the poor moved into older suburbs, perhaps a consequence of gentrification, and contributing to the pattern just described.

Bruce Katz of Brookings writes candidly about the pivotal role of race in our settlement pattern. He says:

Race has fundamentally influenced the policies of exclusion that are practiced by suburbs throughout the country. These policies have exacerbated the concentration of racial poverty in the central cities and helped construct the metropolitan dividing lines that separate areas of wealth and opportunity from areas of poverty and distress . . . In many respects, sprawl is the inevitable flip side of racial segregation and social exclusion. *Race shapes growth patterns and drives business and residential decisions in ways that no single other factor can match.* (Our emphasis.)[11]

Meanwhile, there is business as usual among many builders. But with this difference: In 2003 you are selling not just a house but a stab at a community. "Home Town Living" is how a real estate supplement to *The Washington Post* of March 7, 2003 was headlined. "The Allure of a True Home Town" was the next pitch. "People remember places," it reads. "The allure of a great home town is simple: A warm, inviting house, a choice of interesting places to gather outside the home, nice neighbors to gather with, and convenient shops and services nearby."

Another trend is to make subdivison developments feel somewhat urban, the thrust of neotraditional town planning or new urbanism. The hybrid combination of retail and residential has seized the imagination, it is said, of the shopping center industry. Thus we have a "lifestyle village" such as Santana Row in San Jose, California, where apartments were being built over the stores of the shopping mall. They are an obvious attempt to market to the affluent young professionals who might otherwise move to a real city location or a traditional suburb, or perhaps more likely, to older baby boomers who have lived for years in the suburbs and for whom this mix might seem attractive. In any case, it is a reaction against the more sterile subdivision and reflects the dissatisfaction many express about the traffic they experience. It's also an attempt to breathe life into older malls, 18 percent of which were reported by PricewaterhouseCoopers to be dying.[12]

At least one person sees a moral dimension to the prevailing land use pattern of the country. Roman Catholic Bishop Anthony Pilla of Cleveland watched his city and his parishioners drain out into the suburbs, losing half of its population from 1950, for all the usual reasons: crime, racial discord, better schools, better housing, and jobs. Pilla has taken on the "unbalanced investment" that occurs, noting: "Public policies and subsidies have aggravated urban problems by facilitating and encouraging the development of new, more distant suburbs. Support for the maintenance and redevelopment of central cities—and now the inner-ring suburbs—has simply not been comparable to the underwriting of sprawl." Pilla called for "a change of heart, a real change of attitude to motivate people to address this issue" and proceeded into the diocese at large to explain that he wasn't critical of suburbanites; he wanted to engage them in rebuilding the city. To do so he talked with the business community as well as with other religious leaders. As a result, some 90 partnerships between city and suburb were formed in what came to be called The Church in the City program.[13]

TRAFFIC

Highway congestion is the breaking point of the subdivision pattern. There are those who say their hour in the car two times a day commuting is their private time, when they can think and enjoy quiet and listen to the radio, but for most, the commute and the daily car runs to the stores/mall are a chore at best, agonizing at worst.

Why do they do it? It's the schools (usually first-listed), the nice home, and then backyards and the malls. The price? An increasing amount of time spent stuck in traffic, that is, not moving. It's up to fifty-six hours a year in Los Angeles and fifty-three hours in Atlanta, double the amount just seven years ago.

This is from the Texas Transportation Institute in its annual congestion report: Overall, Americans spent an average of thirty-six hours not moving in 1999, up from eleven hours in 1982. Motorists seem willing to endure the traffic for the sense of freedom the car brings, Texas Institute researcher Tim Lomax said, noting that cheap gas and often free parking contribute.[14]

A study by two anti-sprawl nonprofits that support mass transit, walking, and biking as alternatives determined that Americans on the average spend more on their cars than on food. In Houston and Atlanta, households spend 22 percent of their income on transportation. Dallas is right behind at 20 percent. The national average annual cost for transportation was put at $6,312. The places where people spend the least—New York and Honolulu—are dense, compact, and have good public transit, the study noted.[15] The report quoted came from the Surface Transportation Policy Project and the Center for Neighborhood Technology.

It's not the commuting so much, it's the nonwork trips in the land of subdivisions that are time-consuming. Jane Holz Kay, in her book *Asphalt Nation,* puts it well: "What sets the odometer reeling is . . . something less critical than life, liberty, or the pursuit of happiness. And that is errands."[16] A study found that running errands constitutes 85 percent of all trips—the grocery, drugstore, mall, church, and taking children to birthday parties, movies, roller rink, soccer, and friends' houses. Some of this is done during rush hours, contributing to congestion, but it also means midday and weekend traffic jams. The average of such errands is four miles, a U.S. Department of Transportation study determined.[17] And that has an adverse impact on air quality compared to the longer commuting journey because frequent engine starts generate more exhaust.

This kind of car use confounds transportation planners who urge carpooling and transit use, which won't work for the side trip to the grocery. Representative is Katy Joseph of Crofton, outside Washington, D.C., for whom the closest grocery is five miles away on back roads without sidewalks. She also drives the children short distances because she's not comfortable with them out at night, including a 15-year-old daughter visiting a friend two blocks away.[18]

It's clear this is where the breakdown is occurring. Only now are the traffic planners coming to grips with the implications of people having to take the car all the time for personal business, church, doctors, recreation, and the like. People can, and do, log up to three hours a day taking kids to school, running errands, taking someone to ballet class or gym, and seeing friends. That can include young children who are hauled along because there is no one at home to care for them.

In the commuting world, what's happening to some is that the treks are ever longer. That's because home prices in an area like San Francisco propel the need for long commutes. It's estimated that every mile east of the city takes $5,000 off the cost of housing. And so people buy houses in Tracy, California, about sixty miles east of the city, where houses go for an average of $225,000. It means workers get up at 5:00 A.M. to begin the commute. Fully 90 percent of the homes in Tracy are bought by commuters. The pricing in the area is such that in San Carlos, a traditional suburb roughly midway between San Francisco and San Jose, the average home price is $600,000. The mayor there announced he was leaving—couldn't afford it any more.[19]

Decentralization affects the job world as well, meaning more people are unable to take transit even if they want to because it doesn't take them from their subdivision to their office park in an adjoining neighborhood. This adds to the three-hour rush congestion at the beginning and end of each workday.

Nonetheless in the Washington, D.C. area, transit use is up. For the region as a whole the increase was 13.2 percent from 1999 to 2000, across the board, on commuter rail, subway, and bus. Helping is a transit subsidy for all federal workers. The national average transit increase was just 3.5 percent, but at least it's up and reverses years of decline. This is from an American Public Transportation Association report that showed Los Angeles with the largest percentage increase in transit use, followed by the BART system in the San Francisco Bay area. Highway lobbyists remind us in the meantime that most transportation is still on roadways, by way of asking for more funds to build more highways.[20]

HEALTH AND LIFESTYLE

Americans are fat. Nearly 65 percent of the population is overweight, including the 31 percent who are classified as obese, meaning over thirty pounds above what they should weigh. And this despite the proliferation of health clubs, best-selling diet books, marathons drawing thousands, and general health-consciousness by many.

The culprit, no surprise here, is lack of exercise. And the people who study this, like the Centers for Disease Control (CDC) in Atlanta, are focusing on the subdivision layout as a basic contributor. A researcher at CDC's National Center for Environmental Health, Richard Jackson, says, "We are coming to the conclusion that land use, urban design and the built environment are much larger factors in public health than people have really appreciated." Landmark studies published in 2003 by the *American Journal of Health Promotion,* the Surface Transportation Policy Project, and Smart Growth America concluded that there is a direct link between community forms and inhabitants' health, namely that in car-dependent areas people don't walk as much, and they weigh more and have higher blood pressure.[21]

Typical subdivisions are designed strictly for the automobile, and even if people wanted to walk, it's made difficult for them. Everything in a sprawl suburbia is spread out, there may be six-lane arterials slicing through, and sidewalks are rare. Like the young woman who took to walking for exercise in her subdivision in Germantown, Maryland, north of Washington, D.C. She was about five blocks from her house on a deserted sidewalk and one neighbor after another pulled their minivans to the curb and asked if she was alright. "They said, 'What's wrong? What are you doing here? Do you need a ride?'" The woman said she was embarrassed and didn't want to walk anymore.[22] Journalist Laura Pappano, relating an anecdote about how America was different in the 1930s and earlier, compared to the generations of Boomers and GenXers, said an older woman she interviewed thought a while and came up with the near-universal recollection of walking everywhere: "Nobody went to Betty [*sic*] Craig or whatever to lose weight or get in shape. All you had to do was walk. You never heard of a diet. You ate."[23]

Another researcher at CDC reports that 25 percent of all trips by Americans are under one mile and 75 percent of those are made by car. Only a third of the schoolchildren who live within a mile of school walk, Dr. William Dietz, director of the Division of Nutrition and Physical Activity, reported. Overall, only 13 percent of schoolchildren walk.[24] A study done by the Georgia Institute of Technology found that Americans use their feet far less than others, walking and biking only 10 percent of the time versus over 50 percent in Italy and just under that mark in Sweden.[25]

Efforts to build more walkable subdivisions encounter hurdles. The building community says walkable developments are expensive to construct, hard to get past local planning agencies, and difficult to finance, says Clayton Traylor for the National Association of Home Builders.[26] Even if we had the sidewalks in the subdivisions and the schools were within a mile of home, many Americans have become so fearful for their children's safety in the last twenty-five or thirty years, they probably wouldn't let them walk.

Also contributing to increasing obesity is the trend to eat in restaurants and do take-out more, brought about in part by the strung-out lives people lead driving around for hours at a time. Americans now get 35 percent of their food from restaurants and the percentage is climbing, reports Susan Roberts of the Department of Agriculture's Human Nutrition Research Center on Aging at Tufts University. "Restaurant food has more fat, saturated fat, sodium, carbohydrates and calories and less calcium than food prepared at home," she says. "Everything about restaurants encourages over-eating," she adds, because high-fat food tastes good.[27]

Obesity is costly to the economy. An employers' group, the Washington Business Group on Health, which provides benefits for 40 million people, says that obesity adds $7.7 billion to insurance costs, part of an overall loss of $12.7 billion put to serious overweight. The group reports that businesses small and large are mounting programs for their workers to encourage fitness, including providing incentives like a day's vacation for a cumulative 1,000 miles of walking.[28]

A spate of articles in popular magazines and newspapers notes that studies indicate that we are a nation suffering sleep deprivation for a host of reasons. One is surely the long commute forcing people to rise early to get to work. A college president we interviewed who had moved from the suburbs to downtown near his university observed that he was able to sleep an hour longer and get to work earlier.

There are two groups especially for whom the spread-out, automobile-dominated subdivision can hurt psychologically: teenagers and the elderly. For the teenager, the subdivision often means alienation. The irony is that their parents chose to live in a subdivision for the health and safety of their children, many of whom can't wait to get out. "Typical of the Denver metro area are the new suburbs, where 'downtown' is a four-way intersection with three centers and a condo development," says Charles Blosten, community services director for Littleton, Colorado. He says of the largest subdivision, Highlands Ranch, it's "nothing but rooftops and miles and miles of nothing" in describing a numbing vista of houses. "It's got to affect people." Columbine High School is out here. In Atlanta we quote a onetime suburban developer who thinks the psychological problems of the young can be laid in part to the fact that their home is identical to everyone else's.

Analysts see sprawl subdivisions creating their own neuroses: "Lack of character and the grounding principles of identity; lack of diversity or the tolerance it engenders; lack of attachment to shared, civic ideals." The sprawl pattern may lead to disassociation from the reality of contact with other people. Of the teenager, William Morrish, director of the Center for American Urban Landscape at the University of Minnesota says, "They're basically an unseen population until they pierce their noses." One specific problem is that the subdivision culture has no real place for teens, where they can play out their sense of awkwardness.[29]

The other group is the elderly, who are car-dependent in a subdivision world. When they reach an age when they no longer can drive, their lives grind to a halt. When a woman in her eighties with severe memory impairment was advised to give up driving, she began crying and said, "You might as well shoot me." Retirement is planned for, but not the reality of reaching a point where retirees can't get behind the wheel, effectively stranding them.[30]

There's a reaction setting in to the dominance of the Internet that now emphasizes human contact. One indicator is that even with video teleconferencing, the convention/conference business was booming, at least before 9/11. The growth in meetings during the 1990s was striking, especially in technology-related fields. Conventions, conferences, and expositions are a huge $82 billion industry. Says Ken Sommer of the American Society of Association Executives, "It boils down to the fact that nothing will ever replace the face-to-face peer interplay for which meetings are famous. The networking, the high-level learning, interacting with colleagues, exchanging information, doing business. Technology is merely enhancing meetings, not decreasing them."[31]

As business executives are seeking personal contract, so is another, more surprising group—Generation X. The first PC age group was fixated on computer games, spending hours with them. Now, reaching their thirties, they are turning to board games at the homes of friends. Michael Megalli is one of these, recalling how he used to spend nine hours a night playing Age of Empires. Now he and his colleagues have discovered real people. "This is really a return of how people can be social rather than staring at a screen," he says.[32]

What these trends have in common is that they are expressions of people seeking human contact, a sense of community in a society that emphasizes separation and distance, embodied in the subdivison. This is the thesis of Robert Putnam's recent popular book, *Bowling Alone: The Collapse and Revival of American Community*.[33] In it he recounts the breakdown across the board of various associations, from the PTA to political organizations to clubs to churches. He calls this social capital and says we've been spending less of it than ever. He charts the growth into the 1950s of an array of groups, and then traces their declining participation, as with PTAs, whose attendance peaked in 1959. He reports that we even visit each other less, with home entertainment in decline since 1975. Sports for spectators grows, but active participation, as in bowling leagues, has plummeted.

The subdivision is part of the reason, Putnam says, noting the introvertism of gated communities and how they contrast with extroverted urban neighborhoods. People tend to stay in their houses when they are not spending their average 72 minutes a day in the car. He sees longer commuting times as affecting, among other things, the time available for community participation. We join him in seeing that sprawl disrupts community "boundedness," as he calls it, which makes the subdivision less attractive than the central city or smaller towns.

A big culprit is TV, which the average American watches four hours per day, and not, he points out, so much for news anymore, strictly for entertainment. More TV spells less involvement and less interaction, even within the home because there are often multiple sets tuned to different shows. The time pressure on the two-wage couple is another contributor to the breakdown in group participation.

Putnam concludes by saying that in the end Americans will largely get the kind of physical space we demand, and that if people resist policies that underwrite segregated subdivisions, perhaps they will change. It is a powerful case for the tight-knit urban neighborhood, where human contact is a regular part of the rhythm of the day and where, especially in newly settled neighborhoods, community participation is high.

SMART GROWTH

Sprawl has been identified as a problem, as we noted, since 1974. So thirty years later, how are we doing? We're going to suggest only fair, given the amount of analysis and discussion devoted to the ill effects of sprawl. Smart Growth is the moniker given for the solution, which is said to lie with state governments because sprawl is obviously beyond the capabilities of local jurisdictions and people seem unwilling to tackle the problem at the federal level. Smart Growth has taken on aspects of a movement. It is backed by some of the country's largest foundations (Ford, MacArthur, Turner, Packard, and others) who have formed a Funders' Network for Smart Growth and Livable Communities. Besides coordinating their efforts, the network focuses on the effects that unplanned sprawl growth has on social inequality.[34]

An early leader, former Maryland Governor Parris Glendening, became a hero of the movement when he advocated and then signed into law a package of measures designed to stop unwanted growth, particularly those types that were chewing up remaining farmland. The trouble is, he was replaced by a new governor of a different persuasion who has set about dismantling the Smart Growth Office Glendening established.

Essentially what's called for here is to direct state funding and regulations toward keeping growth from continuing to eat up the landscape, as with allocations of highway, sewer, and other construction grants. States like Colorado give communities grants to help plan to contain growth, but funding was down in 2003 with state budget difficulties. Governor James McGreevey in New Jersey has set up a Smart Growth Policy Council to guide agencies in such decisions as whether to withhold water permits in fragile areas. McGreevey also wants to promote development in cities and older suburbs with incentives.[35]

A survey of voters in New Jersey points up the essential difficulty in implementing a Smart Growth policy. In the country's densest state, there is support for the general proposition that the state should encourage development in built-up areas and limit it in farm areas. When pressed, however, the 71 percent support dropped to 48 percent if the policy meant that "people like you" would not be able to move into homes in undeveloped parts of the state. The same results occurred when people were asked if they wanted to give up local control over growth issues. Concluded this columnist: "To truly implement a 'smart growth' initiative would require tremendous cooperation by state and local officials as well as developers and environmentalists . . . No choice is easy when it comes to dealing with the sprawl problem in this state."[36]

The limitations of Smart Growth policies were brought home by a proposed Wal-Mart on Kent Island outside of Annapolis, Maryland. The store, it turned out, was located outside the "priority funding area" where there was existing infrastructure. Maryland's program forbids state funding for roads, sewers, or anything else outside the area. The trouble is, a behemoth like Wal-Mart doesn't depend on state subsidies. There's nothing to prevent it from building its own roads and sewage treatment. The same applies to subdivisions outside designated growth areas, in what is seen as an inherent weakness of Maryland's approach, and this was under Governor Glendening.[37]

A major piece in *The Washington Post* pointed up another problem with Smart Growth–type efforts. Entitled "Density Limits Only Add To Sprawl," the analysis discussed the impact of larger-lot zoning, enacted to preserve open space. More than half of the land surrounding Washington, D.C. in suburban Virginia and Maryland is under restrictions that limit development to one house per three acres or even more. But the effects of these well-meaning restrictions are twofold: One effect is that they create enclaves of spread-out housing. Under traditional suburban zoning, where there is one house now there could have been thirty clustered homes. The second effect is that developers simply skip past the restricted areas to build subdivisions still farther afield, into West Virginia, for example.[38]

Resistance to Smart Growth restrictions comes from a seemingly unlikely source: advocates of low-income housing. Their fear is that restrictions on growth will drive up the price of land, and thereby housing, at a time when housing affordability is a problem. Development interests have adopted the concerns of the affordable housing advocates and use their arguments to try to curb restrictions. But anti-sprawl forces counter that housing prices are up just as sharply in areas without growth restrictions as they are in areas with them. Debate will continue.[39]

Some conservative organizations are on the warpath with regard to Smart Growth. Columnist Neal Peirce reported from a meeting organized by the Thoreau Institute of Oregon, entitled "Preserving the American Dream of Mobility and Homeownership," that speakers railed against rail transit "boondoggles" and "coercive social engineering" and described Smart Growth advocates as "quacks" and "a bunch of elitist, Volvo-driving, brie-cheese eating blowhards." The group says only 2.6 percent of the land area in the country is urbanized, so what's the problem?[40]

Efforts to curb sprawl are obviously complicated in a system with multiple layers of government and where, traditionally, land use decisions are made at the local level. In chapter 9 we look at the pioneering effort in Oregon to take meaningful intergovernmental action.

DOWNTOWNS

Amid the ever-widening circles of sprawl and ringed by highways are the nation's downtowns. "Downtown" was once the happening place of our cities, large and small. What occurred to largely empty them except for the poor since the 1950s? And did the burgeoning economy of the 1990s help bring many center cities back to life?

In 1999 the FannieMae Foundation commissioned a survey of urban scholars to come up with the ten major influences on cities in the past fifty years. What it produced underscores the profound influence the federal government has had—almost all of it negative—on cities, perhaps reflecting the general public's distrust of them. Reading this list can't help but give rise to the notion that the same federal government has got to be part of the solution. (See Recommendations.)

The number one influence is the 1956 Interstate Highway Act and the dominance of the car as the primary mode of transportation that this vast public works program accelerated. City leaders petitioned to extend the interstate highway program into their core areas, under the wrongheaded assumption that it would help the growing suburban population to speed into downtown. It had the opposite effect, namely helping residents to leave. Urban beltways turned into the main streets of the suburbs, and our decentralized, car-dominated settlement pattern was launched. The further tragedy is that cities have bent over backwards to accommodate the car, to the detriment of safe, attractive, walkable neighborhoods.

The federal government's second major influence was that Federal Housing Administration (and Veterans Administration) mortgage financing underwrote the subdivision explosion after World War II that continues today (note FannieMae ad cited earlier). The formula of low down payment and long-term payout made housing affordable. And it did not finance the purchase of existing houses in urban neighborhoods. These had to be financed with high rates and short terms, which had been the tradition until FHA changed the rules.

Deindustrialization is seen as the third major influence hitting cities and their centers. Changes in technology, the gradual shift to trucks over rail, the availability of cheap labor outside cities, suburban tax breaks, and the trend toward large-lot, single-story factories and warehouses all spelled a flight of manufacturing from the city, first to the suburbs, then to the Sunbelt, and finally overseas. Hurt the worst were blacks and blue-collar whites who had looked to city factories for work and who found it difficult to access suburban job centers.

Urban renewal is the fourth villain, coupled with the first public housing programs. Here too the business and political leaders of cities made a wrongheaded and profoundly anti-urban decision. They decided that the solution to city problems was to level areas seen as "blighted" so they could be rebuilt along clean-cut suburban lines. The conventional architectural wisdom of the time (still much with us) called for high-rises, usually offices, to be built on super blocks. Many a black or poor neighborhood too close to the center city and troubling to the white downtown leadership was lost in this era. This leadership, along with the urban planners of the day, understood not a whit about the vitality of these neighborhoods and how close-knit they were, or the rich street life of a section like West Boston, an Italian neighborhood lost to the bulldozer. Public housing quickly turned into black ghettos in isolated high-rises with no middle-class role models.

The number five influence is the subdivision discussed earlier. Combined with FHA-backed financing, sprawl was on its way in a country with wide open spaces and increasingly productive agriculture that required less land.

Racial segregation is number six on the list, as more blacks left the South for jobs in northern cities. Job discrimination left only the lowest-paying positions open. There was what sociologists call "hypersegregation," meaning that blacks were effectively excluded from white urban and subdivision America and instead were trapped in ghettos that were high in poverty rates, crime, and other signs of social disintegration such as the breakdown of the family.

The impact of the shopping mall amid the subdivisions spelled the end to downtown retail. This is seventh on the FannieMae list. The first enclosed, air-conditioned mall opened outside Minneapolis in 1956, providing easy access, free parking, a homogeneous environment (i.e., no panhandlers, and probably few black people if any, at first). By the 1990s the allure of the mall was fading a bit with the rise of the big-box discounters and the Internet, along with a generation that was bored with them and interested in the more exciting urban venues, now that city crime rates had come down.

Eighth on the FannieMae list is the spread of subdivision sprawl into the Sunbelt. And as we saw in the census numbers from 2000 to 2002, it's happening today. It's our sense that a sizeable number of the empty-nesters who do sell their subdivision homes will go to the Sunbelt rather than, as many demographers have suggested, into urban neighborhoods.

Ninth is the role air conditioning has played in making the Sunbelt habitable. It came into widespread use in the 1950s and '60s as the subdivision boom was taking off and which it helped along.

Number ten, the urban riots of the 1960s, emptied out many a center city. Watts in Los Angeles in 1965, followed by the violent riots in places such as Newark, New Jersey, in 1967 and Detroit and Washington, D.C. in 1968 after Dr. Martin Luther King Jr.'s assassination deeply frightened the middle class and sent them fleeing to the suburbs. The scars, physical and psychological, remain today in a place such as Memphis, Tennessee, which we talk about in chapter 6.

With this recitation, it is no wonder that center cities were left for dead by the 1970s. Most were devoid of significant retail, emptied of residents except for the poor, and home to workers in isolated office towers who by and large drove to work and parked free or cheaply before emptying out at 5:00 P.M. It is a tribute to the resilience of our center cities, and their continued vital function as a nexus, that they have come back as far as many of them have in the past twenty-five years or so.

The same FannieMae panel was asked to name the ten major influences the analysts foresaw for the next fifty years. We'll not run through them all except to say there are more negatives than positive. Income disparity and the political dominance of subdivision voters (read anti-urban) top the list. The scholars foresee a perpetual underclass in cities as well as in inner-ring suburbs, which suburbs they think will deteriorate. On the up side are listed anti-sprawl efforts and urban neighborhoods supporting racial as well as cultural integration, such as Adams-Morgan in Washington, D.C., West Mount Airy in Philadelphia, and South Pasadena in Los Angeles.[41]

We've talked about what brought American cities down; now let's look at examples of comebacks in places large and small. These rebounds must either precede a residential expansion or occur along with it to sustain it, as our case examples will illustrate. But let's look at what a sampling of city centers are attempting or have accomplished. This is only a sampling of the comeback stories that crowd our files, chosen for their range of geography and city size.

Chicago. State Street, once the dominant downtown retail district, is a classic tale of misguided city building. It went into decline in the 1970s as suburban malls opened and North Michigan Avenue replaced it. In 1979, in a mistaken attempt to imitate the suburban approach, traffic was taken off in favor of making it a pedestrian mall. In bad shape, it went steadily downhill afterwards and, as a real estate executive was quoted, was "kept alive on a ventilator." In 1996, after a housing boom downtown added thousands of new residents, the city came up with $44 million in incentives to developers to restore retail, plus other developments including a hotel, and $25 million in streetscape improvements to undo the earlier damage. Cars were brought back to the street. As of the year 2000, a resuscitated State Street had 2.5 million square feet of retail space and more planned. It has now become a community center for area residents.[42]

Harlem, New York. With the revival of the fortunes of New York's principal black neighborhood, with restored buildings and new businesses, have come new residents—some of them are white. This gentrification has some worried that there will inevitably be displacement of the poor. Others see diversity and new investment and the chance for an integrated neighborhood. Along 129th Street, once so fearsome that police dispatchers gave warnings before sending officers in, where poverty, drugs and unemployment prevailed, there is now transformation. As of 2001, seventeen buildings in one block alone had been rehabilitated, and they housed a mix of black, white, and Hispanic young professionals.[43]

Northampton, Massachusetts. Described as an amenity-rich town and very comfortable to live in, Northampton is attracting young professionals, baby boomers, and retirees in such numbers that the population remains steady even as the birthrate declines. It has a well-preserved nineteenth-century downtown, the kind of place many are nostalgic for. Restoration began in the 1970s led by creative real estate developers, and eventually Main Street came to house entertainment-oriented businesses with apartments above. Working in its favor is the cluster of colleges and universities in the area, including its own Smith College. A major negative in an otherwise charming setting is a relative lack of jobs.[44]

Cincinnati. At the turn of the century, the Over-the-Rhine neighborhood near the center city was enjoying a renaissance, fueled by the dot-com industry at first but remaining strong after its crash. About 150,000 square feet of office space along the area's Main Street was occupied or under renovation as of 2001. Earlier it had suffered a period of neglect and crime that kept investors out, but intrepid artists began moving in, followed by restaurants, nightspots, and galleries. Internet startups saw a vibrant neighborhood with affordable office space in the second and third stories of historic buildings and began moving in around 1999. Part of the appeal for the young entrepreneurs was being able to network with peers in an urban environment.[45]

Downers Grove, Illinois. This small community outside Chicago had gone the way of most others, looking to "big box" and strip retail on the outskirts of town for commercial development (and tax ratables). Downers Grove thinks that this model has played out, and it has set about reviving its Main Street for specialty retailers. This includes a new streetscape to make it more attractive as the outlying malls run into difficulties, reflecting in part the impact of Internet shopping. There are said to be 200 huge, empty store buildings in this region, surrounded by acres of macadam.[46]

Newark, New Jersey. The Ironbound section of this city, a working-class Portuguese section, remained stable while much of the rest of the city was abandoned after riots in 1967. Now a bustling neighborhood of about 45,000 and newly popular, its restaurants are packed and its real estate prices are soaring, so much so that there is tension between the Portuguese who have been here and the new immigrants from places like Brazil for whom housing is being built at the rate of 300 units a year. Working in its favor is ready access to jobs and public transportation and relative safety. While Newark as a whole has intense poverty, it also is attracting young artists, writers, and musicians said to be drawn to the "realness" of the city, giving it a new bohemian flavor. Contributing is a dramatic drop in crime since 1995, a new New Jersey Performing Arts Center, a new minor league baseball park, and a major art museum.[47]

Indianapolis. A huge downtown mall, integrating historic building facades into its design, is said to have sparked a downtown revival. Before the 800,000-square-foot Circle Center project opened in 1996, business was leaving downtown to decay. Indianapolis Downtown Inc. reports that since the mall's opening, more retail and restaurants have opened, and more conventions are meeting in the city, staying in its expanded number of hotel rooms. The city also has a successful minor league baseball park downtown and a renovated performing arts venue. And crime is down.[48]

Suisin City, California. When the *San Francisco Examiner* in 1989 labeled this city the worst in the Bay Area, city leaders took action. They set up a renewal agency and took aim at the rotting warehouses and oil tanks along the silted-up Suisin Channel that connects it to the Sacramento River. In an approach clearly not for everyone, they proceeded to level 500 structures to make way for new housing and a new marina. Historic buildings on Main Street have been renovated and the harbor dredged. An old drug-infested neighborhood has been replaced with a Victorian-style middle-class project whose former residents were given rent subsidies if they relocated in the region.[49]

Millville, New Jersey. This blue-collar city in southern New Jersey, population 26,000, set about to revive itself by establishing a Glasstown Center Arts District and putting out a call to artists and craftspeople to settle there. Incentives such as low- or no-interest loans are offered, and zoning regulations have been modified to encourage the rehabilitation of

High Street buildings. The artists themselves are given a $5,000 no-interest loan to help with moving and setting up their studios and shops, over which they live. The revival has encouraged new manufacturers and other businesses to locate in the area. Downtown has a monthly third Friday event when the galleries stay open, attracting as many as 800 people.[50]

Detroit. Long the sickest of large American cities, Detroit now shows some positive signs. Crime and unemployment are down as of 2003, property values and housing starts are up, and there's renewed interest in its vacant office buildings. The city's bond rating has gone from junk status in 1993 to A-minus. The city hopes to attract more workers into downtown and is looking to casinos and stadiums to pull people in. There have been a number of earlier suggestions that Detroit was reviving, but a 19 percent drop in serious crime and the health of the auto industry give some hope that this current revival will finally stick.[51]

Jacksonville Beach, Florida. At first leaders here tried the blockbuster approach to downtown revival—namely, looking for a developer to come in and build a mall or something similar to cover a large area of dereliction. Failing that, they went with a Plan B, relying on their own resources, looking to shop owners, residents, and businesses there to invest in improvements. A seven-year, multimillion-dollar redevelopment was nearing completion in 2002, including a Sea Walk Pavilion, a stage for the symphony orchestra. There's a landscaped parking area and seven condominium projects in the works. The boardwalk and municipal pier were to be upgraded as well. Is it working? Store owners complain there's not enough parking.[52]

A sample of other cities in our files includes: Huntsville, Alabama; Troy, New York; Oakland, California; Helena, Montana; Kansas City, Missouri; Asheville, North Carolina; Portland, Maine; Manning, Iowa; Sioux Falls, South Dakota; Newberry, South Carolina; and Jersey City, New Jersey.

DEMOGRAPHICS

The focus of our research is detailed examinations of neighborhoods in center cities where residential growth has taken place. Before going into the case cities we need to look for a moment at the proverbial bigger picture of what's happening to cities, older suburbs, subdivisions, and rural areas.

We have to continually remind ourselves that the United States is a huge place where contradictory trends can and do take place without any difficulty. America's largest cities grew in the 1990s at a higher rate than in the previous decade, with some like our case city of Minneapolis reversing a steady decline for the first time since 1950. Researchers at the Brookings Institution found that seventy-two of the largest cities grew from 1990 to 2000, but only 55 percent of the neighborhoods in those cities expanded.

Alan Berube and Benjamin Forman found that the "outer-ring" neighborhoods of the cities was where growth was concentrated, not in the center. But, in another of those wonderful contradictions that census data tends to yield, two-thirds of all downtown census tracts gained population in the period under study, albeit in small numbers and often offset by overall decline. In looking at 232 downtown census tracts, Berube and Forman found that 65 percent had population increases for an overall growth rate of 13 percent. And sixty-eight of the ninety-eight cities they looked at had growth in the central business district—in cities that were declining overall. This suggests that the idea that central cities are enjoying a revival is not just a case of wishful thinking.

By analyzing neighborhoods, they found an uneven pattern in big city data for the 1990s, where growth in city neighborhoods outstripped the overall population increases, 22 percent to 13 percent. At the same time, they found one third of all center city census tracts lost population. Cities with the largest number of declining neighborhoods that were still growing overall were Columbus, Ohio; El Paso, Texas; Indianapolis, Indiana, and Montgomery, Alabama.[53]

Adding to the health of center cities in the 1990s was that concentrations of poverty were declining. These were districts where over 40 percent of the population was below poverty level, and these areas declined by 24 percent or 2.5 million people in the last decade. In Detroit the decline was 75 percent. Some inner-ring suburbs actually experienced increases in poverty over the last ten years, researcher Paul Jargowsky, University of Texas at Dallas, declared. He attributed the change, reversing decades of increases in the numbers of poor, to the robust economy of the 1990s. Among our case study cities, Houston had a drop in its high-poverty neighborhoods of 48 percent, Memphis 44 percent, Dallas 45 percent, and Minneapolis (plus St. Paul), 41 percent. Jargowsky cautions that while reductions in high-poverty neighborhoods are welcome news, there are warning signs that our society is still vulnerable to increasing concentrations of poverty, pointing to the weaker economy in the years since the census data was compiled.[54]

In the role of naysayer, Joel Kotkin, author of *The New Geography: How the Digital Revolution Is Reshaping the American Landscape,* says reports of an urban renaissance are exaggerated and that the 1990s were a period of urban decline.

Recognizing the reality of the 1990's decline—and the greater forces that are driving people, jobs and wealth away from urban centers—represents a critical first step for cities interested in staging a true long-term recovery. A belief that history is on their side, or even that the tide has turned, is a dangerous illusion that could lead urban officials to adopt strategies that will be ineffective at best and downright damaging at worst.

He sees as the underlying cause that Americans prefer suburbs to cities by the wide margin of nine to one (citing a 1997 FannieMae survey). And, he reports, only one city had its skyline "transformed" in the 1990s, Charlotte, North Carolina.[55]

CREATIVE FORCES

When we were first starting our research, initially visiting Atlanta, New Orleans, and Minneapolis, we were told we should look into Richard Florida's book *The Rise of the Creative Class*. We did and were struck that what we were observing on the ground in these cities and the others was described and analyzed there. We were seeing what Florida was telling us was happening.

In Florida's classification, the Creative Class numbers over 38 million, fully 30 percent of the workforce, second only to service workers. At the top are the super-creatives: the scientists, engineers, university professors, poets, novelists, artists, entertainers, designers and architects, nonfiction writers, editors, cultural figures, researchers, analysts, opinion-makers, and of course software programmers. This group does creative work that produces new forms or designs that are commercially useful. He argues they are the driving force of the economy today.

The other component of the Creative Class are professionals in knowledge-intense industries such as the high-tech sector, financial services, legal services, health care, and business management. The unifying element among all these people is that they are required to think on their own.[56]

It's what Hewlett Packard CEO Carly Florina was talking about when she told a governors' conference: "Keep your tax incentives and highway interchanges, we'll go where the highly skilled people are."[57]

Florida says these skilled people make location and job choices based on their lifestyle preferences, which turn out to differ from the suburban quality of life amenities (adequate parking, closeness to a mall). What they seek is an openness, a tolerance for differences, nightlife, the presence of gays and artists. It's reasons like this that graduates of Carnegie-Mellon where Florida teaches choose Austin, Texas, rather than staying in Pittsburgh. Among the reasons: "Lots of young people, a tremendous lot to do, thriving music scene, ethnic and cultural diversity, fabulous outdoor recreation and great nightlife."[58]

This is fundamentally different from how jobs, employers, and a place to live were selected in the past, where generally the company dictated the place. Today people pick where they want to live and trust they will find jobs, even in the down economy of the early 2000s. We interviewed a thirty-ish couple relocating from Los Angeles to come back East. They did a Web search (naturally) of places between North Carolina and New England. They looked strictly at cities ("the suburbs make me nervous," the woman stated flatly) and chose Providence, Rhode Island, which they love and where they soon found work (she is a Web page designer, he's a freelance writer). Things they looked for: not too big a city but proximity to same, near the ocean, schools for continuing education, an arts scene, good restaurants, affordability, outdoor recreational opportunities, diversity of population, and some charm.

Florida finds that the high-tech, knowledge-based, and creative-content industries tend to concentrate in specific places, which is where the talented want to be. In the knowledge age, he finds, "place and community are more critical factors than ever before." It leads to a clustering of creative human capital in what are turning out to be the winning cities in the competition to recruit the bright talent needed to power today's businesses.

Here are the factors he says play in the location choices of the Creative Class:

Thick Labor Markets. A place with multiple employment opportunities.

Lifestyle. A music scene, an art scene, technology scene, outdoor recreation, and the like. Nightlife is an important part of the mix, the most highly valued venues being for music, neighborhood art galleries, performance spaces, and theaters. These are seen as indicating that a city "gets it."

Social Interaction. This entails having the "third places" in the memorable phrase of Ray Oldenburg in his classic work, *The Great Good Place*. These are the cafes, coffee shops, bars, and bookstores—places midway between home and office where socializing takes place.[59]

Diversity. A diversity of population is a sign that a place is open to outsiders (part of the perceived problem with Pittsburgh, where its elite is seen as a closed society). A visible gay presence is taken as a signal of openness. Diversity also means excitement and energy. A place can be small, but it must be cosmopolitan.

Authenticity. A place with real buildings and a real history is appreciated. Chain stores/nightclubs are off-putting. The role of local music in establishing a community identity for the Creative Class is probably more important than downtown business leaders realize. An authentic place has a distinct "buzz," in this group's terminology.

Identity. Place is increasingly important in establishing a person's identity, in fact more important than place of work, in another of those flip-flops from the way business was conducted in the past. Members of the Creative Class like to get involved in their communities, to preserve and enhance the authenticity of the place, to nurture the arts, and make the city better.

Quality of Place. This is Florida's summary of what's involved in the decision making of the Creative Class: the combination of the built and natural environments, the diversity of the people, and the vibrancy of the street life and cultural scene.

Florida ranks cities according to a Creativity Index. We were more taken with the analysis than the number-crunching. But it produced interesting results. Of our case city regions with over one million people, Houston ranked seventh, Dallas and Minneapolis tied at tenth, Atlanta thirteenth, Portland, Oregon, sixteenth, New Orleans forty-second and Memphis forty-ninth, at the bottom. It seems a little arbitrary to say that Atlanta is a more creative place than Portland, Oregon or New Orleans, but numeric analysis is what academics do in part.[60]

That Memphis realizes it has a "brain drain" problem is very real, we found. Efforts to better market the city to young talent are under way there by the Regional Chamber of Commerce. (See chapter 6).

Robert Cushing, a retired researcher at the University of Texas, analyzed 2000 census data showing that a great migration was taking place. He examined the nation's 318 metropolitan regions to identify the places gaining the most in the 20-to-34-year-old generation, as well as those losing the most. "Many mobile young men and women are heading for places that match their interests, talents and even politics." New York was number one, gaining 452,966 young people from 1990. Atlanta was next, up 54 percent. Dallas was third, up 46 percent. Houston was eighth nationally (ahead of Austin, incidentally) of our case cities. Ranked at the bottom were Dayton and Youngstown, Ohio, Springfield, Massachusetts, and Cleveland, Buffalo, Syracuse, and Pittsburgh.[61]

Others are catching on to Florida's insights into the predilections of bright young professionals. A report in the Lansing, Michigan, *State Journal* confirmed the trend. "Wake up and smell the double mocha, Michigan: Our young people are bored and leaving this state to a future of Geritol," it began. "The post-college and pre-parenthood groups are fleeing in droves to hip, cool cities such as Chicago, Minneapolis, Boston and Austin, Tex." The report quoted John Austin of Public Policy Associates, a research firm, "They don't want the white picket fences of the suburbs. They want street life and culture and entertainment. They want to be constantly stimulated by their neighborhood." He went on to warn that Michigan had to develop lively cities to compete. To do so will require a change in the way chambers of commerce function. "The old chamber of commerce focus on courting businesses that will bring workers must change to courting a new generation of workers, thinkers and creators that will bring businesses." Says Lou Glazer, president of Michigan Future, a think tank, "It's a whole new way of thinking, but the places doing this are the ones that are growing and prospering."[62]

Here's a story suggesting the power inherent in the interest in street life and nighttime activity, from Tampa, Florida. After years of blight and failed urban redevelopment, the Ybor City neighborhood is alive with nightlife, attracting millions of dollars of investment, private and public. A struggling cafe apparently started the rebound by staying open late at night with a local band, after the city loosened restrictions on bars. College students poured in. "Suddenly, brick buildings colonized only by pigeons were converted to bars." It started a night scene that now attracts as many as 20,000 young people on a Friday evening, coming from a 100-mile radius (Orlando to St. Petersburg). Developers have pumped in millions to capitalize on what has been a natural evolvement, building offices as well as bars. There's now a "mix of Mediterranean bistros, Cuban sandwich shops and throbbing dance clubs spiced with cigar stores and tattoo parlors" that has made Ybor City a huge draw. This is in contrast with downtown Tampa, where a $200-million, twenty-year effort to create vitality downtown (with a standard-issue convention center and isolated aquarium) still lacks walkability, among other things. "The ability to promenade ten blocks, to see and be seen—that's Main Street USA," says Del Acosta about the street scene in Ybor City. He administers an architectural review board there.[63]

Cities are awakening to the challenge of attracting bright young talent to the extent that they are helping their colleges and universities market themselves, on the theory that if they come to school in Philadelphia, for example, they'll learn to love the place and stay. A regional coalition (The Knowledge Industry Partnership) put up $8 million to attract and keep students in the greater Philadelphia area. Pittsburgh now calls itself "The College City," and St. Paul likewise is "A City of Colleges and Universities." As the economy is increasingly fueled by ideas and knowledge produced in universities, cities see their importance to the local economy.

The coalition in Philadelphia is marketing itself with brochures about its "student zones," such as the lively and slightly sketchy South Street area of bars and clubs. There's a fall annual downtown music festival planned for students and, to encourage students to stay, the coalition is working with businesses to develop internship programs. Leaders in Philadelphia recognize that competing with areas such as San Francisco is an uphill effort to win the hearts and minds of the next generation that will power the business world.[64]

There are naysayers, naturally. Like Rob Atkinson, director, Technology and New Economy Project, Progressive Policy Institute in Washington, D.C., who says the information technology revolution is contributing to deconcentration (sprawl) and decentralization (moving to smaller places), that it is a greater force for dispersal than toward the center, where people can avoid the "disamenities of core urban areas, such as poor government services, high costs, a decrepit built environment and traffic congestion." This observation came during a panel discussion convened on Nov. 9, 2000, by the Lincoln Institute of Land Policy, Cambridge Massachusetts. He then contradicted himself a bit, saying there are forces for concentration, that people in the knowledge industry need to be in a particular place to be effective. "There also seems to be a rising need for people to value community . . . in a knowledge economy people want to be in a place that frees the mind and to be part of a community. That certainly describes a lot of urban places."

Others in the roundtable agreed more with the latter point. Like Mitchell Moss, director, Taub Urban Research Center, New York University, who said,

There are some cities that are going to get worse, losing people and jobs, while others will improve. Western Massachusetts is a good example. Springfield was once an important business center, but it is being superceded by Northampton, which is a much more culturally innovative and creative area. These two cities are not far apart geographically, but they are miles apart culturally and economically. Why is one thriving and one not? Springfield is an agricultural and industrial capital, while Northampton is a hub of creativity, culture and education.

Added Ceasar McDowell, director, Center for Reflective Community Practice, Massachusetts Institute of Technology, after saying the technological revolution had not helped the most vulnerable of the population, "I do believe the urban environment is the most promising environment in this country. It is what I term 'The New American Heartland.' It is the place where the new ideas that are shaping the United States emerge. It is the place where culture, race and identity are being redefined for the country. It is the spatial and cultural form that has the most promise for this nation."[65]

Arguing to the contrary again is Joel Kotkin, senior fellow at the Davenport Institute for Public Policy at Pepperdine University, who thinks Florida's analysis is a product of the 1990s bubble economy and represents liberal wishful thinking. Kotkin says it's a stretch to say there's a connection between bohemians and economic development, or that Silicon Valley developed because of gay people. His solution to cities seeking centers of the New Economy? Constructing lofts and apartments is a good place to start, he says.[66]

Kotkin agrees with Florida that the new information industry makes place more important than ever. "Today, high-technology and other information-age firms must go where the talented engineers, designers, scientists, and other creative workers are, and increasingly that means to places offering a quality of life this 'ascendant new middle class' finds attractive," according to a review of Kotkin's book that summarizes his argument, in what seems a partial endorsement of Florida's analysis. He finds, however, that technology jobs are clustered in suburban "Nerdistans" separate from cities, places like Irvine, California, as distinct from San Francisco, say, or Austin.[67] Florida counters that this model is out-of-date.

Another southern California researcher has a different tack. Ross DuVal, director of regional studies at the Milken Institute in Santa Monica, advises communities there to: "Stop sprawling into the suburban fringe and work on building hip downtown centers with dense housing mixed alongside cafes, shops and theaters."[68]

Putting the importance of creativity in a historical context is Peter Hall, professor of planning at University College, London, and author of *Cities in Civilization*. In looking back as many as five thousand years and asking why certain cities prospered and some have been able to reinvent themselves, while others had a period of prosperity but have fallen back, Hall attributes it to creativity. Artistic and intellectual genius in the first instance, creativity in technological and then in commercial organizations, all distinctly urban, from Manchester to Silicon Valley. What's happened now is the convergence of artistic and technological creativity; interestingly he cites Memphis and the birth of rock and roll as an example.

Cities around the world, Hall argues, now have to compete with each other over quality of urban life.

Not for nothing have Singapore and Hong Kong invested heavily in new rapid transit systems, new residential areas, and extensive park and waterfront areas. But it is not just a matter of a clean and well-planned modern environment, for this could produce a sterile city. Significantly, Asian and Latin American cities are increasingly protecting and restoring their historic urban patrimony; conservation is high on the agenda, in a way that would have been unthinkable twenty years ago.

Of course, urban quality does not guarantee creative genius. Nobel Prizes can and do come out of slum laboratories, and great undiscovered artists will always languish in garrets. But increasingly, universities build laboratories to retain and attract international star scientists, while the garrets of the starving artists soon become immensely fashionable and expensive. Creativity is no longer an incidental miracle that happens occasionally in exceptionally favored cities; in a globalized economy where no place can rest on its laurels for long, it is now a central part of the business of being a successful city. And this is a principle no city can safely ignore.[69]

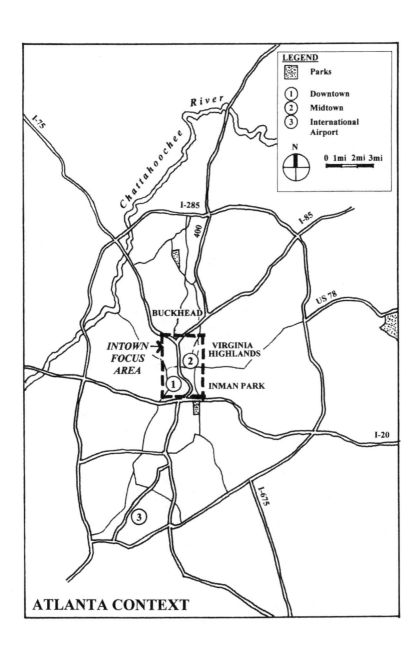

LEGEND

Parks

① Downtown

② Midtown

③ International Airport

N

0 1mi 2mi 3mi

River

Chattahoochee

I-75

I-285

400

I-85

US 78

BUCKHEAD

INTOWN FOCUS AREA

②

VIRGINIA HIGHLANDS

①

INMAN PARK

I-20

I-675

③

ATLANTA CONTEXT

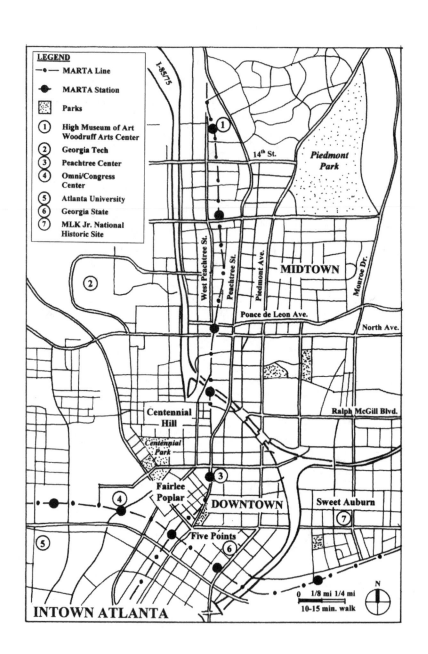

I-85/75

14th St.

Piedmont Park

West Peachtree St.

Peachtree St.

Piedmont Ave.

MIDTOWN

Monroe Dr.

Ponce de Leon Ave.

North Ave.

Centennial Hill

Ralph McGill Blvd.

Centennial Park

Fairlee Poplar

③

DOWNTOWN

Sweet Auburn

④

⑤

Five Points

⑥

0   1/8 mi 1/4 mi
10-15 min. walk

N

INTOWN ATLANTA

Atlanta

> In the early 1980's the Midtown area . . . looked like a bombed out war zone with boarded up buildings and graffiti-sprayed walls. Today it is a bustling business and residential district with its own distinctive skyline.
>
> —*Don O'Briant*, Atlanta

ATLANTA'S MIDTOWN

Dubbed "The Sprawl Capital of the World" by *The Wall Street Journal* in late 1997, metropolitan Atlanta covers a vast area containing over four million people, only one tenth of whom live in the city itself.

The center city is distinguished by tall, glitzy skyscrapers marching down the central spine of Peachtree Street, with clusters in Buckhead, Midtown, and Downtown. Atlanta has a well-deserved reputation as being a car-oriented, pedestrian-unfriendly place, with a sterile center core. "The utter failure to create any meaningful pedestrian environment (that is, a rewarding public realm) defines the heart of Atlanta today," writes James Howard Kunstler in *The City in Mind*.[1]

Our focus will be on a new, more urban style of Atlanta that is beginning to emerge. Scratch the surface of the city's Midtown section, between the Arts District with the High Museum and other major cultural institutions to the north, to the restored Fox Theater near the southern boundary, and you have an area that has a chance to become a great urban neighborhood in the center of Atlanta's sprawl. But it will be an Atlanta-style urban center.

It will never be as dense or intense as, say, Chicago's Michigan Avenue corridor or Boston's Newberry Street. Rather, Midtown will be its own distinctive, jumbled self, with traditional urban values gradually being instilled in a suburban-feeling place—if all goes well.

Midtown comprises several different sections offering great contrast in character and style. Close by gracious Piedmont Park on the eastern boundary is a distinctly old-fashioned residential area with tree-lined streets, big old homes, garden apartments, and townhouses. In contrast are pockets of high-rise office towers with some mixed-use and retail, hotels and apartments, mostly along Peachtree Street, which runs north-south through the middle of the district. Many of the towers are solitary, insulated, inwardly oriented and boring to the pedestrian. Also in the Midtown central spine are the Federal Reserve and Bell South office campuses, bringing major employment to Midtown but architecturally more imposing than welcoming.

On the west is a section with loft and condo buildings, both conversions and new construction, along with emerging cafes, bars, restaurants, and shops, most of which are street-oriented and pedestrian friendly. Here one gets a hint at what more of Midtown can look like in the future as the vacant parking lots and old buildings are reclaimed. On the westernmost edge, abutting an interstate highway, is an old industrial area, gradually being converted. Scattered throughout are some nightclubs and sandwich joints, plus incongruous billboards and signage.

To some this mix spells an interesting, quirky diversity. Others call it disjointed. A *New York Times* writer found Peachtree Street a "crazy salad of architectural styles as dizzying as any Surrealist construction."[2]

Powering the urban push in Midtown as of early 2003 was an accelerating addition of new residents, buyers as well as renters. The three 2000 census tracts at the core of Midtown show 10,661 residents, up 2,706 from 1990 or 39 percent. Perhaps better capturing the spurt in the late 1990s is this statistic: In a plan developed in 1997 by the Midtown Alliance, a business-oriented organization, a goal was established to add 4,000 residential units by the year 2017. As of 2002, there were 4,595 new units built, another 1,021 in the planning stages, and more projected. Midtown, it should be noted, has a racial balance that now is 77 percent white, 13 percent black and 10 percent other, a shift from 1990 when 66 percent were white—in a city that is 61 percent black.

We'll return to numbers later, but first we want to round out the picture of the forces at work that could propel Midtown into the fore as a true urban neighborhood.

Midtown Forces

We start with the Midtown Alliance organization. Its leadership is decidedly business establishment. The chairman is Shelton Stanfill, president of the Woodruff Arts Center. He succeeded Jack Guynn, president of the

Federal Reserve Bank of Atlanta, which has a new Midtown headquarters. There is a seventy-five-person board and an executive committee of fifteen to eighteen. Membership starts at $250; large companies pay $10,000. The annual budget is over $3 million.

The Alliance has grown along with the area, starting from a staff of three in 1996, growing to thirteen in 2003. This coincides with the growth spurt in the neighborhood. The Alliance dates back to 1981 when downtown business leaders set up a group to help combat the area's seediness. In the 1970s Midtown was Atlanta's red light district. When the city did crack down on the sex business in Midtown and closed most adult businesses, it left the place largely deserted, recalls Alliance President Susan Mendheim.[3] After a speculative burst in the early to mid-1980s, producing high-rise towers on the area's northern stretches (also at North Avenue), and leveling numerous structures, leaving many lots still vacant, Midtown went on hold.

With an economic resurgence beginning in the mid-1990s, the leadership of the Alliance realized that they needed a plan and that they had to articulate what they did—and did not—want to see happen. A huge planning outreach followed, involving as many as 2,000 people over time, including meeting one-on-one in homes, and at sixty-seven public presentations. The product was called "Blueprint Midtown" and embodied many sensible urban planning principles, such as: Mid-rise was the desired height of buildings, after the unfortunate high-rise experience. A "pedestrian-scale environment" was said to be key and in fact underscores much of what is sought. Sidewalks were to be wider, trees planted along them, and streets and highways tamed. Offices concentrated to the north, retail foreseen to the south. More residential units contemplated.

After this effort, a zoning ordinance embodying the principles was hammered out and passed at the last minute just before a City Council change in November 2001. It took effect on January 1, 2002, and basically aims to recast the previous suburban-style zoning into a more urban expression. Instead of viewing Midtown as a pathway through which cars pour in and out of the suburbs growing to the north, Midtown wants to to slow the traffic and assert itself as a destination.

Together with its partner, the Midtown Improvement District (MID), the Alliance has raised funds to undertake street improvements that will enhance the pedestrian experience. The business community has raised a total of $8.1 million for this effort to date. The target completion date is 2005, when all major corridors are to have new sidewalks, landscaping, uniform lighting, and street furniture to unify the disparate sections.

Two other initiatives of MID stand out. One is "Midtown Blue," an armed private police force on duty twenty-four hours a day since the fall of 2000. It is staffed by off-duty Atlanta police who have full arrest powers. The budget is $1.2 million a year. (There is also a Midtown-Ponce

Security Alliance supported by a neighbors' association which aims to help security in the area and "clean up Ponce de Leon Ave.")[4]

The second initiative is Midtown Green, a cleanup and outdoor maintenance effort run by two full-time staff people and one part-time. Uniformed crews collect trash, attend to graffiti, sweep up, and try to get the City of Atlanta to attend to broken sidewalks or potholes. The annual budget is $125,000.

The true significance of the Alliance and its partner MID is that the business leadership sees the need to establish an attractive and hip urban neighborhood. Why? To recruit the young talent needed in their businesses, the talent that will help propel them forward in today's rapidly changing business climate, where knowledge and speed are key ingredients. The suburbs hold no interest for many of this group, unless and until children come and even then, not necessarily. The physical Midtown improvements, then, are as much business self-interest as conversion by the leaders to the tenets of quality urban design. Businesses in cities like Atlanta realize that to compete for young talent with attractive destinations such as San Francisco, Seattle, and Boston, they have to provide the urbanity this population looks for. This competitiveness will turn out to be a driving factor in all of our case cities.

Arts District

Another major force at work in Midtown is the Woodruff Arts Center, home to the Atlanta Symphony, High Museum of Art, Atlanta College of Art, and the Alliance Theater, clustered in a campus-like setting on Peachtree. This major cultural presence in all of Atlanta is growing significantly. Under construction in early 2003 was the first of four projected new buildings, designed by Italian architect Renzo Piano. First in place is to be a new dormitory for the Atlanta School of the Arts, plus a sculpture studio. Next are to come an addition to the High Museum that more than doubles its exhibit space, another building housing two floors of gallery space, an office structure plus parking, a central piazza, and a newly designed MARTA subway station ("Arts District" stop).

To this may be added a new symphony hall to be designed by Santiago Calatrava of Spain. The project involves the development firm, Hines Interests LLP, that would buy six acres from the Woodruff Center and then donate three back for the new music facility, while erecting a twenty-story-plus tower on the other acres, to be called Symphony Center. The present symphony space, in a large, box-like structure, would house a "lyric hall" with ballet, jazz, and musical theater.

In addition, the area contains a number of other cultural and artistic venues. The Museum of Contemporary Art Georgia is two blocks north of the Woodruff campus, opening in February 2002 with the 250-work collection of David Garden, a real estate developer. Nearby is the Center for Puppetry Arts Museum in an old school, the Margaret Mitchell House and "Gone With the Wind" Movie Museum, the William Brennan Jewish Heritage Museum, and 14th Street Playhouse. In all, the Midtown Alliance tallies thirteen new cultural attractions coming to Midtown since 1997. Even without the Hines project, the expanded upper Midtown area is the heart of Atlanta's cultural world.

A major downtown law firm announced in early 2003 that it contemplated moving into the prospective new Hines building.[5] King & Spalding has four hundred lawyers, and its move to Midtown would continue a pattern of businesses leaving downtown locations for Midtown. Last year AGL Resources did the same. The first to do so was C&S Bank ten years ago, to North Avenue at Peachtree to what is now called Bank of America Plaza, Midtown's first high-rise.

An idea exciting to us that the Alliance is proposing is to establish an art walk. This would tie together a number of the facilities mentioned above with galleries, studios, and a cluster of restaurants and bars in a funky nearby neighborhood called the Crescent District. If promoted with outdoor artists' displays on weekends, for instance, such a walk would draw people to Midtown's cultural venues and contribute to the street life that is being sought.

Not proximate to the Woodruff campus, but a major performance venue, is the Fox Theater on Peachtree near Midtown's southern boundary, mercifully saved from the wrecker's ball and which now features plays, musical performances, and dance.

There are two additional features of the Midtown renaissance deserving mention as they are part of the area's attractiveness—to young people especially.

Nearly everyone we interviewed mentioned Piedmont Park, Atlanta's largest at 189 acres. This green open space forms the eastern boundary of Midtown, north of 10th Street. Apparently it had a period of unsavoriness that is now gone or greatly diminished, so that it is presently a much used and cherished public space. The Piedmont Park Conservancy is refurbishing it in a $25 million effort. New trees, shrubs, and lawns are added as each section is restored. New lighting, benches, and fountains are also being installed. Magnolia Hall was recently restored and is a special events venue. A former American Legion building will become a community center, and Lake Clara Meer will be restored to health. The park is host to major civic events, including a major Gay Pride festival of three days, to which businesses and politicians alike pay attention, and a major Dogwood Festival, among others.

A second factor of keen interest to the young families in Midtown are the public schools that serve it. They are Morningside Elementary, S.M. Inman Middle School, and Grady High School. The latter two are the highest rated among their counterpart institutions in the city, and by wide margins. Morningside is the third-ranked elementary school, behind by small margins in test scores among third and fifth graders. The cluster of the three is the city's best.[6]

One mother we talked with, an interior designer whose 13-year-old attends Inman, moved to Midtown recently from a university town. There, she related, at a school twice the size of Inman, perhaps five parents would show up for a PTA meeting. At Inman she was astounded to see three hundred. Absent any galvanizing event (she was aware of none), this speaks to the parents' commitment, which no doubt translates into support for a good faculty, provision of extras to the school, donations of equipment, and other augmentations that help place the school at the top. The racial breakdown at the school was roughly 50-50 black and white as of 2002. To attract and keep families with children intown, the availability of good schools, whether public or private, is perhaps the key.

Who is attracted to live in Midtown? The census tells the story. In the three tracts at the core of the area, the age profile is striking: The largest age group is from 25 to 34, not quite double the size of the next largest age cluster, the 35-to-44-year-olds. Fully two-thirds of the population is under 39. In the dominant age group, men number 2,770, women 1,733. The census further tells us that in the center of Midtown, the empty nesters have yet to arrive in large numbers. The older group that is there includes long-standing residents from earlier days.

During our site visit in early 2003, a phenomenon in Midtown residential sales was occurring. In the face of a slumping residential market, as Atlanta's overall economy suffered—where a glut of 2,000 condominium units were on the Midtown market requiring, a real estate agent told us, from 1 1/2 to 3 years to find buyers—one new building was selling out. The sleek Metropolis, a twenty-story steel and glass twin-tower complex, takes up an entire block. Situated at Eighth Street and Peachtree, close to a MARTA stop, it was perfectly designed for its market. Floor-to-ceiling windows with ten-foot ceilings offer stunning panoramic views of the city skyline, especially at night. Units as small as studios with 700 square feet at prices around $165,000, or one-bedroom units of 919 square feet, $212,000, plus larger offerings, clearly suited a largely single, young, and often gay clientele. The first tower sold 212 of 249 units in less than a year, while the south tower had seventy-seven pledge documents in nine days. The south tower was originally to be rental apartments, but is now going condominium as well, even though this form of real estate is relatively new to Atlanta. One real estate broker who had high praise for the developers here said he toured the building and was struck by how small the units were. "Where do you put the bed?" he asked.

Listen to the promotion of the Metropolis:

But of course the world outside your door is pretty cool too, and you haven't even made it out of the building . . . Club M on Seven. Lux and low-key, it's your place to relax and recover your groove . . . Extremely hip shopping and dining is only an elevator ride away. Just press G—very cool stuff awaits you on the ground floor.

Clearly not the older, empty-nester market here. In fact, an agent showing us sample units told how his grandmother looked at the concrete walls, open ductwork and other "loft"-style features and asked when they were going to finish the building!

Traditional Neighborhood

A few blocks from the Metropolis is another Midtown story, of the traditional residential neighborhood that spreads eastward from Piedmont Avenue (which runs parallel to the Peachtree central artery). The first homes were built in the 1890s, rambling, spacious, but relatively close together (compared with, say, Inman Park, Atlanta's first suburb, another thriving intown neighborhood). Development at the turn of the century took place along the next street, Myrtle, the homes not quite as large. And then Penn Avenue and finally, in the 1930s, small bungalows were built five or so blocks away.

This roughly ten-block-by-ten-block neighborhood, featuring a heavy tree cover, is the core of the Midtown Neighbors' Association, a volunteer civic group with approximately two hundred members working to protect itself from inappropriate development within and keeping a watchful eye on nearby projects, such as restaurants and clubs. The group is wary of spillover parking, and is still experiencing the impacts from a long-standing twenty-four-hour nightclub in its midst, a holdover from the area's wilder days.

The census profile of this neighborhood shows that it is the slowest growing of Midtown's three subareas, up 15 percent between 1990 and 2000 while the area between 10th and 14th was up by 80 percent. Some two hundred of the 3,897 residents are older people who hung in during the area's rough days in the 1970s, when novelist Fred Willard described it as a haven for the homeless, the lawless, and the restless.[7] While drug dealing, crime, and prostitution (especially male) have diminished, they have not been eliminated from Midtown.

The hippie period had people piling into the rooming houses carved out of the large homes to satisfy post–World War II housing needs. Some remain. Gays moved in gradually. We talked with one couple who bought their house in 1993 when the area was, in their word, "dismal." The front yard in the morning would have needles, condoms, and other detritus from the evening, near as they are to a commercial corner that once featured a very active club scene. The turnaround in the immediate neighborhood began in 1993 when a gay bookstore, Outwrite, at 10th Street and Piedmont, replaced a late-night club. Now this intersection is a small commercial district with a grocery store and a number of lively, moderate-priced cafes and restaurants in addition to the bookstore/cafe.

We interviewed another resident, a young mother of two small children, who plans to stay and send her children to the public schools. Further, she advised, there are nine kids on her small block, indicative of another segment of Midtown's population. A professional working in Midtown, she and her husband moved here in 1995. She finds the current house pricing "astronomical" and related that her real estate taxes doubled in one year, as a strapped City of Atlanta leans on the property tax. She grew up in the suburbs, her family is there, but she and her husband were attracted to Intown Living for its convenience and liveliness.

Steve Brinkley, former president of the Neighbors' Association from 1992 to 1997, says,

One big difference in Midtown is that there are a lot more children. It's a sign that we've been able to overcome some of the problems down on Ponce (Ponce de Leon Avenue has an unsavory reputation), and at the park (Piedmont). Now, it's not necessarily the place to move out of when you have a child, but a place to stay because of the culture and the diversity. It (departures) still happens, but not to the degree it once did.[8]

The rooming houses carved from the old homes in this neighborhood are gradually disappearing. The couple we talked to expressed some regret over this trend, feeling that the diversity of the area is lessening, that fewer blue collar workers, fewer artists, and for that matter, fewer gays are living there. Within five blocks of a rooming house where an apartment rents for $600 a month, a home sold for $945,000, indicative of the trend here.

Westside Area

On the western side, along West Peachtree and Spring Streets (also running parallel to the Peachtree central avenue), something else is happening to add to the crazy quilt that is today's Midtown. First, the Biltmore Hotel, a charming old brick hulk opened in 1924, was restored in 1999 after sitting vacant for years, casting a large shadow. A brave developer converted the main building to offices, and put an apartment wing up for sale for residences. It was an instant sellout.

This turnaround helped set the stage for the addition of new housing. A Realtor we talked with lives in one of the new projects, Midcity Lofts. She purchased one of the two-story live/work units and spoke of marketing the building armed only with project drawings while vagrants lurked in the next-door vacant lots. Midcity Lofts emulates an industrial feel, with concrete columns punctuating the block-long hallways. Big glass windows look out on the streets. The roof has a pool, a stepped-down seating/viewing area, and a cozy clubhouse and fitness center, all with fabulous views of the city.

A wine bar is moving into one of the live/work spaces, soon to join nearby Chez Ami with its welcoming sidewalk cafe and Halo, said to be the hippest bar in Atlanta—so hot there is no sign on the door. The Realtor reports that the people buying in the building are in their late twenties to early forties and that an increasingly straight male population is evident. Prices here, too, are skyrocketing. Four years ago she took the plunge on the then-unbuilt project for $305,000. Now it might fetch $500,000.

Next door is one of the engines of Midtown's prospective ascendancy as a great Atlanta urban neighborhood. Well on their way toward completion in early 2003 were two related projects. One, being built by Georgia Tech University, is a 600,000-square-foot, multiple-building undertaking. It is labeled Technology Square, and occupies eight acres across from the Biltmore that had been vacant for years. It will house the school's DuPree College of Management, a Global Learning Center, an Economic Development Institute, and the Center for Quality Growth and Regional Development. A 250-room hotel/conference center is to be included. The Fifth Street Project, as it is also called, will include the university bookstore, joined by a chain coffee shop.

Next door is a complementary, privately financed project called Centergy, with another 625,000 square feet of space. Here will be offices for high-tech firms and others, plus residential and retail spaces. Two more phases are planned, doubling the size. Included is a hotel component, and envisioned down the road are additional residential units (this is the developer of the Midcity Lofts described previously). Georgia Tech's Advanced Technology Development Center, an incubator for high-tech firms, is to lease space in Centergy. The Yamacraw Design Center will also locate in a Centergy building being constructed.

The significance of such a high-technology center here, beyond the students, researchers, visitors, and faculty, is that Georgia Tech will become a major presence in Midtown, whereas before it was totally isolated across a major interstate expressway. A bridge at Fifth Street existed, but with vacant lots and a boarded-up Biltmore, not much interaction occurred.

Wayne Clough, president of Georgia Tech, relates that when he arrived in 1994, advisors told him to erect a wall around the campus to protect it from the surrounding neighborhoods and their crime. Clough knew this wasn't the answer, and he commissioned a master plan exercise modeled on Stanford and the University of Washington, both centers of thriving communities.[9] The result included working with the neighboring communities as well as taking the big leap over Interstate 75/85, the infamous "Downtown Connector." As part of the plan, the Fifth Street Bridge will be enhanced to handle the projected new traffic. A shuttle service is to be offered.

Rising from abandonment on the central western portion of Midtown, then, is a significant, dynamic new presence. When the market returns it would seem that there is every prospect that additional housing units will be constructed in some of the still-vacant lots that populate this area. This future housing would no doubt be attractive to the Georgia Tech and technology/research community.

BIGGER PICTURE

The Midtown Alliance in its overall planning ranges beyond its core area past the Georgia Tech campus to Howell Mill Road. Included here are industrial areas that seem far removed from Midtown proper. The population here reflects the student body of Georgia Tech; fully 74 percent are students, according to a graduate student analysis.[10]

To give an idea of what's entailed in a larger Midtown, the Alliance has prepared population estimates. Within a one-mile radius from 10th Street and Peachtree are said to be 26,849 residents (2000 census), with an average income of $56,836 (source: Georgia Power/National Decision Systems April 2001) and average household property value of $163,922. Nearly half are college graduates. The daytime workforce is nearly 60,000.

But this larger view gives a better sense of the significance of Midtown— or lack of it, if you will—in the larger context of the city. Atlanta as a whole has 416,474 people, up 5.7 percent from 1990 to 2000 for its first growth in decades.

Midtown's core 10,600 people—our preferred definition and number for the area—do not loom large numerically. Yet our sense is that numbers belie the potential impact here. Many Midtown residents are leaders in the professions, business, the arts, the design world, and other creative endeavors, and soon in technology research. If in fact the neighborhood burgeons as we sense it might, more and more Atlantans will discover it, come to its multiple attractions, and begin to appreciate this emerging neighborhood and perhaps be tempted to move intown.

Problem Areas

With all the positive forces for change, there are, however, problematic areas for us in assessing how well Midtown will continue to attract bright new residents. Assuming that important factors like crime, noise and general messiness remain under control, one worrisome note is the presence of huge office towers. A spurt of development occurred in the 1990s, and coming as it did with the economic downturn, it has produced a glut of office space. Atlanta as a whole experienced an abandonment of

4.5 million square feet worth of office tenants, a commercial real estate broker told us.

In 2001, three projects were built in Midtown with a total of 1.5 million square feet of office space. Atlantic Center Plaza opened in the fall at 14th between Spring and West Peachtree, twenty-two stories with half a million square feet of space. A law firm occupies nearly half, and the building was said to be 75 percent leased as of fall 2002. Millennium in Midtown at 10th and West Peachtree opened in December 2001 and is described as a mixed-use building with retail, a market, fitness center, and a fourteen-story office structure, a total of 410,000 square feet. The Proscenium at 14th and Peachtree opened in spring of the same year, is twenty-four stories and contains 527,000 square feet. As of fall 2002, nearly three-quarters leased.

Aside from vacancy, projects like this are a mixed blessing for a residential Midtown. On the one hand, there's a large population five days a week that at midday might visit local shops and restaurants. Absent ground-floor retail, restaurants, or any other off-hour attractions, which most of them lack, they are dead at night and on weekends. Typical: A restaurant in one office tower has to announce its presence with a sandwich board on the sidewalk because it is otherwise tucked invisibly inside. Lunch only.

The office tower design approach here has traditionally favored the stand-alone, isolated presence, frequently back from the street. The Midtown Alliance is working to reform this style, but it is of course too late with the buildings already in place. It will have its work cut out to bring about reform here. Only in 2002 did they achieve zoning to require buildings to be built to the sidewalk and for first-floor retail to be encouraged—standard urban design guidelines that characterize many other downtowns.

One example of the problem: A chain supermarket was recently built just outside the southern edge of Midtown, and an effort was made to get the store to build to the sidewalk. This is not how it is done in the suburbs, where the parking is in front. The developer, unused to urban retail, was no doubt afraid that if the motorists didn't see the parking, they wouldn't necessarily know it was in the back.

Offsetting this, on Peachtree a national chain pharmacy has been successfully tamed, its signs made modest, parking put beneath it, and a friendly face on the street. No small achievement as chain drugstores are notorious for imposing lackluster, formulaic designs no matter the context; so much so that the National Trust for Historic Preservation has made them the object of a national campaign.

Retail Scene

While residential growth outstripped the projections of 1997 as we have seen, retail is behind. The "Blueprint Midtown" goal was to add

2.4 million square feet of retail in twenty years. In the first five years, only 300,000 square feet were added, a pace far short of the goal.

In early 2003 there were indications that new shops and restaurants might be about to take off. In fact, we heard one projection that by fall of 2003, 190,000 square feet of retail would be committed, meaning that the marketplace had caught on to the potential of Midtown and that enough developers/investors were seeing the potential. We heard that this was the only growth sector in real estate in 2003 because residential and commercial sectors were overbuilt.

To succeed, the suburban development community will have to learn new ways. As our commercial broker told us, Atlanta developers "don't know urban." He was speaking particularly of the retail market, but it obviously has broader application. Most developers in Atlanta have made their millions in the suburbs. This was confirmed by Bob Silverman, who was planning a mixed-use project at Spring and 17th Street (near the High Museum): "No one who's from here gets it; we don't understand retail on the street. We understand strip centers. We understand big box, but we don't get street-level retail."[11]

Leading the way in bucking the tide are three businessmen who have prospered in Buckhead and who apparently do get it. (Buckhead is the wealthy area to the north with two major, upscale shopping malls. Buckhead is ranked in one accounting as the twenty-sixth wealthiest neighborhood in the United States, and Midtown is ranked twenty-eighth.)[12] Charlie Loudermilk, his son Robin, and their partner George Rohig purchased key intersections along Peachtree between 10th and Fifth, the projected retail core of Midtown, and had already installed high-end, designer furnishing stores in the Fifth/Peachtree area. Five pioneering stores were here in 2003. The area has already acquired a name, Midtown Design District.

The president of Central Atlanta Progress, the downtown business group, concedes that his area has long lost the battle over retail space. "The planned Midtown retail will be a frontal assault on Buckhead," says Rick Reinhard. "It will be a battle for the middle class and relatively affluent shoppers."[13]

Another sign of what might come: A women's fashion store, FrenchKiss, opened in 2003. The manager was quoted as saying she and her partner considered Buckhead, the traditional high-end retail stronghold, before settling on Midtown. "Buckhead's too congested and stuffy," says Bridget Cunningham. "Midtown is growing, and we want to grow with it."[14] A stylish men's store has also opened, as has a sleek restaurant/wine bar and wine and cheese shop and a fashion boutique for men and women featuring a water bar of twenty beverages plus monthly events. Another sure sign of the times: The upscale grocery Whole Foods opened a branch on Ponce de Leon Avenue on March 10, 2003. These high-end stores seek trendy neighborhoods like the Pearl District in Portland, Oregon. Amid all the trendiness, one person we interviewed wished aloud for a place where he could buy a regular pair of jeans. Rumored to be interested in Midtown: a Target store to be located on the western side in a projected high-rise.

More restaurants are beginning to settle into Midtown as well, after a number of casualties that apparently were too expensive and pretentious. The market preference is for casual, moderately priced places with good, innovative cooking—real neighborhood places. The Midtown Alliance reports there are over sixty restaurants in the area, defined as serving dinner. One in the planning stages that will occupy a historic firehouse built in 1907 just off Peachtree gives a flavor of the scene. Its projected cuisine is "American brasserie-style, live-fire foods" from a grille, oven, and rotisserie, with an emphasis on seafood. Casual lunch spots are opening also.

In June 2003 the Midtown Alliance scheduled meetings about "Blueprint Midtown II," an update of its master plan. After the meetings, online voting was sought between June 1 and 20, with retail the first-listed area of emphasis. The questions being asked were whether Midtown needed more shops and if yes, what kind? Green space and transit were the other areas of inquiry, in the latter case, the idea of a trolley along Peachtree being advanced by some. Participants were shown a series of images and asked to rank them; the preferences were to be put together in an updated plan document.[15]

Traffic Issues

The biggest negative in Midtown are the main arterial highways that allow traffic to roar through. This is particularly true for Spring Street and West Peachtree on the west side, a one-way pair with multiple lanes running north-south. Walking along either is unpleasant, and they are no fun to cross. Peachtree is such a main artery that it has, unbelievably, interstate-standard billboards along it. The new Midtown zoning bars further such intrusions.

Given, then, the presence of high-speed roadways especially on the west, inimical to pedestrian use, plus the pedestrian-unfriendly office towers of the 1980s and 1990s, Midtown has two strikes against it. The good news is that the Midtown Alliance knows it full well, and hence the streetscape improvement program, with a total budget of $42 million covering 25 miles of streets eventually, designed to make the pedestrian more comfortable.

A first effort by the Midtown Alliance to see if Spring and West Peachtree could be returned to two-way traffic, which is more comfortable for pedestrians, struck out. The engineering firm it hired to look at the issue concluded that the large-scale infrastructure investment required was too much, and that losing left-turn lanes would "significantly reduce traffic flow"—which is exactly what the Alliance might want. The root trouble here is that these are state highway department arteries. If there is an institution in this country more damaging to urban street life than state highway departments, we have not found it.

Likewise, the Alliance looked into whether the one-way pair on the east of Juniper and Piedmont could be returned to two-way traffic. These streets run through significant residential areas that would benefit from traffic slowing. Another engineering firm was used, looking into whether there could be wider sidewalks and parallel parking. The study concluded that, "to maintain an acceptable level of service" if the streets were made two-way, parallel parking would have to be removed. The adjoining neighbors objected, and this idea, too, is dead for the time being. You have to ask who the acceptable level of service is for, the neighborhoods or the through traffic?

Midtown has other traffic problems. One is busy 14th Street with heavy rush-hour congestion, we were told. A new bridge at 17th Street is coming into Midtown to serve a huge new development west of the interstate, Atlantic Station (see later discussion). The Alliance has been working to modify the design, cut some lanes, and to have a lane for a jitney-type service, trying to make it pedestrian-friendly—a tough assignment given the enormous distance it takes to cross the interstate.

To our minds, the Alliance and its allies must succeed in reducing traffic lanes and reversing its one-way pairs to fully benefit from the presence of an expanding residential population that would appear to be ready to support area shops, cafes, restaurants, and clubs—the core of what could be a vital urban neighborhood. Absent this, it will likely fall short of the desired ambiance.

We chose Midtown as our case example in Atlanta because it seemed to have come the furthest and it seemed to be dynamic and diverse. But it is not the only Intown Living example in Atlanta. (There's even a free "Atlanta Intown" newspaper.)

OTHER AREAS

At least four other areas near the center of Atlanta are currently experiencing a residential resurgence, including instances of gentrification. We looked most closely at downtown and will discuss it in a little detail, but other areas to note in passing include historic Inman Park, two miles or so from the city center, with its edgy commercial neighborhood, Little Five Points; Virginia Highland, with a more middle-class, middle-income, and comfortable commercial core surrounded by a large residential area (that adjoins Midtown); Grant Park, south of the rail lines and Interstate 20 that separate north, white Atlanta from south, black Atlanta, where housing prices are skyrocketing and rehabilitation abounds; and the newest hip area, East Atlanta, where a traditional blue-collar neighborhood that has attracted artists appeared to be in for significant changes.

The areas are by no means alike, but they have in common big and/or growing middle-class populations in what can be fairly called intown neighborhoods. *Atlanta* magazine, for instance, includes the restaurants of Inman Park, Virginia Highlands, and East Atlanta in its "Intown" grouping.[16]

The growing market for Intown Living in Atlanta is epitomized in a mixed-use development taking place on the edge of Inman Park. In a plan worked out with the neighborhood association, a developer will convert a former Mead Corporation plant on twenty-one acres to 520 apartments and nineteen single-family homes plus retail and restaurants, some of which was taking place in early 2003. The plant, which produced notebooks and envelopes, shut down in fall 2001. The Mead Corporation worked with the neighborhood in selecting the developer, Wood Partners, from the two dozen offers it received. The concern in Inman Park was that an outsized project would ignore its historic, Victorian character. The association supports the Wood plan.[17]

Downtown itself lies immediately to the south of Midtown. There is one area, in fact, that is in both, the Overlap District, which features institutional buildings. The full definition of downtown has North Avenue on the north, Northside Drive on the west, Interstate 20 on the south, and Boulevard on the east. This is an expansive, not to say misleading view, leaping as it does over Interstate 75/85 as it cuts a swath through the core of the city, to the east into the historic black neighborhood of Sweet Auburn where Dr. Martin Luther King Jr.'s church and that of Walter Abernathy exist. Likewise, the western boundary encompasses the Georgia Dome and the huge Georgia World Congress Center, the convention center.

With Peachtree Street as its spine, what's at the center of downtown are primarily office structures, some oriented to the state capitol here, others to the major corporate interests that make Atlanta home, such as Coca-Cola, CNN, Delta Airlines, Home Depot, and SunTrust Bank, plus the major sports venues, Phillips Arena and Turner Stadium.

Three forces are at work on the residential aspect of downtown. One is the popularity of lofts, as we found everywhere. While in Midtown they are being built new, in downtown there are warehouses being converted into more traditional loft spaces. Central Atlanta Progress, the downtown business group, reports that its annual loft tours attract several thousand people who pay $20 each. (The Midtown tour of homes in 2003 grossed $25,000, the neighborhood association reported in an e-mail.)

There are three clusters of these lofts in downtown, located in Castleberry Hill to the southwest, Fairlie-Poplar between Peachtree and the CNN Center, and Marietta along a street of that name. Representative of the conversions taking place are a former General Electric factory, Deere Lofts in an old John Deere factory, and the Swift Building Lofts combining three buildings into twenty-nine rental units. All told there are twenty-eight downtown apartments, some as small as fifteen units (Baltimore Row), some as large as 798 (Centennial Place), and sixty-three condominiums, ranging from 3 units in Lofts at 560 to 330 units in Peachtree Tower, as listed by Central Atlanta Progress. The tightest downtown population estimate, from Research Atlanta, is that three thousand lived in the core area in 2000, with more possibly moving in by the end of 2003.

The new residents are true urban pioneers, living in a section of the city that, as one candid Realtor said, has too many derelicts and panhandlers. Residents in the Fairlie-Poplar neighborhood, self-described liberals, complain about the homeless in the area and say it scares people away from downtown. There is an estimated homeless population of 15,000, far in excess of the available shelter spaces. Aggressive panhandling is also said to be a problem.[18]

But downtown residents also speak positively of the relative safety of the area, its neighborhood feel, the walk to work. And for now they don't begrudge the lack of convenient shopping, as markets are apparently getting ready to open nearby.

A second positive force, one of the lasting additions to the city from the 1996 Olympics, is Centennial Olympic Park, a large greensward three blocks to the west of Peachtree straddling International Boulevard. It provides the setting for new condominium construction, adding to downtown's residential population. It cleared an apparently run-down section as part of Atlanta's push to ready itself for the Olympic visitation. From all accounts, that event meant as much or more psychologically to Atlantans than the specific facilities that are its physical legacy.

Further, an interviewee related, the Olympics was the event around which was wrapped a citywide neighborhood revitalization effort. The major capital improvements and planning energy were concentrated in the "Empowerment Zone" neighborhoods, enabling the city to accomplish a major leap forward.

Several residential projects adjoin the park and another cluster exists at Centennial Hill. Centennial Park West is a new condominium associated with a nearby hotel, for example. Another boost for the area came in 2002 when Coca-Cola and the Marcus Foundation donated land just north of the park for Atlanta's proposed new aquarium. Coca-Cola's museum will be relocated here also.

The third force downtown is Georgia State University, with a student body of 27,000 at its downtown campus, plus several thousand faculty. New student housing for two thousand is planned in the area. University President Carl Patton, who has an urban planning background, has spearheaded an effort to create an "urban village" campus. The Main Street Master Plan calls for, among other things, converting a street that runs under a viaduct into the "university village center," providing connections to the main campus areas; changing the principal street, Decatur, by reducing the traffic lanes and providing tree-lined sidewalks and distinctive paving; and altering the design of the central gathering place by lowering it to street level from its current platform.

Georgia State will thus gain a coherent intown campus. It is responsible for such downtown acts as the restoration in 1992 of the Rialto Theater and is establishing new centers of activity west of its central campus.[19]

Another aspect of Atlanta's downtown deserves mention, namely the large amount of public art that is displayed here. The city has had a percent for art program since 1977, and the Bureau of Cultural Affairs that administers the program says the city has two hundred such works, fifty of which are downtown. Folk Art Park is above Interstate 75/85 and features some "outside" artists. A bridge by Daniel Chester French from 1910 (the Lincoln Memorial sculptor) is counted, as is a large metal sculpture at Five Points by George Beasley, completed in 1996. Many works are featured around the state capitol building.

There's an underlying reality about real estate in downtown versus Midtown, an interviewee pointed out to us. Downtown land is often three times as expensive, $60 a square foot versus $20 a square foot, which is why Midtown has "taken off," in this person's phrase. Downtown land is valued for its commercial potential, namely for high-rise offices. But that generally prices it out of consideration for housing, something officials in Atlanta will have to confront if they make it public policy to induce more residential development in the downtown.

Before we turn to a brief discussion about Atlanta's burgeoning suburbs, there is a project under way in early 2003 that should be mentioned because it will have some bearing on both Midtown and downtown. Initial funding of $155 million in public and private funds enabled the developer, Jacoby Development Inc., to start on a three-level parking deck that is to be under the first phase of a planned $2 billion mixed-use project called Atlantic Station. The site is huge, 138 acres, lying to the northwest of Midtown (and within the large definition of same). The site is the former Atlanta Steel factory and was a "brownfield" project requiring remediation of the soil.

The project, which has been long delayed with one developer or another backing out along the way, is nothing if not ambitious. Envisioned are 6 million square feet of office space, 1.5 million square feet of retail and entertainment, 3,000 residential units and 1,200 hotel rooms, to be built in three phases. To be included are a Wal-Mart and a Sam's Club, stacked on top of each other in what's called an "urban design," with housing on top, small stores and cafes at the street level, and parking below. One commentator we talked with described the first phase as having a distinctly suburban feel. Be that as it may, Atlantic Station will certainly bring additional residents into greater Midtown and will provide nearby shopping of a kind not readily available now nor likely to appear (unless a Target is built). How the marketplace will absorb all of this projected space remains to be seen. Our sense is that the type of neighborhood that is to be created will not really divert people from Midtown, and that Atlantic Station's retail will complement rather than duplicate what's likely to locate in Midtown proper.

What worries some observers is whether the office space projected can fill, given the three large buildings we mentioned previously that were built in Midtown in 2001, with nearly 1.5 million square feet of space. These skeptics note there was vacancy rate of 23 percent in 2002 in Midtown and rents were dropping. But Atlantic Station was pushing ahead with a seventeen-story office in the face of this.[20]

THE 'BURBS

Thus far we have considered only the city of Atlanta, and indeed only its central portions. Looming outside its borders is a suburban phenomenon of staggering proportions. To the city's 417,000 people, the metropolitan area contains 4,112,198 people scattered over the landscape among ten counties.

The Census Bureau reports that between April 1, 2000 and July 1, 2001, three of the five fastest-growing counties in the nation were Paulding, Henry, and Forsyth Counties, all within the Atlanta metropolitan area and growing at a rate of 11 percent each, as sprawl continues unabated.

Metropolitan Atlanta is either the fastest-growing area in the country or second fastest, depending on who is counting. The largest growth is taking place on the north of Atlanta, both in employment, housing, and retail. A researcher at Clark Atlanta University reports that the suburbs outgrew the city by 100 percent in 1998. Further, the boundaries of the metropolitan area have doubled. In 1990, the region measured 65 miles from north to south. In 2000 it was 110 miles.[21]

How did it happen? An editorial in the *The Atlanta Journal-Constitution* suggests the answer:

If you are stewing in traffic from all the Cherokee County subdivisions that funnel into the same road, searching for an escape from the cul-de-sac maze of South DeKalb or pushing baby carriages in the road in Gwinnett for want of sidewalks, you might reasonably ask: Was there any planning involved in this mess?

Not really. Metro Atlanta's development over the past 30 years has been a land grab. Developers threw up houses, counties scrambled to provide services and schools and malls sprang up overnight in cow pastures.

A few voices in the rapidly vanishing wilderness urged smarter growth, but they were demonized as environmental loons whose real goal was no growth. Georgia road builders even aired TV ads warning soccer moms that their Grand Caravans and cathedral ceilings were at risk. "Don't let Atlanta's environmental activists take away your right to live where you want and drive when you want," the ads threatened. "They're trying to use laws and lawsuits to move families out of the suburbs and into downtown."

So, the asphalt flowed relentlessly, leading to the congestion, pollution and sprawl that's become Atlanta's calling card. Now, many concrete-heavy communities are trying to figure out how to create neighborhoods rather than subdivisions. And, surprisingly, they're being sabotaged by their own elected officials.[22]

So what is it like in the "Sprawl City" outside of the intown areas we've discussed? Here are two indications. One is the presence in Gwinnett County, in the north, of the Mall of Georgia. Located on one hundred acres, it contains 1.7 million square feet of space arrayed in what appear from a sketch to be eleven somewhat interconnected buildings. It is fully thirty-five miles from the center of the city, cast as a new type of mall complete with a nature park and "open air village" that you walk around. There is macadam everywhere for an unbelievable 8,600 cars! Then there is "Perimeter Mall," in a place so faceless that even its geographic designation refers to its being far away.

Let's hear from a developer who has helped make the sprawl happen, John Williams of Post Properties. In the 1970s and '80s he turned thousands of acres of suburban forest into garden apartments, hitting the market with the right product at the right time. He sensed that more women would be at home and that they would want gardens. Now Williams, although semiretired, preaches the value of the city. Not only preaching it but building in it, before backing off several years ago when he perceived, correctly it turned out, that the marketplace in Atlanta and elsewhere was overbuilt.

After constructing some 36,000 garden apartments in a dozen cities, Williams in the 1990s undertook such projects as helping in the restoration of the old Rice Hotel in downtown Houston into 312 loft apartments (see chapter 5) and numerous townhouses in Uptown Dallas (see chapter 4). In Atlanta he's built several intown projects, including Post Parkside near Piedmont Park, within walking distance of the BellSouth office campus, and Post Biltimore near the restored hotel.

"The suburbs, frankly, are just sort of ugly," says Williams. "People can't live in that environment and feel good about themselves. Children who grow up in a suburb where you can't tell one house from the other. It's just an unfortunate experience. I think it's related to the neuroses we are seeing," he adds.[23] Williams, incidentally, has served as chairman of the Metropolitan Atlanta Chamber of Commerce.

Sprawl-bashing has become somewhat "in," and there are reports that people in the Atlanta suburbs don't like to admit where they live. But still they pour into new suburban developments, for the reasons outlined in chapter 2.

The one factor, however, that is beginning to take its toll in Atlanta is its horrific traffic. Metro Atlantans drive an average of thirty-four miles a day to work, 50 percent more than in Los Angeles, reports Robert Bullard of Clark Atlanta University. Atlanta is fourth in congestion, behind Los Angeles, Washington D.C., and Seattle in time spent stopped in grid-lock, sixty-eight hours annually.[24]

Our files fairly bulge with Atlanta newspaper stories with headlines like these: "Commute Spoiling Sweet Life in the 'Burbs? Suburbanites get up early to beat traffic, arrive home late, and find there's not much time left in between for living."[25] Or: "Price of Sprawl Shows in Commuting Costs. Transportation Can Outstrip Housing."[26] Air quality is second worst in the nation, behind only Houston. There were sixty-nine smog alert days in 1999, reports Bullard.

Everyone in Atlanta knows a commuting horror story. Inman Park residents told us about a friend of theirs who worked at Georgia Pacific in the city. His commute used to be 45 minutes. In 2002, four years later, it is 1 1/2 hours, each way. The newspapers are replete with accounts of people pulling up stakes and moving nearer to their workplaces. Carl Patton at Georgia State University relates how when he moved into downtown from Buckhead in the northern part of the city, he could sleep one hour later and be in his office earlier every day, walking.

The prospect of reducing the commuting time, stress, and expense provides a powerful incentive for many to think about joining their more adventurous counterparts taking up residence in Midtown, Virginia Highlands, or some other Intown Living location. As mentioned in the preface, any predictions about cities have to be made with caution and caveats. And this is so here. But there is every indication that, with the perception that an area such as Midtown is, one, safe and two, fun, and three, somewhat affordable, young people especially will choose to come here. And while the numbers moving to Atlanta's intown neighborhoods will be relatively small, they say something hopeful about America's cities.

So we must part company with our friend James Howard Kunstler, who found Atlanta such an appalling mess that he felt nothing could be done to redeem it as a human habitat. Jim, it's happening.

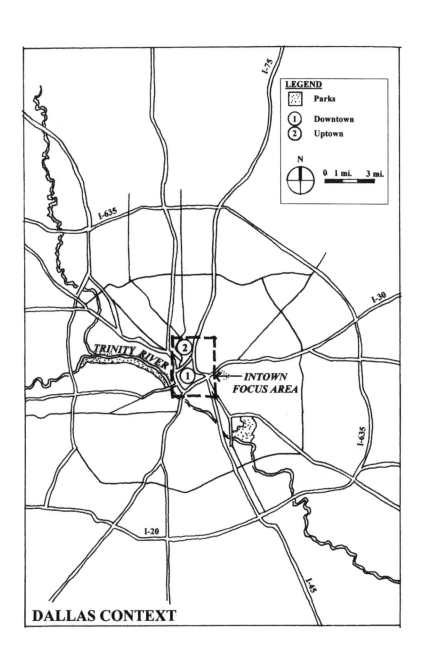

LEGEND

Parks

① Downtown

② Uptown

N

0 1 mi.   3 mi.

I-75

I-635

I-30

TRINITY RIVER

② ①

INTOWN FOCUS AREA

I-635

I-20

I-45

DALLAS CONTEXT

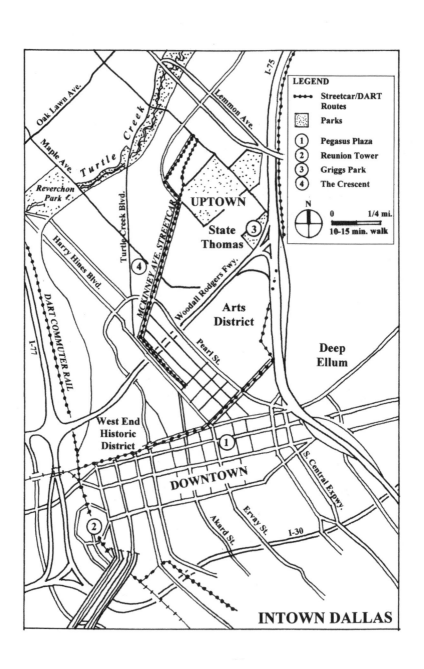

INTOWN DALLAS

LEGEND
- Streetcar/DART Routes
- Parks
- ① Pegasus Plaza
- ② Reunion Tower
- ③ Griggs Park
- ④ The Crescent

N
0   1/4 mi.
10-15 min. walk

UPTOWN

State Thomas

Arts District

Deep Ellum

West End Historic District

DOWNTOWN

Reverchon Park

Turtle Creek

Oak Lawn Ave.

Maple Ave.

Lemmon Ave.

I-75

Turtle Creek Blvd.

Harry Hines Blvd.

DART COMMUTER RAIL

I-77

McKINNEY AVE. STREETCAR

Woodall Rodgers Fwy.

Pearl St.

S. Central Expwy.

Akard St.

Ervay St.

I-30

4

Dallas

The community mosaic needs linked movement systems whereby people have more than one option to negotiate the city. There needs to be more freedom for the third of the population that does not drive, either because it is too old or too young; this would give these people more control of their lives . . .

—*James Pratt,* Imagining Dallas

Dallas looms large in all of our imaginations. Sleek, a bit brassy, Neiman-Marcus sophisticated, with a downtown skyline of glass-walled towers, this Texan city sprawls in all directions. From the top of landmark Reunion Tower, you look out across the city's 331-square-mile spread (Chicago is a mere 228 square miles) and the channelized Trinity River running through it. The Dallas we will talk about is a bit different—populated largely by young professionals, hardworking, somewhat hip, many from elsewhere, who represent a newer face of "Big D."

From the tower you can see the infamous grassy knoll and the Texas School Book Depository Building forever to be associated with John F. Kennedy's assassination—a tragic event for the nation and one that deeply affected the spirit of this city for many years. Gail Thomas, of the Dallas Institute of Humanities and Culture, described it this way: "After the city suffered that horror and the further horror of being blamed for it all over the world, Mayor Erik Jonsson led the rebuilding of Dallas . . . to overcome the blight on Dallas's name."[1] It's one of a string of misfortunes that have hit the city and from which it has struggled back.

Dallas points to its city hall, new public library, and striking office towers that make up its dramatic skyline stemming from this rebuilding period and extending into the early 1980s. We note that while several of the skyscrapers have beautiful plazas and in one case, Fountain Plaza, a gorgeous water garden, in most cases the buildings are alienating to pedestrians, typical of the architecture of the period. To make matters worse, a network of underground tunnels connecting these towers destroyed a vital downtown street scene by sucking people below grade.

From the accounts of several we interviewed plus a contemporary history of Dallas, a more recent catastrophe—economic this time—occurred when the savings and loan scandal struck in the mid-1980s. The collapse of savings and loan institutions in the U.S. began in Dallas. The first bank to go under was in a suburb here, where speculation on real estate was at a high pitch. One immediate result was the emptying of Dallas's downtown. Fully forty million square feet of office space was vacant in 1987, an amount equal to Boston's entire office market.[2] The seriousness of this for Dallas can be seen in the fact that fully fifteen years later, in 2001, downtown still was experiencing a high vacancy rate, an overall rate of 27.9 percent by one account, and it suffered that year what is termed a "negative net absorption" of 290,490 square feet, or emptying.[3] *The Dallas Business Journal*, quoting Integra Realty Resources Inc., a national firm, put the vacancy rate slightly lower, at 22.7 percent in 2001, but noted that this amounted to 6.8 million square feet of empty space, a huge amount.[4]

RESIDENTIAL IMPETUS

Ironically this downturn was the impetus to the Intown Living phenomenon in today's downtown and nearby neighborhoods. What you had in Dallas at the end of the 1980s and early 1990s were the combined interests of the downtown business community, real estate developers, preservationists, the Dallas Institute, and the City of Dallas in bringing downtown back to life, including building or restoring residences.

The real estate development community approached the City of Dallas in the late 1980s, a development attorney related in an interview, saying in effect we can't build offices anymore, the market is glutted, and the only alternative for us is to build housing. They further said, if we're to build housing, we've got to have incentives. That was the impetus for what became the Intown Housing Program of the City of Dallas, put in place in 1991. The major component was a ten-year across-the-board tax abatement on city and county real estate taxes (Texas is a non–income tax state, meaning that property taxes are high). Other benefits included forgiving permit and other fees, which were reimbursed when the certificate of occupancy was issued. An affordable housing component was required, namely 20 percent of the units set aside for persons with an income 80 percent of the city's median. The Real Estate Council, a nonprofit advocacy group with 1,200 members, was also pushing for neighborhood revitalization during this period.

A survey undertaken in 1989 of the downtown workforce determined that there was interest in Intown Living and that the area with the most potential was the State-Thomas neighborhood immediately adjacent to downtown, an executive told us. Another look was taken in 1992 by the Central Dallas Association, which hired the market analysis firm M/PF. This study determined that there was a market for as many as 24,500 intown residential units.[5]

Meanwhile, another group was at work in Dallas promoting residential neighborhoods in the city. This was the preservation movement, started, we were told, by three women who were upset at the teardowns of stately Georgian mansions on the eastern edge of the city, along Swiss Avenue and environs. The activism here led to the establishment of the Historic Preservation League over twenty-five years ago. A Neighborhood Conservation District was established for the area also.

Later called Preservation Dallas, the organization set up an Intown Living Center in 1994. This was a resource for people interested in possibly living inside the "Loop 12" area, with both inhouse data and staff available for neighborhood tours. Loop 12—not to be confused with the Inner Loop, which circles the tightly knit downtown—measures 15 miles wide by 18 miles north to south, a giant territory of 270 square miles. The aim, of course, was to stabilize neighborhoods with new residents and thereby to keep houses from disappearing with the resulting loss of neighborhood character. The organization's approach, according to a person active with the group, was to emphasize neighborhoods as distinct from individual buildings, and further to recognize that all near-city neighborhoods, historic or not, needed assistance, that they would sink or swim together.[6]

Another factor at work then and now is the Downtown Improvement District (DID), working with a special assessment that results in an annual budget of $2 million currently. Created to promote safety, maintenance, communications/events, and capital improvement projects, DID's priorities, according to a fact sheet, are "The Clean Team" working on litter, the "Dallas Ambassadors" seen as a helpful safety presence, enhanced street lighting, a newly designed "wayfinding" sign system, improved parks and open space, and new "entry portals." The "Ambassadors" number twenty-three, are equipped with maps and radios, and serve as additional eyes and ears for the police. Two huge murals over parking lots are another initiative to brighten otherwise drab areas. DID also makes available matching grants for storefront improvements, and it helped to fund a pedestrian connection between the Pearl Street rail station and the Eastern Transfer Center, a bus hub.

Still another factor in reviving the downtown is the Center City Tax Increment Financing District (TIF). In 2002 the City council increased its budget from $62 million to $109 million. The TIF board in 2002 funded thirty-three projects, including the renovation of a furniture building for a restaurant/nightclub, the rehabilitation of 1407 Main Street for residential (sixty units) and retail and 1414 Elm for a small residential/retail project, and the conversion of a Dallas Power and Light Building for residential (147 units) with parking and retail, as described in the Central Dallas Association 2002 Annual Report.

The success of the rapid transit system, Dallas Area Regional Transit (DART), is but one of several elements key to a potential rebound not only in downtown but for the region as a whole. As of 2001, twenty-three miles of rail had been opened, with twenty-two stations serving thirteen cities in the region. Ridership has exceeded projections from the time it opened. On June 14, 1996, the first cars rolled along twenty miles. Ridership was 18,000 where 15,000 had been anticipated. Even before major extensions in 2002, including to Plano, approximately twenty miles from downtown, there were 40,000 riders a day. DART has also installed train service between Dallas and Fort Worth, all of which has received voter approval at various junctures.[7]

Deserving of special mention in the story of Dallas's rejuvenation is the Arts District at the northern edge of downtown, a 1980s urban renewal vision slowly becoming reality. Major facilities include the Dallas Museum of Art (strong on French Impressionists); the new $34 million Nasher Sculpture Garden; the Crow Collection of Asian Art, housed in the Trammel Crow Center office tower and featuring six hundred pieces; the restored Belo Mansion, home of the Dallas Legal Education Center; the Dallas Black Dance Theater; Myerson Symphony Center; Cathedral Santuario de Guadalupe; an Arts District Theater in temporary quarters; Annette Strauss Artist Square; and the Booker T. Washington High School for the Performing and Visual Arts. Followers of popular music will recognize graduate Norah Jones, a Grammy winner in 2002.

DOWNTOWN CORE

The core of Downtown Dallas, surrounded by freeways, is but 1.3 square miles in size, a tiny fraction of the total. It is nonetheless a major employment center, with a daily workforce put at 120,000. The big employment sectors are services (41 percent), finance/insurance/real estate (27 percent) and transportation/communications/utilities (12 percent). Big employers are Southwestern Bell, the City of Dallas, Bank of America, Blockbuster, and Neiman Marcus.[8]

In contrast to Houston and Atlanta, we find in downtown Dallas a traditional core where a significant number of older buildings have fortunately been retained. Other inviting areas of the downtown include a historic West End warehouse district full of restaurants, the aforementioned Arts District and its civic buildings, and Pioneer Plaza with its life-size sculpture of cowboys and a thundering herd of cattle that lets you know you are definitely not in New York. Immediately adjoining the eastern edge is a funky area of clubs and bars called Deep Ellum that we discuss later in this chapter.

These features combine to make downtown Dallas a potentially exciting urban neighborhood. At its center is a small area running along the three principal avenues with six cross streets that feature a cluster of older buildings, mostly offices, some dating to the 1920s and more than a few of distinctive architecture. It is these that have been and are being converted to residential uses. It is notable that only the Manor House at twenty-six stories and 252 apartments, built in 1966, had a downtown residential presence until conversions of old, empty office buildings began in the late 1990s.

Writes Darwin Payne about this period:

The torpor of the late 1980s and early 1990s that had momentarily enveloped Dallas and made it lament the fact that its downtown streets were empty after 5:00 P.M. was giving way to a more positive mood in the late 1990s. Almost without warning, the idea of living downtown had become trendy. Historic old buildings that had been deserted for many years, such as the Wilson Building, the Adams Hat Building (originally the Ford Motor Co. Building), the Kirby Building (originally Busch), the old Titche-Goettinger Department Store and many other structures were reconfigured by imaginative developers and sold or rented as expensive lofts, condos and apartments.[9]

The conversion at 1900 Elm, formerly the Titche-Goettinger department store, was the first, creating 129 apartments at a cost of $12 million. There was a $4 million low-interest federal loan involved, for which the city required that 40 percent of the units be set aside for "lower income" tenants, defined as under $29,300 for a single and $41,480 for a family. The less expensive apartments are as low as $520 a month, and these attracted office workers, bartenders, and beauticians. Executives and lawyers are said to be in the larger spaces. Other subsidies the city provides in its conscious effort to encourage Intown Living include waiving fees and covering utility costs.

The developer, Jack McJunkin, said it was the most complicated project he had ever worked on. A hole was cut into the center of the building to allow windows for the interior units, requiring approval from the U.S. Department of the Interior as the building is a designated landmark. Interior columns with Italian Renaissance moldings were retained, as were many of the architectural details. The apartments rented quickly. A downtown executive recalls that on opening day there was a crowd on hand waving deposit checks.

Here's an account by one of the urban residential pioneers attracted to the old department store:

"I wanted to downsize my life," says Realtor Kitty Dusek, who after a divorce traded in a three-bedroom house in Rockwall for a loft apartment at 1900 Elm. "Six acres of mowing was too much for me, so now I'm living in what used to be Titche's linen and fine china department, I feel I'm so 'in.'"[10]

Another conversion is the Kirby Residences on Main Street that we visited, originally named for its St. Louis developer Busch of the Budweiser beer family. It was picked up in a distress sale from a developer who lost millions on the transaction, a resident active in the transformation told us. A number of subsidies played a role in the conversion, including a fifteen-year property tax abatement from the city for historic restoration work, a $5 million low-interest loan, a sum from the downtown tax increment finance district for sidewalk work, and funds from the U.S. Department of Housing and Urban Development.

The building was faithfully restored, and walls and doors have their original appearances. At the same time, a pool was added on the roof. The project is four years old as of 2003 and took $22 million to rehabilitate. The biggest problem is said to be a lack of parking for the residents and visitors.

A 1999 newspaper story offers an account of life in the Kirby:

Dorcy Siegel grew up in North Dallas in a spacious home with a generous yard and a short drive to shopping malls and movie theaters.

Now she lives in a 600-square-foot apartment with no yard, far from the nearest mall. She wouldn't have it any other way.

"It's a completely unique experience," she says. "I can walk to work. I can walk to the gym. Last Saturday night, I had about 35 people over and we walked to the Gold Bar in the Titche-Goettinger building. . . . It was a novelty for them to actually walk somewhere in Dallas."

An urban planner, she lives in downtown Dallas in the Kirby Residences, one of many loft developments that, along with dozens of more conventional townhouse and apartment units sprouting just outside the central business district, are beginning to remake the face and culture of a city that once seemed hell-bent on escaping from itself.

"I can't imagine living anywhere else," Siegel says. "It's like a campus feel. I have a rooftop pool. Two of my friends live two stories above me. Everything's familiar and comfortable."[11]

Downtown residential is mostly rental. A condominium in the West End is reported to be having difficulty, which hasn't prevented another developer from tackling a homely 1950s-looking building for downtown condominiums.

For the urban pioneers here, the first years had to be lonely, without much in the way of restaurants or convenience shopping. That began to change, however, with the opening of a popular restaurant, Jeroboam, at 1501 Main Street and the conversion of Stone Alley into a string of urbane cafes, plus the restoration of the grand old Magnolia Hotel, a key, symbolic redevelopment.

Pegasus Reborn

Which leads us to the story of the Magnolia, Pegasus Plaza, and the great neon Pegasus—once the most visible icon of Dallas that soared atop the hotel. Built in 1922, the Magnolia was the tallest building in Dallas for years. The city sold the hotel to a San Francisco developer in 1979 and there was fear about the fate of the Pegasus.

To give an idea of what Pegasus means to the citizens of Dallas, Gail Thomas noted:

> For those of us who have lived a while in Dallas, Pegasus is more than the myth of the winged horse; Pegasus is Dallas's image, its own symbol, a sign of Dallas's spirit, there brazen-red in the sun and illuminated in the sky at night!
> Until Reunion (Tower), Pegasus has been our Eiffel Tower, our Golden Gate Bridge. The Dallas Pegasus is the largest Pegasus in the world. It is 30-by-40 feet and weighs almost 15 tons. It flies 400 feet above street level. The Flying Red Horse was added to the top of the Magnolia Building in 1934 . . . Though modern buildings have eclipsed the dramatic vision of Pegasus that dominated the Dallas skyline, our citizens have regarded this image as precious.[12]

Fortunately, the city retained ownership of the famed horse. In 1991, after the economic debacle of the 1980s, the city announced a revitalization program for downtown Dallas that included a beautification program for Main Street and the restoration of Pegasus. This initiative built on the work that The Dallas Institute undertook in the late 1980s, namely a "Dallas Visions" project that recommended reviving the downtown. The Institute and a team of consultants became involved in revitalizing Main Street, including the concept of creating a Pegasus Plaza—a public space adjacent to the Magnolia Hotel and across from the Kirby Building to celebrate the myth of Pegasus and symbolize new energy coming to downtown. The plaza is the result of a collaborative effort and includes artfully placed stones representing and celebrating the nine muses. The project boldly reintroduced a natural spring that had been capped off in the early 1960s to create a living fountain in the heart of Dallas. The plaza was dedicated in 1994. It was engineered to work as a performance space as well when the fountains are turned off.[13]

Six years later, on the stroke of midnight at the turn of the century, a magical event occurred when the resurrected Pegasus took its rightful place atop the restored Magnolia Hotel in all its shining, red glory. Sponsors hoped it would augur more auspicious times.

Downtown Numbers

The core downtown area census tract in 2000 showed 1,911 residents—but 812 or 37 percent were classified as "institutional," which are jail or shelter occupants. While there is a middle-class downtown residential population, in a number of beautifully restored buildings, and there are additional buildings in restoration as of early 2003, the population is thin. The demographics show a largely white (73 percent), single (70 percent), young (median age thirty-three) rental population (98 percent). The Central Dallas Association puts the figure at 2,500. The census tract to the north of the downtown core, where office towers dominate, had a total residential population of nine.

There are two ways of looking at the relatively small but growing downtown residential population. One is that it is just that, small, a tiny portion of the 1.2 million who call Dallas home.

The other is that the fact that there is a cluster of residents downtown at all is pretty remarkable in a city that has no urban culture or tradition and which offers little in the way of support facilities. Dallas has been moving to the suburbs since the first rail lines were built beginning in the 1870s. Not only that, but the city has had troubled race relations, as author Darwin Payne catalogues. In his book, *BIG D: Triumphs and Troubles,* he recounts how a race riot broke out downtown in 1993 during a parade for a winning football team. This reflected the sharp racial divide in the city, basically another north-south, white-black dichotomy. This event is relatively recent and has to be in the back of the minds of at least some of the new downtown residents.

We interviewed a downtown pioneer active in a residents' group. He acknowledged that he was uncomfortable at times with the homeless/derelict population. While panhandlers are in evidence, crime downtown as reported by the Downtown Improvement District is said to be down 64 percent from 1990, with a further drop of 8.4 percent in 2002 from 2001. The Police Department has a seventy-four-member unit for the central business district, including officers on foot, bicycle, and horses. A crackdown on public drinking and disorderly conduct was scheduled for 2003.[14]

A survey found that, more than safety, the biggest felt need among downtown residents was for park space. The city was undertaking a study in 2003, looking at four or five potential park locations. In fact, one estimate we read was that fully 30 to 40 percent of downtown consisted of parking or streets, which contributed to its desolateness, something our interviewee spoke about.[15] The city is said to have a very suburban parking standard (a high parking to square foot ratio, in other words). The other aspect is that parking in downtown Dallas is ridiculously cheap: $2.50 all day on a surface lot, for example.

Noise is also an issue for downtown residents, especially at night. A bit of a club scene in the area translates to loud street noises at 2:00 A.M. as they empty and motorcycles rev up. Downtown's streets were receiving a face lift in 2003, and that entailed some nighttime construction work.

Another resident we interviewed said the core area needs an influx of shops, as much as 100,000 to 150,000 square feet of additional retail space. This need is underscored by the vacancy at the street level even in the central core, amid the large empty buildings that dot the landscape. Also, some of the retail that is present is pretty marginal.

The Mercantile Building, one huge example of downtown's problems, takes up an entire block on Main Street and has been empty for years as of 2003. A person knowledgeable about downtown properties said one of the things holding back a conversion is an estimated $9 million worth of asbestos cleanup. A fashion market was proposed in 2003 but was met with skepticism. So the large dead space remained.

What apparently brought its downtown problems home to business interests was losing out to Chicago in 2001 in the competition to acquire the new headquarters of the Boeing Co. The stated reason was that Dallas "did not have an energetic street life." A free translation of this might be that Boeing executives found downtown Dallas boring. The other loser was Denver.[16]

The Dallas Partnership Inc., a public-private group, is trying to force-start a retail surge. It hired a Washington, D.C.–based organization, the Madison Retail Group, to prepare a master lease plan for the core of downtown. In March 2002, a number of firms signed exclusive listing agreements with Madison and a local broker. The next step is to line up tenants. The broker in 2002 said the response was "great" and that better retailers were taking downtown "seriously."[17] Then there are those like a downtown executive we interviewed who see downtown retail as a "tough nut," notwithstanding the presence on Main Street of the flagship Neiman Marcus store, still going strong.

Assessing Downtown

One of the characteristics we sensed about downtown Dallas is that it seems to have a split personality. Full of optimism and looking confidently to the future on the one hand, doubtful, even pessimistic and saying that real revitalization of the area is two decades away on the other. We have a friend here who speaks of her love-hate relationship with the downtown. Here are some sample commentaries:

Bennett Miller, a pioneer in lofts downtown, is cautious. Several years ago he was quoted saying: "A lot of amenities are still missing. There are no good schools downtown, no grocery stores. There is not the kind of street life you see in New York, Chicago or Boston. It will take a generation or two for that to come about."[18]

In an article several years ago discussing office leasing, commercial real estate analysts said on the one hand, "the main obstacle to downtown growth is the fact that few people live there," said Justin Stein. In the next breath, the real estate executives were saying that Dallas is moving toward becoming a "24-hour city" with its lofts. That development was occurring because, the Realtors agreed, the new generation of business executives want an "urban living lifestyle." Carl Ewart of the Staubach Co. said, "The hardest age group to hire is the 22- to 35-year-old. That age group wants to have fun and doesn't want to travel a long distance to work."[19]

Here's still another take, from the editor of the *Dallas Business Journal*:

Many questions (about downtown) remain, however. The biggest one on my list is that of residential growth in and around downtown. We have seen a mini-boom in new apartments, renovated lofts and other projects all around downtown, and (Ross) Perot (Jr.) hopes to add more. But the market for such properties looks very limited and one-dimensional to me. No one with kids is going to move into one of these places. That doesn't mean residential projects aren't worth pursuing. It just means that all the talk about downtown becoming an actual community seems overblown to me. (And until the Dallas Independent School District gets its act together, the entire city of Dallas will continue to lose middle-class families to the suburbs.)[20]

And finally, we have the following commentary by the *Dallas Morning News* architectural critic David Dillon. After excoriating some of the new apartment developments for "slipshod" construction creating "incipient slums," he gives this analysis:

If the metropolitan population does rise to seven million during the next twenty-five years, downtown housing will have to get denser and more diverse—eight stories instead of two, affordable and subsidized as well as luxury. Otherwise, downtown will attract only a narrow segment of newcomers . . .

Likewise, much has been written about the explosion of jobs in technology and finance, and the new Dallas housing certainly tracks that curve. Yet statistically, the biggest job increases will be in the so-called service jobs: cooks, carpenters, janitors, bus drivers. These people keep the new economy humming, but $1,500-a-month apartments are far beyond their means.

"If downtown Dallas is going to succeed, it will have to have mixed housing," says Bennett Miller (quoted above), who pioneered the development of downtown lofts. "You can't cater only to people with disposable income. You need those who have to work for a living."

Dallas has reason to feel good about the downtown revival. The combination of new housing, DART and a revamped Central Expressway has made it more attractive and more accessible. At the same time, the revival remains fragile. The economy could go south; priorities could shift. Instead of a lively mixed urban neighborhood, downtown could end up as just another business and government center, or a sprawling tourist and convention district of interest mainly to visiting cardiologists and fly fishermen.

The first phase of the downtown revival has been led by the private sector. The next phase will likely require more government participation, as well as a different kind of developer—someone interested in neighborhood- and community-building and willing to take on the tough small projects as well as the lucrative big ones.

"Dallas has neglected the inner city for so long that it will take 20 years or more to bring it back," cautions Mr. Miller. "And it's going to be a hard birth. We've done the easy stuff. Now we have to start on the rest."[21]

This leaves us somewhat up in the air about exactly where downtown Dallas is headed. One thing seems certain: The booming success of the next-door Uptown neighborhood has to have cut into the potential market for downtown housing.

UPTOWN RESURGENCE

Today's Uptown residential growth has its roots in and encompasses the area known as State-Thomas, part of which was a historic Freedmen's Town and which lies to the immediate northwest of the central business district, just on the other side of the Woodall Rogers Freeway. This was the section identified by downtown interests as having the best potential, as we mentioned earlier. Uptown itself runs west to the fashionable area of Turtle Creek and north into Oak Lawn. The name is just ten years old, replacing the designations "Quadrangle" for a cluster of shops or "Vineyard" for an old grape-growing section as previous area names.

Preservationists were keen to stabilize the State-Thomas before more demolition occurred, containing as it did a cluster of some of the city's finest Victorian homes, some dating to the 1880s. The area as a whole had deteriorated by the 1970s and '80s, experiencing a high crime rate, use of crack cocaine, and prostitution. An aside: In its very earliest days, the lower end of McKinney Avenue was known as "Frogtown," the city's most notorious red-light district.[22]

New attention became focused on State-Thomas around 1990. Developers including local doctors and lawyers began to purchase land as an investment. In the words of one who moved to Dallas from Chicago: "Gee, here's an area less than a mile from the CBD that no one seems interested in."[23] A portion of the black population had left, but we were told by one of the redevelopers that a number of black families owned their property, meaning they could stay for the rejuvenation or cash out.

To the north of State-Thomas is the Oak Lawn area. It had undergone its own partial revival in the late 1970s as young professionals moved in, including a sizable gay population. It was an offbeat neighborhood according to contemporary accounts, and had a club scene until the early hours.[24] Oak Lawn had established itself as an active, quirky, rejuvenating but still dangerous section. An executive working in the area today reports her parents expressed concern as late as 1990 if she was headed there.

Significant to the State-Thomas/Uptown effort was a grassroots campaign in the early 1980s to chart the course of the redevelopment that activists could see headed their way. Single-family homes were already being replaced in Oak Lawn and what is now Uptown with apartments or condominiums, and some feared the loss of a sense of neighborhood. The feeling was that the residents needed to take action.

The result was the Oak Lawn Forum, established in 1982, with sponsorship from the North Dallas Chamber of Commerce and the city. Its coverage includes much of what is Uptown today. The result after several years of community participation was an ordinance adopted by the city that established some sound urban design principles: that parking should be in the rear, reflective glass prohibited, height limits and setbacks established, sidewalk cafes permitted, offices should plant trees, and Turtle Creek should be kept as an open green space. Architect Philip Henderson spearheaded this effort.[25] And while its coverage did not extend officially to State-Thomas, it established principles that were bound to have influenced what took place there. Ten years later the ordinance was updated and amended, which process took three years, according to a participant.

STATE-THOMAS

The impetus here came from four individuals who banded together and with their own funds began buying and restoring houses and then reselling them, setting up a revolving fund, according to one of the partners. They did about fifteen such rehabilitations, which helped to stabilize an area that was under considerable development pressure and experiencing tear-downs.

Then came a lengthy process of debating the area's future and coming up with a Planned District, which ended up calling for mid-rise housing, a compromise between developers thinking high-rise and the existing neighborhood. A search then ensued to find a developer to tackle this new kind of housing for Dallas. What may be the city's first mid-rises were built here, starting with a project known as the Meridian in 1991. This made developers happy as the area's density was increased. Old Victorians were fixed up rather than being assembled for tearing down. The area comprised sixty-five acres, and its rebirth was the spark that led to Uptown's eventual redevelopment. The Columbus Realty Trust was the main developer, later to be acquired by Post Properties of Atlanta. Today Uptown is home to a large number of garden apartments set amid charming older homes.

Significant to the success of the program was the property tax abatement made available by the City of Dallas, which gave ten years free from paying property taxes and constituted a powerful incentive, particularly when matched with historic renovation credits.

A tax increment financing district was set up, and its funds were used for such improvements as parking, lighting, streetscape improvements, landscaping, and infrastructure upgrades, all in the name of attracting and supporting private development investments. One who was involved in the redevelopment says this fund was key and was the primary mechanism by which infrastructure improvements were accomplished. In this person's account, a pivotal move was to rezone the area for housing where it had been slated for office development, meaning land costs were high. Many of the office developments went to the suburbs, and with a residential zoning classification, the way was opened to build apartments (four-story over parking was the product settled on) aiming at the 30-something professional market. This person mentioned the influence of the *Seinfeld* TV program in creating the market in Uptown, something we heard elsewhere.

Important too, in this person's account, is the reduction in crime and the reporting on same in the media. The generation before had seen a crack epidemic in the area, so it was essential that the streets be perceived as safe in the 1990s for residents to move in.

We thought it important to sketch the earlier days in this area, because the history helps explain today's reality of a lively, largely developed intown neighborhood that embodies the characteristics of a real urban district. Uptown has today what intown neighborhoods aim for: walkability, density, diversity, hipness, and transit. It combines residential, office, retail, cultural offerings, and restaurants. It has a free trolley service running down its main spine street, McKinney Avenue, connecting to downtown, using colorful historic cars, moving along handsome brick paving. McKinney is eminently walkable. The trolley tracks down the middle of the street serve to tame the traffic, the sidewalks are generous, the largely commercial buildings along it are low-rise, varied, and interesting—including a former church now a Hard Rock Cafe. Street-level retail is the norm, the side streets have appeal, and there are trees.

The trolley is an interesting story—actually two stories. First, Uptown businesses and property owners agreed eight years ago to tax themselves as a Public Improvement District, where the city collects money that is turned over to a nonprofit Uptown organization overseen by a broad-based board numbering forty-seven. Over 50 percent of the property owners must sign a petition, but since three large developers who favored the move held half of the area's real estate, this was easy.

The Uptown Public Improvement District had an annual budget of $750,000 in 2003, to be spent on public purposes. They are for "landscaping, lighting, security patrol, recreational and cultural facilities, pocket parks and open space, marketing, retail development, financial support for the McKinney Avenue trolley, trash cans, sidewalk sweeping and maintenance of these and other improvements allowable under State law," the organizing document states. Generally the improvements and services are to augment what the city provides. This fund was the source of the initial capital and operating money for the now-free trolley service. The Downtown Improvement District also contributes as the trolley line is to be extended to loop around downtown; in early 2003 there was a transfer from rail to a jitney-type bus into downtown.

The seven trolleys (two in storage) date variously to 1913 or 1920. Several come from St. Louis. Typical is "Petunia," built for the Dallas Railway Co. in 1920 by the J. G. Brill Co. of St. Louis, part of a fifty-seven-car order. It served several city routes before being sold in 1947 to a rancher. McKinney Avenue Trolley Authority (MATA) cofounder Ed Landrum purchased it in 1980, but it lacked motor, wheels, seats, or controls. He spent eight years restoring it to its original appearance, and it now runs as much as 8,000 miles a year. Another is known as the "Green Dragon," a name given it by Southern Methodist University students in the 1930s. It was retired in 1956 when trolley service ended in Dallas and was also later restored by Ed Landrum.[26]

The trolleys provide a link to such downtown features as the Arts District, with its cluster of major facilities. (It is actually within walking distance for residents of the closest-in Uptown sections.) Also relatively near and served fairly well by the trolley/jitney line is the West End Historic District, an area of old warehouses with clubs and restaurants (twenty-seven in number, many of them chains). And near it is the American Airlines Arena opened in July 2001, for basketball and hockey, adding to the attractiveness of the Uptown neighborhood as a place to live.

In addition to providing transportation, the trolleys are Uptown's signature. They distinguish the area from any other place in Dallas. They immediately say, "This is a special place." The Uptown Association uses a trolley in its logo.

Uptown has twenty-two office buildings that employ 11,000 today, as structures went up in the area during downtown's stumble.[27] Uptown executives told us they do not foresee much additional office development. A developer said the area is effectively built out, and was done in just fifteen years, in what is a dramatic story of Intown Living and related property development.

One developer alone, Post Properties, has thirteen residential projects in Uptown. They range from Post Meridian, described as a "luxury residential community" with "European elegance" to the Post Abbey townhouse project with thirty-four units. Meridian apartments range from 659 square feet to 1,012; the Abbey has larger, two-story units up to 1,454 square feet. The company publishes a newsletter for its thousands of renters.

The area has three distinct retail centers in addition to the shops that line McKinney. The Gallery Walk District is where the antique shops and galleries are clustered and is 30 years old. A glitzy development, The Crescent, contains an upper-end group of shops operated by Korshak and is in its twentieth year. Its retail mix is said to be aimed at mid-30-year-olds. The owners dream of decking over the freeway that separates the project from downtown, which would help link the two neighborhoods and cover up a significant visual intrusion.

The third area, West Village, is a three-year-old mixed-use project in 2003, perhaps a harbinger of things to come as more dense development is forecast. It combines some high-end retail on the first level (Ann Taylor, Design House Stockholm, Polo among twenty-two stores) plus nine restaurants, with 179 apartments above, served by interior parking. As of February 2003, it was 94 percent leased, with an average size of 1,242 square feet. Rents start at $850 per month and go up to $3,150 for a three-bedroom unit. A fitness center and pool are included. The trolley service runs around its perimeter.

Travel+Leisure magazine in June 2003 described it this way:

West Village . . . once appeared to be just another clutch of precious European village-style apartments and stores. Lately, it has become wildly popular, thanks to an eclectic mix of tenants: Arthouse cinema, upscale *taqueria,* gelato shop, noodle house, even a sumptuous flower "gallery."[28]

The demographic profile of Uptown is striking: young, white, single, predominately male, renters with only a small percentage over 60 years of age as of the year 2000. In the old State-Thomas area, the census tract shows a population of 1,870 with a median age of 31. Nonfamily households are 85 percent, and blacks now number only about 7 percent of the total. To the west of the roughly north-south spine of McKinney, the census numbers are very similar: 2,361 population, 55 percent male, median age 30 years, white over 87 percent and singles 73 percent, renters 92 percent, over 60 years of age only 2 percent.

Uptown observers report a slight bump since 2000 in the percentage of owner-occupied housing. While still said to be a small portion, like 10 percent, the increase in condominiums (from an average of about 5 percent) reflects a growing number of empty nesters moving to Uptown, now that its unsavory reputation is long past and the young population has enlivened it. They also report seeing more baby strollers, more young families staying, perhaps sending children to private schools. There is said to be a solid middle school, Travis, serving the area.

The appeal of Uptown is that it offers a balance between an active cafe, bar, and club scene without the edginess of, say, the Deep Ellum neighborhood on the east side of downtown, as a 30-something single professional woman put it.

Uptown had seventy-nine restaurants, counting all types, as of spring 2002. "American-ish" was the dominant style.[29] If you include the adjoining

Oak Lawn neighborhood, at least eight of the forty-three "best" restaurants in the February 2003 issue of the magazine *D* are in the area. In addition, there's a large art gallery and antiques scene in Uptown (thirty-three listings), a number of theaters, at least one major grocery store, and an array of basic shops essential to a viable neighborhood.

One interesting feature of Uptown is its four cemeteries, the focus of one of the trails the Uptown Improvement District maintains. The cemeteries reflect their times. The Greenwood Cemetery, 1874, was strictly for white Protestants. The Calvary Cemetery of 1878 was for Roman Catholics of European ancestry. The Temple Emanu-El Cemetery, 1884, was for Jews, and the Freedman's Memorial, dedicated in 2001, honors thousands of blacks buried there since the 1850s, most of whose graves were paved over by roads. About 1,500 people were later reburied.

OTHER RESIDENTIAL

Beyond Uptown and downtown we should mention the existence of expanding residential developments in other areas surrounding the center city.

Despite its edginess and body-piercing parlors, Deep Ellum has new residential projects, notably Deep Ellum Lofts. These are four historic warehouse buildings that have been updated with amenities. The Web site for the area has an interesting feature: It outlines a typical week in which a resident walks to everything, dropping off the laundry while stopping in a cafe, going to a restaurant in the evening and so forth, Monday through Sunday. *The New York Times* described Deep Ellum as one of the country's "coolest, most exciting neighborhoods." It consists of twenty blocks of "shops, boutiques, bars, restaurants and nightclubs that pulsate with energy." *The Times* calls the choice of restaurants "daunting."[30]

The census tract here covers a larger area than just Deep Ellum, but is nonetheless instructive. The median age is 32, matching the profile established in Uptown. The tract had 2,271 people, 60 percent were male, and fully one quarter were in the 25-to-34 age bracket, far and away the largest group. Next was 35-to-44-year-olds. The majority was nonfamily, and 92 percent rented apartments.

Just to the south of downtown and within the beltway is a garden apartment project with a projected 1,800 units, Camden Farmers' Market. About 1,000 units were built by 2001. And further to the south past the Convention Center is the rehabilitation of a huge Sears warehouse complex into 450 apartments, called Southside on Lamar. There is also an attractive townhouse cluster named Oakcliff on the east side of the city, tucked beside a freeway.

In the West End Historic District, a mixed-use project was under construction in early 2003. It is to have ground-floor retail and 204 apartments above

in a four-story undertaking, at Ross and Lamar, within the central business
district. It is being built by a Canadian company, the Fram Building Group,
which acknowledges it is taking a risk after being turned down for tax abatements. They report interest in their 30,000 square feet of retail space.[31]

We have then in Dallas the Intown Living phenomenon making important beachheads in increasingly urban neighborhoods, from the very core of
Dallas to a cluster of neighborhoods, most notably Uptown, immediately
adjacent to the center. And they are populated in large part by the young
professionals that the business community is eager to recruit to their city.

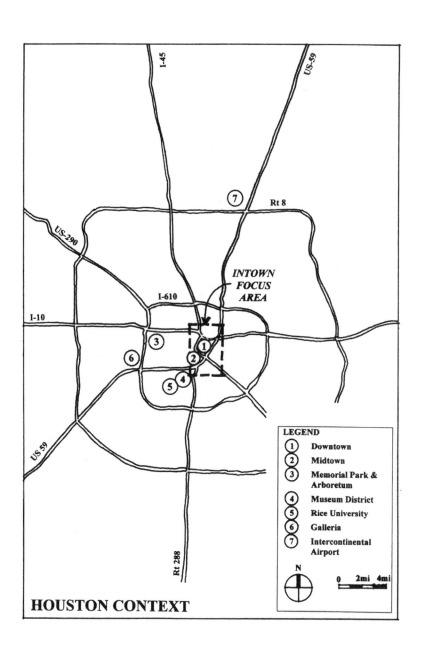

HOUSTON CONTEXT

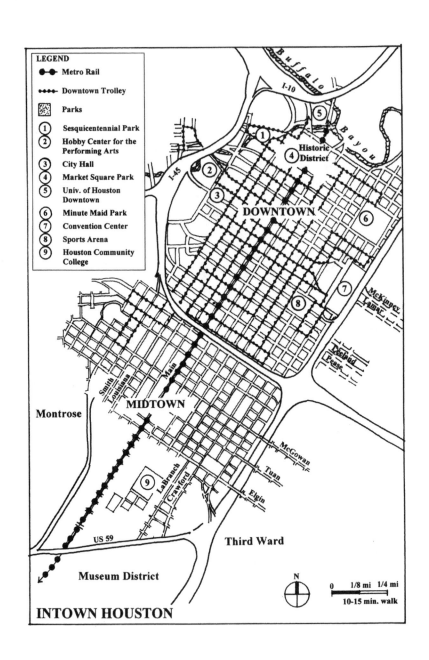

LEGEND

●—● Metro Rail

●●●● Downtown Trolley

▦ Parks

① Sesquicentennial Park
② Hobby Center for the
   Performing Arts
③ City Hall
④ Market Square Park
⑤ Univ. of Houston
   Downtown
⑥ Minute Maid Park
⑦ Convention Center
⑧ Sports Arena
⑨ Houston Community
   College

I-10

Buffalo Bayou

I-45

Historic District

DOWNTOWN

McKinney
Lamar

Field
Pease

MIDTOWN

Montrose

Smith
Louisiana
Main

McGowan

Tuan

LaBranch
Crawford

Elgin

US 59

Third Ward

Museum District

N

0   1/8 mi   1/4 mi
10-15 min. walk

INTOWN HOUSTON

Houston

For Houston to thrive in the 21st century, it must be a place where people from around the world want to live. I believe that our future depends on how Houston's leadership addresses this challenge. I am optimistic about the future outcome . . . but the challenges are formidable . . .

—*Bob Eury, Central Houston Inc.*

Our Intown Living story from Houston comes in three parts.

The first, overriding reality is the ballooning sprawl that is Houston. To anyone not from Los Angeles, the enormity of Houston's spread is hard to believe. And it continues.

Second is the concerted, business-driven effort over the past twenty-plus years to breathe life into the downtown core dominated by high-profile, sleek office towers. Forces combined in the late 1990s to begin to achieve the desired rebirth, but in 2001 the downtown took five blows that set it back. While improved from twenty years ago, downtown Houston still has a major distance to travel to become a true center of urban vitality.

Our third tale is from the Midtown/Fourth Ward areas immediately south and southwest, respectively, of downtown. By immediately we mean on the other side of one of the numerous expressways that circle Houston in concentric rings, namely Interstate 45 (or Pierce Elevated). In these neighborhoods new apartments and townhomes are being erected at a blistering pace to meet a market demand.

Other stories from here as well indicate a countertrend to the predominate sprawl, such as lofts built immediately to the east of downtown, an apartment conversion in a no-man's-land to the northeast of the core city, and apartments marketed fairly successfully at the western edge, along and overlooking Buffalo Bayou. Farther afield is The Heights, a historic neighborhood to the northwest of but fairly close to downtown that has over one hundred structures on the National Register of Historic Places. This area features a cluster of antique shops, art galleries, eateries, and specialty retail and has an active historic preservation movement.

HOUSTON SPRAWL

So far-reaching is Houston that people perceive and describe the area within Highway 610, "The Loop" that circles downtown, as "center city." Mind you the area stretches fully twelve miles from east to west and nine miles north to south. We're talking approximately central Boston to Newton, or downtown Chicago to Winnetka. But in the sprawl that is endemic to Houston, it makes perfectly good sense for people to think they are living close-in for being inside "The Loop."

Outside The Loop we have a second ring road, Highway 8, the Sam Houston Tollway/Parkway, that stretches twenty-five miles north to south and twenty-six miles from east to west. Outside it, around to the western and northern perimeter where the growth is most explosive, another road by various names (Highway 6, Highway 1960, Humble-Hoffman Road) provides a third encircling highway. It is fully seventeen miles west of downtown and by no means constitutes an outer limit. An additional outer beltway has been on the drawing boards since the early 1960s. It would run for 170 miles, passing through seven counties. One segment, near Sugar Land, was opened in 1994.

The growth in these perimeter precincts continues apace. Builders in 2002 sold more than 32,000 new homes in the suburbs.[1] The real estate section of the *Houston Chronicle* on Sunday, February 23, 2003, had telling maps by various home builders. Newark Communities, for instance, placed nothing inside The Loop, one housing development inside Highway 8, seven inside the outer loop or Highway 6, and fifteen beyond it. The map for Royce Builders and its seventy-three projects, some of them "new communities," shows a similar pattern. One project inside The Loop, six inside Highway 8, thirty-three inside Highway 6, and the remainder beyond.

An analysis of the real estate market in the year 2000 showed that only 5.9 percent of sales took place inside The Loop, while 75.5 percent were outside Highway 8. Contributing to this is the relatively higher cost inside The Loop: $128 median per square foot price versus $58 outside Highway 8.[2]

To serve this population, thousands of square feet of new retail space are being added. Twenty-three free-standing drugstores were to be added in 2003 in the area, for instance, and sixteen new grocery stores.[3]

One sidelight to Houston's continuing growth is a trend by developers to try to build some sort of community centers into their subdivisions. It's an attempt to satisfy the stated desire on the part of many for walkable places that have a center, an identity. Carrying this to an extreme are developers at The Woodlands, a planned suburban community twenty-seven miles to the north of Houston that dates to the 1970s. Plans call for a convention center with an "entertainment waterway," plus a hotel and thirty-story office tower, a developer told us. A nearby 400,000-square-foot retail center is to feature two-story buildings with "pedestrian-friendly" streets, shops and restaurants below, offices above. "Developers are creating the Main Street–style centers in suburban areas that have never really had much of a downtown or urban core, such as The Woodlands," wrote *Houston Chronicle* real estate writer Ralph Bivens. The developer, a Fort Worth company called Trademark, said it thought residents were ready for a sophisticated "downtown."[4] We take this as affirmation that even people miles from the actual downtown seek urban values in whatever form they are served up.

Houston's center of gravity is moving away from downtown to the northwest, University of Houston economics professor Barton Smith told a group of realtors in 2001. First, the center moved from downtown out to The Loop or Highway 610. Now it is located on the next circumferential, Highway 8, centered on a place called Spring Branch. What will drive its growth, Smith said, is its accessibility to major employment corridors along Highway 8. It is in the middle of the action as housing continues to spread westward. Its school system is highly rated, and its leaders are prepared for an onslaught of redevelopment.

Smith reported that people weary of heavy traffic were attracted to neighborhoods between Highways 8 and 610 because they are "closer to town" and relatively inexpensive. They are not, he said, willing to pay the high prices of inner-city real estate.[5]

Houston's sprawl has naturally spawned a countermovement by proponents of Smart Growth. Led by David Crossley of the Gulf Coast Institute, backers are quick to say they are not antigrowth, as they must in a city that leads the country in its pro-business, laissez-faire approach. Houston's appeal has traditionally been based on low taxes, low wages, limited government, and weak development controls, including no zoning ordinance. Some in the leadership are seeing that this approach may have to be modified as we'll see in the discussion that follows about downtown.

Smart Growth will be a tough sell in Houston, says Mike O'Brien, president of the Houston Homeowners Association. "We don't embrace things quickly," he observed. The business community seems skeptical, even though the Greater Houston Partnership has formed a "sensible growth committee." Said the organization's president, "The fact is, one person's sprawl is another person's Great American Dream," Jim Kollaer wrote in the organization's newsletter. And Barton Smith of the University of Houston doubts Smart Growth can ever gain wide appeal.[6]

TRAFFIC WOES

Continued trouble with air pollution and traffic frustration may, however, make for converts. Houston's traffic is legendary. For example, *Houston Chronicle* columnist Ken Hoffman wrote:

Last week, the weather warmed up, so I thought I'd drive to the batting cages at Celebration Station on the Southwest Freeway near Hillcroft. It's real close to my house, maybe four or five miles. Just hop on Loop 610 at Bellaire Boulevard, spin around to the Southwest Freeway and double back to the Hillcroft exit. It took me an hour to get there . . . How do people who commute from Sugar Land or The Woodlands keep their sanity? (note: Sugar Land is approximately 20 miles from downtown, Woodlands farther). I've lived in Houston for seventeen years. I know people who have lived here 40-to-50 years. They all agree. This is the worst they've ever seen the traffic mess . . . There's got to be a better way. It's taking the joy out of living in our terrific city. There's so much to do here. It's just too hard to get there."[7]

Five days later Hoffman printed some of the responses. Such as the woman who moved from Highway 8 into the Galleria area beside Highway 610 because, she said, it was taking as much as 1 hour and 45 minutes to commute there. "I had to move, just so I could have a life," Laura Howey wrote. Agreed Cary Coole: "Never has Houston been so unpleasant. The quality of life in our city has gone into the toilet because of the traffic." And chimed in Michael Souther: "If you want to meet me at the batting cages next weekend, let me know. I'll plan on leaving my home on the northwest side of town around noon Thursday. That should put me at Hillcroft sometime Saturday morning."[8]

And still they build. The Katy Freeway, running from the satellite city of Katy 28 miles west of downtown to Highway 610, is being widened. In the memorable phrase of the irreverent Web site www.hobil.com, this "mother of all freeways" is being expanded from eleven to twenty lanes in width, not counting exit and entrance ramps. The right of way is growing from 300 feet to 500, including ripping out a rail line. The Texas Highway Department determined that there was no demand for commuter rail. Guess they've never been to Dallas.

In May 2003 a "Citizen's Congress" was convened to develop Blueprint Houston, for the purpose of establishing a list of priorities for the community. The number one, most urgent goal: for Houston to develop a public transit system to reduce traffic congestion, improve air quality, and permit increased density and mobility options. After the Congress, attended by over 1,000, a phone survey in May of 1,000 voters came up with mobility as the number one issue.[9]

DEMOGRAPHIC PICTURE

Overall, Houston continues to grow rapidly. Houston's home county of Harris has 3.4 million people, up from 2.8 million in 1990, while the city has nearly two million, adding 323,078 people since 1990. A major source of local pride is that Houston is the nation's fourth largest city. Never mind that it contains 575 square miles—making one of its monikers, "Space City," somewhat ironic. For comparison, Rhode Island contains 1,545 square miles and San Francisco, 46.

Here's a closer look at representative Houston growth. An analysis of ten census tracts on the north side of the city, near Highway FM 1960, found a fifteenfold increase in population in three decades going from 6,059 in 1970 to 86,217 by 1999.[10]

Sociologist Stephen Klineberg of Rice University provides an interesting insight about Houston's population: In the boom years of the 1960s and 1970s, Houston's growth was largely from Anglos moving to the city. After the oil-based economy collapsed in the early 1980s, the Anglo percentage of Harris County leveled off and has since declined. Hispanics are now the dominant racial group in Houston, with 37 percent of the population. Anglos are 31 percent, 25 percent are black, and 7 percent are Asian. County figures are similar. The city is also experiencing extraordinary diversity as it attracts immigrants with high levels of technical skills for the new knowledge-based economy from India, China, Taiwan, the Philippines, and Africa. Most Hispanics, however, come with low education levels and are generally confined to service-sector jobs, Klineberg found.[11]

BUSINESS LEADERSHIP

Much as the business community has come to see the importance of a lively downtown as a key to its future economic well-being, it may come to recognize that unfettered sprawl may damage the city's image and livability. The difficulty reported in recruiting the bright talent it needs, a talent that is looking for vibrant, urban centers, prompted a business-led effort to create an attractive, lively downtown, with activity on the streets day and night as in competing cities. Does this sound familiar? We turn now to that business-driven effort.

A quick and necessarily superficial history of the downtown begins in the 1970s, a boom time for the economy that spurred signature office tower construction—"trophy towers," as a veteran in commercial real estate called them. The "Skyline District" was born. About the liveliest thing on the streets are the banners telling you you are in the Skyline District. The negative side was that fine old buildings were torn down to make room for still more towers, and the central city lost much of its historic fabric.

As one reporter observed:

> They don't erect tombstones for fallen buildings. But you can find the former sites of some of Houston's most magnificent old structures just the same.
>
> Just look for the parking lots.
>
> For decades, Houston—the world's "Space City"—gleefully spurned its past to embrace the future. Landmarks tumbled under cover of darkness. . . . Build it up, use it up, tear it up and start over. That was the Houston way.[12]

Today, around artfully restored Market Square Park in the remaining historic section of downtown, you can see the results. Only half of two sides of the square are intact, housing restaurants and bars in two- and three-story brick buildings, some with decorative iron. Everything else is gone. On the other two sides and elsewhere around the square is parking, either a surface lot, a ramp, or a garage. One historic building came down at night after a permit was mistakenly issued—the developer gave the address as the back side of the building, not the classic front, we were told (and have read about). Further, downtown lost population in this period, dropping about 40 percent. There was a net loss of housing units as well and only one new project, on the top floors of the Four Seasons Hotel (1982).

Another blow to the downtown scene came in 1969 with the opening of the glamorous Galleria shopping mall on the western edge of The Loop. An instant sensation, it succeeded in draining much of the retail life from downtown and over the years also took the attention away, shifting the focus of the city to the west, according to downtown restaurateurs. The Galleria is more than a huge, high-end shopping mall; it centers a massive, high-rise hotel and residential complex that is still expanding. Before addition four was done, Galleria already had 330 shops and restaurants plus an ice skating rink. It receives sixteen million visitors a year.[13]

Houston was a true boomtown in this period. Ada Louise Huxtable, architecture critic of *The New York Times* in 1976, pronounced Houston "THE city of the second half of the 20th century."

The bottom fell out of the oil market in May 1982, devastating the economy. A sea of vacant lots remain today, on the east side of downtown especially, from this boom/bust period. During the resulting slump through 1996, downtown property lost significant value. One of the consequences is the huge amount of surface parking present in downtown today. In the core, which measures 20 blocks by 16 blocks, there are over 110 such lots, 25 of which cover an entire block! Beyond are numerous garages.[14]

Here's a description of what downtown felt like in its bleak period:

> It's 9 o'clock at night in downtown Houston—the 1984 version—and the heart of the nation's fourth largest city is barely beating. Workers who make downtown a thriving place by day have vanished to outlying areas. The world's largest sculpture garden (a reference to Hermann Square beside City Hall, we believe) is instead populated by winos and derelicts, a smattering of conventioneers, a few free-spirited roller skaters and theatergoers who scurry to their automobiles as soon as the curtain goes down.[15]

To promote general downtown improvement, the business leadership formed Central Houston Inc. in the early 1980s to tackle, among other things, the homeless/derelict issue that was thwarting improvement. A close link was forged with the police that remains in place today, and over time, armed with new laws banning open bottles, for instance, the derelict factor in downtown has been reduced, but by no means erased. After ten years of effort, a newspaper account in 1992 talked about the situation on the east side of downtown that still had derelicts, litter, instances of urinating and defecating in public, drinking, and panhandling. Women coming to the numerous court-related facilities located downtown reported being afraid to get out of their cars because of aggressive panhandling.[16] Overall, despite the continued presence of the homeless, major crime is now significantly reduced in the downtown. From 1991 to 1998, violent crimes dropped 82.1 percent and nonviolent crimes dropped 58.9 percent.[17]

Meanwhile, one positive effect of the oil bust was to halt some demolition and to give the budding historic preservation movement a chance to take hold. A few activists seized the moment to establish a historic district in 1983 in the north end of downtown where the majority of historic buildings remained. It is nine blocks wide and six blocks north to south, centered on Main Street. It was home in 2003 to seven restored loft projects that are the heart of the new residential movement into downtown. Two earlier projects paved the way, the restored Beaconsfield (18 units), originally built in 1908, and Houston House with 403 units built in 1962. But historic preservation is difficult in Houston, an activist told us, in that development interests still have the ear of the city council. An effort to toughen an admittedly weak preservation ordinance was defeated in 1993 because developers opposed it, we were told.

THE 1990s

Except for the Four Seasons mentioned previously, residential development was dormant until 1993 when Dakota Lofts developed by Randall Davis came into being, with fifty-three units. This property is a bit north of downtown, out of the historic area, in a section of warehouses and

low-rise industrial buildings populated by a number of artists and a few
scattered residents. Some call the area "NoHo," but it's otherwise called
the North Warehouse District. The area is hip and casual with avant-garde
theater, galleries, and studios. Its potential will get a considerable boost
when a nearby postal facility is relocated and a rail line moved, both in the
works in 2003. The ambitious *Buffalo Bayou and Beyond* master plan prepared in August 2002, calls for building a new canal through the district,
effectively creating a new waterfront.[18]

By everyone's account that we interviewed, the restoration in 1998 by
Randall Davis and Post Properties of the old Rice Hotel on the edge of
the historic district was the galvanizing moment for the "quality of life"
advocates in downtown. A Houston landmark, the Rice was built in 1913
only to close in 1977 after serving as a major social center of the city. Its
renovation cost an estimated $32 million. After lying abandoned for
twenty years, the Rice, with complicated financial arrangements that
included setting up a tax increment financing district (value: $6 million),
brought 312 apartments onto the market that moved fairly quickly. Top
rental is $3,800 per month.[19]

In 1997 a *Houston Chronicle* article reported what was attracting
people to the Rice.

Amy Alford-Cote is a product of Houston's suburbs. She attended public schools
in Deer Park, then moved to Clear Lake for college and life afterward.

At 23, Alford-Cote wants more spice in her life.

She and her husband are eagerly waiting to rent one of the 312 loft apartments
in the downtown Rice Hotel, undergoing a major renovation in anticipation of a
deluge of people like her.

Forget backyard barbecues and traffic-choked commutes. Downtown living—
with its varied activities, eclectic street life and proximity to work—appeals to this
young couple with no children.

"When I was growing up in white suburbia, people said that downtown wasn't
safe, it was dirty," says Alford-Cote, a fraud investigator for Texas Commerce
Bank. "But I work downtown and know that it is not only safe, but is real nice.
I can't wait to move downtown because that's where the action is."[20]

Since the opening of the Rice, additional residential projects have been
completed, ranging in size from three units to 315 (the latter outside the
official downtown boundary, the Lofts at the Ballpark—three low-rise
buildings). Strictly within downtown's boundaries and completed as of
March 2003 were a total of twenty residential projects, including three
New Hope housing units sponsored by the U.S. Department of Housing
and Urban Development, with a total of 2,176 units and an estimated
population of 2,574. There were another 288 apartments in the works or
under construction in 2003.[21] The one attempt at a high-end condominium
project downtown, Commerce Towers on Main Street, was moving slowly,

according to two people we interviewed. It had sold only a small number of its 135 units as of early 2003. A commercial real estate broker explained that Houston does not have an established condominium resale market, and he felt the city was not ready for them, but rather that there was a huge market for rental apartments, serving, as he put it, the 50,000 secretaries who come downtown every day.

Six loft projects can be found just outside the downtown boundary, but in Houston's context, they could be considered part of the district. One is an ambitious third attempt to make over what was first a failed, government-backed project, the Mercado del Sol, on the eastern edge of downtown in an old furniture manufacturing plant comprised of six buildings on Buffalo Bayou. A city investment of $13 million went for nothing, and the market closed two years after opening in 1985. Millions were then sunk into an effort to establish apartments plus offices and retail in a project called the Americas after a developer picked it up at a city auction for $610,000.[22]

Now Trammel Crow Residential has taken over the buildings, and the first units were open for inspection in early 2003. Known now as Alexam Lofts, the 244 units are being promoted as luxury rentals at prices from $1,000 a month to $2,600. One-bedroom units are as small as 696 square feet. While it is within sight of downtown, the project feels isolated, with no amenities around it. Even so, Trammel Crow, one of the nation's largest developers, obviously sees a market for intown residential in what would otherwise seem to be a hard sell. Perry Homes, another major developer, was to construct a townhouse project next door.

Lending credence to the suggestion that there is a demand for close-in housing is a startling project farther to the east in a starkly industrial area. With the unlikely name of Ballpark Plaza (the ballpark is far away), small townhomes were being sold before they were completed, despite being next to a public housing project and near a scrap yard. A majority of the buyers were said to be 20-something-year-old Anglo females, we were told by a person familiar with the development. The homes are cute, the location somewhat bizarre.

Another development, Sabine Lofts, along the Buffalo Bayou on the western edge of downtown, was reported to be 94 percent leased. One-bedroom lofts started at $1,189 a month up to $1,549, and two-bedroom units ranged from $1,979 to $2,349 as of January 2003.

BOOM AND BUST

Spurred by the successful and symbolic comeback of the Rice, by the late 1990s there was an emerging residential scene, attracting generally young urban pioneers. A developer told us in an interview that a very hot club, bar, and restaurant district on the west side of town in the Shepherd area, appealing to 30-year-olds, began to relocate to downtown, sensing that this was going to be the next great neighborhood. So beginning around 1999, downtown nightlife began to sparkle. Thus we have stories on file with headlines like: "Something Is Cooking On Main—New Restaurants Rush to Downtown Street." This from an August 2, 2000 article:

Restaurateurs are flocking downtown to Main Street, reviving the traditional core of Houston retailing with a smorgasbord of eating and entertainment venues. The restaurants are attracted to the architectural characteristics of the old buildings on Main Street. And the presence of other eateries and nightclubs creates an environment that makes walking down Main Street a popular site for dining and bar-hopping.

"Main Street is getting a lot of attention," said Ed Page of Boyd Page & Associates, a real estate firm that leases retail space. "It has definitely become a new center of entertainment and restaurant activity."

"The restaurants are tapping into a national trend of Americans longing for the 'urban experience' and a pedestrian environment," Page said.[23]

Between 1998 and 2000 there were thirty-eight new restaurants reported opening downtown, according to the downtown management district. At its peak, it's clear downtown was a happening place, as this story suggests:

It's 4 A.M. and lime bombs are dropping onto Main Street.

Lime bombs.

A member of the human race, having scaled the fire escape on a building at Main and Preston, has been hurling large, succulent restaurant-quality citrus balls at pedestrians below. Two have been hit, and this is not funny, they inform Houston cops called to the scene . . .

It's another wee hour of the morning on a downtown corner where, one senses, anything could happen to fill in the blanks. As the city sleeps off its single-minded ambitions, the nocturnal curtain parts for a curious bohemian rhapsody.[24]

"It's incredible." said downtown pioneer Dan Tidwell, who opened Treebeard's restaurant with Jamie Mize more than twenty years ago. "On Thursday, Friday and Saturday nights, people are everywhere," he was quoted at the height of the boom in 1999 in an article titled: "Destination: Downtown After Dark."[25]

For a brief, shining moment around the turn of the century, then, downtown Houston seemed, finally, after years of effort, to have momentum. Residents were growing in number, a restaurant/club/bar scene was evident, a new baseball stadium opened in spring 2000, a rail line was to be installed on Main—a number of factors seemed to be coming together to bring downtown Houston to life after 5:00 P.M. and on weekends. In short, it was beginning to achieve the quality of life many of the business leaders dreamed of.

FIVE WHAMMIES

Then came 2001 and five blows befell the city and the downtown, three particular to Houston and two national.

First on June 8 and 9 came tropical storm Allison, the most damaging tropical storm in U.S. history, causing Buffalo Bayou to come out of its banks to flood downtown and the medical district. The storm cost $5 billion, destroyed 70,000 vehicles, and put as much as 56 feet of water in office tower basements as well as flooding underground tunnels. The Texas Medical Center, one of the world's largest, alone had $2 billion in damages. Some researchers lost their life's work when the water rushed in.[26]

Number two was the attack on the World Trade Center in New York on September 11.

Number three was the Enron debacle, still being played out. The instant impact was the loss in November of thousands of top-paying jobs, both at Enron, Arthur Anderson, and others. It was a civic and psychological blow of major proportions, as Enron was one of the city's most visible companies and its president, Ken Lay, an intimate of President George W. Bush. Lay has, of course, been roundly criticized for not knowing more about off-book financial arrangements and the like at Enron and for spending too much time on civic affairs. Not to defend Lay, but he was experiencing firsthand what others in the city knew, namely that it's hard to recruit bright young talent to come to Houston. This is true for law firms, accountants, medical researchers, and consultants as well as the high-tech fields, a downtown Realtor told us. Houston has to compete with Austin, Boston, Seattle, and other highly desirable places. Its lovely, suburban-style neighborhoods hold little charm for the young. Lay's civic work was less altruism than sound business as he worked to make downtown a livelier, more appealing place.

Enron Field, now renamed Minute Maid Stadium, the new Houston Astros baseball park downtown, was a Ken Lay special. He worked diligently to make it happen, helping to organize the Houston Sports Facilities Partnership to generate $33 million toward the $265 million park. He and fellow backers had to overcome the considerable resistance to putting tax money into downtown, resistance from people like Peggy Hamric, who lived in the northern suburbs and who had this to say:

"People in my area support the theater district downtown, but that's about it," Hamric said (in an interview in 1996). "The truth is, the suburbs have enough amenities to keep people close to home. Why would they want to drive 35 miles to downtown?"[27]

The hope, of course, was that the ballpark would spur new development nearby, and specifically, lure new residents. As of early 2003, the area around the ballpark was deserted, with surface parking lots and boarded-up buildings predominating. One new hotel was under construction across the street from the Union Station portion of the ballpark project.

Whammy number four was the recession, the fallout from the dot.com decline as well as other national and international factors.

The fifth and final blow was of the city's making. It was a decision to get all its downtown roadwork done at once between 1998 and 2004. The urgency, we were told, was to try to get as much done before Houston hosted the Super Bowl and baseball All-Star Game in 2004.

Whatever the reason, for several years the center of the city was completely torn up. One project was to install rail along Main Street, opened early in 2004, running from the University of Houston Downtown complex on the north 7 1/2 miles south to the Medical Center and Reliant Stadium (football). Water and sewer infrastructure work was also being undertaken. The METRO bus system was at work repaving key bus lanes, and finally, a streetscape improvement project in the historic district, called the Cotswold project, was under way (see the description that follows). METRO has been at work on its $300 million in improvements since 1998.

The result of all this? Just as the downtown was on the verge of blossoming, the restaurant and club scene downtown wilted. Some still hung on, waiting for the day when the street work would be done, the rail running, and perhaps more residents arriving, but most called it quits.

Amid the street reconstruction and all-night bulldozers some of the new residents also found aspects of downtown living unsettling. Occupants at the Rice are across from the Houston Chronicle's printing plant and had taken to dropping water or marbles to protest its nighttime noise. One irate resident tossed a twenty-pound frozen turkey onto an idling newspaper delivery truck, causing $3,000 in damage. A Realtor told us the construction was too much for some and they recently had sold their lofts, sometimes at a loss, a further setback to downtown's comeback. Other residents expressed concern that more retail was not opening, and that simple institutions such as coffee shops or non-trendy restaurants weren't available. The pioneer Treebeard's restaurant was no longer open evenings, for instance.[28]

In a sharp contrast to the upbeat newspaper stories in 1999 and 2000 about the bustling downtown scene, we come to this:

Shortly after 8 on a recent Thursday night, bartender Anne Hinds cast a weary eye over the virtually empty pub where she works.

A year ago, this place would have been jammed with customers ordering frothy pints of Guinness and plates of fish and chips. But now, like many restaurants and bars in downtown Houston, the Irish pub called Slainte is in a deep funk. On this night, there are only six patrons in the place. By contrast, there were eight employees on hand, including a cook who must have been dying of boredom . . .

"When downtown started its renaissance a little more than three years ago (1999), restaurants and bars were in the vanguard of the rebirth. They sprouted by the dozens, and rivals bid against one another to get prime locations. It was almost a gold-rush mentality—those bold enough to stake their claim were sure they were getting in on the ground floor of something big."

One restaurant, Cabo, invested $1.8 million into its facility and for a while was hot, taking in $30,000 on a good weekend. Most attribute the decline to the non-stop road construction creating a sea of mud, gravel and broken concrete. Other factors mentioned are the declining economy and the suggestion that there was an over-estimation of the size of the market.[29]

Jeffrey Yarborough, president of the Texas Restaurant Association and owner of Liberty Noodles in the Rice said, prophetically: "You are going to see a shakeout in the first quarter of 2002—absolutely. We can't survive two more years of this."[30] On our visit in early 2003 a sign was posted on the door of Liberty Noodles stating that after three years, the last day of operation was January 16, 2003. "We expect to reopen when the construction on Main Street is finished," the notice said.

The Enron collapse was also part of the restaurant decline downtown. Restaurateurs we interviewed referred to the "Enron kids" who helped populate the downtown for a few bright years and who helped make it lively. Carryouts and coffee bars likewise suffered when 4,700 employees from Enron alone were dropped in late 2001.

TRAFFIC THOROUGHFARES

A major negative that we found in downtown Houston was that the streets are made for speeding vehicles into and out of downtown. Five lanes of one-way pairs serve as north-south arteries, four lanes on crosstown streets, also one-way pairs. They make for an uncomfortable pedestrian experience. Adding to this discomfort is that most of the office towers on the downtown's west side have totally blank, not to say forbidding, walls on the street. Street-level retail is rare in downtown Houston today.

One reason for this is that there is a 6.2-mile interconnected tunnel system below ground. There's a type of restaurant and retail scene underground, at least on weekdays and especially at lunchtime. We came to understand that the tunnels are seen as adding value to the buildings above as privately owned and controlled space. You enter through an office lobby past considerable security. There will be no derelicts in the tunnels and that, it seems, is what propelled the system. A list of retail establishments found underground prepared by the Downtown Management District numbers 162. It includes the types of shops, restaurants, and services that normally would be on the streets above: a bank, candy shop, coffee bar, newsstand, dentist, cafes and carryout, gift shop, watch repair, shoe repair, sundries, hairdresser, card shop, McDonald's and Starbucks, bakery, printer, and the like. When the offices shut, so do the tunnels. That the homeless and the panhandlers have had such an impact on the development pattern in downtown Houston is suggestive of how significant a problem this element is, and how difficult to humanely resolve.

Running counter to these two major strikes against a hospitable downtown is a friendly, free trolley service. Run by the METRO bus system, the jitneys run six basic routes criss-crossing downtown and extending outside to the south and east. It means someone can park on the perimeter and take the jitney in to work, even though parking charges are relatively low.

2003 MOMENTUM

No matter how discouraging these various developments might be, Houstonians point to a variety of projects built or under construction downtown as of 2003 as evidence of a continuing move toward creating a more vibrant core.

Here are some of the new installations in downtown Houston:

- Bayou Place opened in 1997 after some delay as an entertainment venue at the front end of an old convention center in a key location. Included is a Hard Rock Café, a billiards parlor called Slick Willie's, Sake Lounge, Mingalone Italian Bar and Grill, Bar Houston, and Have a Nice Day Café. The complex also houses the Verizon Wireless Theater and the Angelika Film Center, which residents confirm is a very good movie complex but say is lightly attended. The promised second phase of Bayou Place was nowhere in sight in early 2003, suggesting it is less than a roaring success.

- Work is under way along Buffalo Bayou to enhance its contribution to the open space of the downtown, with Sesquicentennial Park in place and making a notable contribution. A stunning artwork here features massive pylons by artist Mel Chin that dramatize the otherwise huge blank wall of the Wortham Center (the performing arts hall). Allen's Landing, where the city was founded in 1836, has been remade with new docks along a formerly abandoned stretch of bayou.

- Harris County has built a Criminal Justice Center high-rise and plans to duplicate it with a Civil Justice Center. This will free up a number of handsome older structures for possible residential conversion if the market will support it.

- Still more offices are being built, such as 5 Houston Center on McKinney, twenty-seven stories including eight levels of parking, completed in fall 2002 at a cost of $115+ million. The office vacancy rate as of February 2003 was 14.45 percent for class A space. The total workforce in the downtown is 153,482, down a little from earlier but still strong.[31]

- The Hobby Center for the Performing Arts, a new addition to the already significant cultural district, houses two theaters (one of 2,650 seats, the other 500). Attendees report that they are excellent performance spaces. Several said to us the architectural style of the building looks like it is out of the 1950s. Whatever the merits of this comment, what is clearly unfortunate is a huge 500-car, multiple-level garage to the rear, overwhelming—and ignoring—a stretch of Buffalo Bayou.

- Houston traditionally has had relatively few downtown hotel rooms for a city of its size, less than smaller Dallas and Austin, for instance. Several new facilities have opened in the historic district, such as the remodeled Magnolia and Sam Houston Hotels, the latter a boutique facility with 102 rooms. The city is building a 1,200-room convention center hotel to be operated by Hilton after failing to get national firms to undertake the project despite major incentives, a downtown executive told us. The Downtown Management District reports that, in response to the city's incentives of tax breaks and abatements, the hotel room supply will soon near 5,000, up from 1,800 in 1999.

- The biggest single project and source of pride is the Minute Maid Stadium discussed previously, seating 40,950 under a retractable roof.

- A new basketball and hockey arena, under construction in 2003 and due to open in the fall, was to seat 18,500 for basketball, less for hockey, and 19,300 for concerts. The Harris County Houston Sports Authority was the developer, and the price was $175 million.

- The other big initiative is the rail line along Main Street, mentioned previously, opened in January 2004. The $300 million investment includes significant streetscape improvements that include handsome gray clay bricks, among other features. This idea, too, came from the private sector, under the auspices of the Urban Land Institute's Houston chapter, the local arm of a national developer organization. In aiming to establish "The New Economic Corridor" for Houston, the plan brochure states that the objective is create a framework for development and redevelopment and "to present a positive image of Houston to the world." It points to other cities combining transit and pedestrian-friendly streets, such as Uptown Dallas and Portland, Oregon. Mention is made of creating a more urban environment in a suburban setting.[32]

DIFFERING APPROACHES

Two schools of thought about how to revive a downtown have been competing in Houston. It's a tug of war between those who tend to the "Big Bang" approach, generally singular, isolated projects, the flashier the better. It's a view of downtown as an entertainment center with a series of attractions to lure people. The contrasting view we would characterize as not necessarily spurning performance venues and museums, but taking a more gradual, organic approach, emphasizing smaller initiatives with a heavier dose of residential projects with neighborhood amenities. This might be termed the "Quality of Life" approach. One of its adherents in Houston estimated that they represented about 25 percent of the voices, large enough to be heard but a minority. This person also characterized the difference as between one group looking to make Houston like Santa Barbara and another looking to Las Vegas for inspiration, with the latter group usually the winner.

We side with authors Roberta Gratz and Norman Mintz, who write in *Cities Back from the Edge:* "A collection of visitor attractions does not add up to a city."[33]

We can sum up the basic difference of approach this way: The entertainment approach will attract expense-account-type restaurants and clubs that close down at night unless a convention is in town. The quality-of-life approach would result in a more well-rounded, twenty-four-hour downtown neighborhood filled with cafes, bars, and retail, working in tandem with the cultural facilities and trendy but not necessarily expensive restaurants that are open nights to serve a neighborhood.

Two projects ongoing in 2003 embody the different philosophical approaches to downtown's revival.

First is the Cotswold streetspace improvements in the ninety blocks of the historic district, a city undertaking costing $62 million. Around 1995 local businessmen developed a vision of a canal down Congress Street, a water park at Market Square, and shrinking traffic on Travis Street, a principal north/south artery. After being kicked around for several years, the water elements were modified, but the "big idea" of angle parking to increase spaces, reducing traffic by a lane and creating a safer pedestrian feeling was adopted.

In early 2003 it was well along, with handsome new mounted wayfinding maps, new lighting fixtures, artful paving stones and trees installed on many of the streets. In lieu of the canal-in-the-street idea, numerous fountains were being placed along the signature corridor of Preston Street, an east-west crosstown street in the middle of the district, as well as along Main. Pillars with flowers have been added to Preston as well. Public art is to be integrated. Marble mosaics have already been placed along Texas Avenue. Portals (gateways) on Commerce Street will lead people down to a to-be-enhanced Buffalo Bayou.

Part of the work was also to improve the infrastructure, namely new water mains, new sanitary sewers, and storm water collection systems. Meaning the streets were significantly torn up and would be into 2004.

The stated purpose was to make the entire district a hospitable place for pedestrians, in sharp contrast to the inhospitable Skyline District. When completed, it would enhance the value of the remaining historic structures in the district and should, if the market demand were there, result in additional residential conversions, which in turn could reignite the lively restaurant/club scene of the late 1990s. Were all this to come to pass, there is a prospect that a viable residential sector of downtown Houston will really take root.

The other approach to downtown—building attractions—is embodied in the selection of "Downtown Aquarium—An Underwater Adventure" over a proposed mixed-use project that included housing for six acres of prime downtown land right on the Buffalo Bayou. The Downtown Aquarium project was opened in early 2003 by the highly successful Landry Restaurant chain, which has 279 outlets in 36 states under various names. The family entertainment package here features a restaurant with a huge, 150,000 gallon aquarium, a tiny train that takes you under a shark tank, Ferris wheel, carousel, boardwalk-like games, plus lounge and cafe.

The first thing to say about the Downtown Aquarium on the Bayou is that it is not an aquarium in the established sense. Landry's owner Tilman Fertitta has been quoted as likening it to the aquariums of Baltimore and Boston, but that is hyperbole squared. These aquariums are primarily nonprofit educational institutions with a strong conservation mission. In contrast, Downtown Aquarium is a commercial venture using fish as its motif. In March 2003, Fertitta bought the bankrupt Denver Aquarium for $13.6 million and announced he had "big plans for it," suggesting more cities will see combinations like that in Houston.[34]

The location of the Downtown Aquarium in the Theater District, Houston's performing arts center, is incongruous. It sits between the Hobby and Wortham Centers. Its garish architecture makes much of fake rocks and blue neon. Will it succeed commercially? Bets are yes. On a beautiful spring Saturday in 2003, the place was mobbed, and people were lined up to get in. Will it put pedestrians on the streets of Houston? Doubtful, with onsite parking available and nearby. Roads in the area are wide and traffic fast, not encouraging pedestrians to meander about. And there's not much to meander to.

In the end, the question that must be asked is whether a collection of singular attractions—cultural, sports, urban entertainment venues—add up to a cohesive, lively downtown. Or will people simply go to a game, a concert, a restaurant/entertainment venue, and then go home?

Under another scenario, could forces come together to create an urbane, lively downtown with real neighborhoods of residents, interspersed with the attractions? The vacant land is here to allow this to happen—and lots of it—but the market for new residential construction was unproven in 2003.

We wind up our discussion about downtown with two developments, one that could alter the way the city does business and the other that could transform the downtown residential picture.

First is an initiative coming, again, from the private sector to enact what are being called "area plan ordinances" that would impose certain building standards. Being careful to avoid the word "zoning," taboo in Houston, the idea does nonetheless smack of the institution of regulations that would guide future development. We first heard about this in an interview and then read about it while in Houston in February 2003 ("New Concept Promoted for City Planning").[35]

The plans, which the city would adopt, would be particular to individual neighborhoods and could alter basic city rules about parking, lot sizes, and so forth. While other cities are examining their zoning ordinances to see if they are too restrictive, Houston is coming at it from the other direction, giving developers a neighborhood blueprint so they know in advance what's expected of them.

The initiative, which still has numerous hurdles before enactment, stemmed from recommendations of the Urban Land Institute Main Street initiative. That group wanted to alter the rules along the corridor to allow, for example, buildings to be built to the sidewalk instead of adhering to the city's basic twenty-five-foot setback rule, thus giving the street a more urban feel. About twelve neighborhoods are expected to take part if the initiative makes it through City Planning Commission hearings. Individual plans would require approval by both the planning body and the city council. If adopted, the new approach could have a positive effect on the urban fabric of Houston, allowing denser and more pedestrian-oriented development than now takes place.

The second development that could make a major difference one way or the other is a proposed apartment tower near the baseball stadium planned by Trammel Crow Residential. It is a rethinking of an earlier thirty-four-story mixed-use proposal called Ballpark Place. The demise of Enron killed that project.

In its stead is planned a twenty-nine-story tower of apartments, average size around 1,100 square feet. If this new project is built and it succeeds in filling its 331 units, it will be the shot in the arm that downtown residential Houston needs. If, on the other hand, financing is not forthcoming or the project is built and does not succeed, the fledgling downtown residential movement will suffer a blow. It would state that there is not in fact a market now, that there are not enough young people interested in central-city living to fill an apartment tower. If it does fill up, a broker showed us a sketch of a thirty-four-story building planned for an adjoining lot full of small apartments. This developer is awaiting the results of the Trammel Crow move. As of September 2003, the project was on hold because of general market conditions and because the rental market was suffering from people buying properties aided by historically low mortgage rates.

MIDTOWN/FOURTH WARD

There is nothing conjectural about the residential growth in the Midtown and Fourth Ward areas. Nearly deserted just six or so years ago, with marginal commercial and office spaces plus major vacancy (one third of the Midtown area, according to the Houston Planning and Development Department), with only scattered, multifamily housing in Midtown and low-income places in Fourth Ward, both neighborhoods have exploded with new housing.

While they are hardly evident driving down the rather dismal-looking, roughly thirty-block stretch of Main Street between downtown and the

Museum District in 2003, one has only to travel a few blocks to the east or west to discover burgeoning developments of garden apartments and townhomes housing an estimated 7,500 people, up from 490 a decade ago, according to the Midtown Redevelopment Authority. The authority in January 2003 reported that 2,007 apartments units had been constructed in the area from 1997 through 2002.[36]

The Midtown story in capsule is one of early glory days, decline, and now, rediscovery. At the turn of the century, Midtown was a "silk stocking" district with fine, large homes. Once the area was known as Southside Place, where the wealth of Houston was displayed along Main Street in big Victorian mansions and Colonial Revival homes replete with large columns. A few, shadows of their former selves, still can be found here. The neighborhood thrived until the advent of the highways in the 1950s when families were drained off to the suburbs and the gradual decline began.

In the 1970s, the Environmental Protection Agency imposed a sewer moratorium on the city. The city then allowed for the sale of "sewer rights" so that existing connections could be bought and sold. House by house, block after block, properties in the once-beautiful neighborhood were sold to provide the sewer capacity for downtown high-rise developments. To add to the devastation, the city taxed these empty old houses as if they were occupied. This resulted in their demolition, especially on the east side, to lower taxes. This is an acute example of the Law of Unintended Consequences. The nearby Fourth Ward, a Freedmen's Town, a historic black district, was quietly ignored.

From two people we interviewed who took part in the transformation, it was a local parish priest, Steve Bancroft, who, working with an activist architect in the late 1980s, coalesced a group of citizens to try to stem the tide of blight, prostitution, and drugs that characterized the area. In 1991 a nonprofit volunteer group, Midtown Redevelopment Association, was formed. The University of Houston School of Architecture students helped create a "vision" for the area. A major objective was to change the image and get the press to acknowledge the area as "Midtown" rather than "south of downtown," which has succeeded. An early effort to try to encourage redevelopment failed, and the leaders realized they had to make tangible improvements before private investment would take hold.

This led to a petition to the city in the mid-1990s to establish a Midtown Redevelopment Authority able to derive revenue from property tax assessments and begin a full-scale effort at improving the quality of life with streetlights, sidewalks, irrigation, and a bicycle patrol. And in 1999 the Midtown Management District was formed, modeled on the downtown management district, more of a promotional entity than a bricks-and-mortar agency, with image enhancement and creation of a safe environment for residents and businesses its top priorities.

Paralleling this came the strong economy of the 1990s and the growing interest in Intown Living, primarily by young people, including many newly moved to Houston. The vacancy of Midtown and its low land prices attracted the development community, starting first on the west side of Main Street.

Major developers, including a well-known local firm, Perry Homes, became active in the neighborhood, which one downtown executive told us was a signal to others in the development community that this was a place to be. Perry builds townhomes ranging in size from 1,684 to 2,600 square feet and in price range from $150,000 to $232,000, well targeted to a young market. The firm built its first homes on the east side of Main Street in 1998, selling most before the concrete was poured, and had another fifty-four under construction (thirty-one of which were presold) plus enough land for two hundred more homes. This paved the way for other builders to expand into the rougher eastern portion of Midtown where street people traditionally hung out.[37] By 2003 there were far fewer homeless in the area. A representative of the firm was quoted by a downtown business leader as saying sales of units priced over $250,000 had fallen off, but that units in the $100,000-to-$200,000 category couldn't be built fast enough to satisfy demand. Further, these apartments were said to be appealing to teachers and firemen, the middle of the market.

The national development firm, Post Properties, based in Atlanta, also has a project here, called Post Midtown Square, with 674 apartments and townhomes. Just off the boundary street of Bagby, it features an urbane two-block section with brick sidewalks, first-floor retail including a cafe, and striking views of nearby downtown. It is next to a traditional soul food restaurant that speaks to the Fourth Ward's heritage as a Freedmen's Town, where newly freed slaves were housed after the Civil War.

Some of the other new projects in the area include Ventana at Midtown, a large rental project with one-bedroom units starting at $850 per month; Camden Midtown, prices starting at $845 per month; Amli Midtown with 419 units on an old estate site, prices starting at $942 per month and served by the free downtown trolley; Oakwood Houston Midtown (actually in the Fourth Ward), built in 1999 with 243 one- and two-bedroom apartments starting at $895 per month; the Calais, 356 apartments announced in February 2003 for completion in spring 2004; and another type of product, "Villa Serena," three-story townhome units with over 2,000 square feet, selling as low as $145,000 on up to $392,500. Some units work out to $1,600 per month, meaning that a two-income couple would be able to build equity. The agent here told us the firm is marketing to young people, including allowing no down payments, and had sold or had sales pending on nine of the twelve units in a matter of weeks in early 2003. Phase two next door was to begin soon. The developer, HHN Homes, was also said to be looking outside the area as Midtown land prices had shot up.

Here is a description of how the market is perceived in Midtown (and the Fourth Ward as well) by architect/urban planner Peter Brown of Peter Hoyt Brown Civic Design:

"The phenomenon of Midtown is an outgrowth of the 21st-century economy. In designing South End (four-story townhouses marketed as lofts) we were very sensitive to what appeals to this new buyer," says Brown, one of the leading advocates of Houston's Main Street redevelopment. "The 'techies' who make up the new job force are the 21st-century buyers," he says, "and they don't want to live in the suburbs."

"They want to live near their work in an active, urban setting. Light rail will make it even more exciting," Brown says. "It's the new 21st-century lifestyle."[38]

The architecture of Midtown is an interesting mix considering that most of the development is low-rise townhomes and only a few projects are very large. Townhouses vary from a modern industrial look of corrugated metal to adobe stucco to the more traditional styles in brick, stone, and wood. Oak trees and lush landscaping coupled with the public realm enhancements of attractive benches and lamps installed by the Redevelopment Authority add to the ambiance. The omnipresence of fences and gates suggests the need to provide a feeling of security in a pioneering area.

As of early 2003 Midtown lacked what you would call a true commercial center. Commerce and light industry, including retail serving an Asian community as well as a noodle factory, were scattered along either side of Main Street, not especially attractive or generally inviting. There are small strip retail centers, the Midtown Square cited previously, and, in a major breakthrough for the area, a new grocery store, Randall's, opened in fall 2002. It contains 38,000 square feet and features underground parking but is well designed to serve pedestrians. Randall's is a division of Safeway, Inc. One of the city's major liquor stores is in the area and expanding. There's a bit of a gallery scene beginning to take shape, using some of the old industrial stock. The Art Car Museum is opening a satellite in Midtown in an old auto body shop, and the Gallery Sonja Roesch, featuring European artists, is opening in a new three-story metal structure with living spaces above, a trend taking root in the neighborhood.

Midtown nightlife is beginning to take hold. Hot spots are said to include the Seven Lounge and Farrago and The Fish restaurants, attracting people from outside the neighborhood.[39]

One factor in the area's emergence is the location here of Houston Community College with approximately 14,000 students. Its administrative offices have six hundred employees.[40]

In early 2003 a proposal surfaced that would make a huge contribution to Midtown, a major, four-block park between Travis and Main on a now-vacant "super bloc." Under it would be parking for 3,700 cars aimed at increasing the area's density, according to proponent Daniel Barnum, an architect who is one of the area's first visionaries. The cost was put at $67 million, and the question of where such funding would come from was under discussion in spring 2003.

There is every indication that, with a burgeoning population of young professionals, and the relative lack of services for this population in early 2003, the retail picture will change, that the dreary maze that now runs along the central corridor will be altered. In fact, it was already beginning to take place as of early 2003. Many feel that the opening of the light rail along Main Street and the cessation of messy construction will be catalytic, spurring commercial development and helping to create a real neighborhood feeling.

Opened in 2004, the light rail is to travel at an average speed of 17 miles per hour and is to run every six minutes in peak hours, at twelve- to fifteen-minute intervals otherwise.[41] It will run through the middle of Midtown, connecting to the Arts District, Medical Center, and football stadium to the south, and the Theater District, sports facilities, and other offerings downtown to the north. METRORail will have three Midtown stations. There are skeptics, of course, but our take is that this line will be wildly successful and will lead to a demand for extensions; an east-west crossing line was in the planning stage in 2003.

Two factors playing a role in the comeback of Midtown are changes in city regulations and a tax increment finance district. In the first instance, the city realized its regulations did not encourage sidewalks, a major objective of the area. Adopted in 1999, the rules now require front-facing garages to be set back seventeen feet, for instance. This is so that parked cars will not block the sidewalk. The regulations also encourage shared driveways by having townhouses behind one another instead of side-by-side. The second factor operating is the Midtown Redevelopment Authority, created in 1995 by the city council to finance public improvements.

A third possible force is a newly formed residents' organization. The Downtown and Midtown Resident's Association was formed in July 2002 to address common concerns of the population in the two areas. For instance, it will campaign for a single, fixed place to vote downtown, instead of shifting around as it has in recent years. It will also work on image enhancement. It was in its formative stages and developing an active membership as of early 2003.[42]

Midtown Demographics

An analysis done for the *Houston Chronicle* by researchers at the University of Houston's Center for Public Policy recorded the following changes for the Midtown and Fourth Ward based on the 2000 census compared with 1990:

Midtown: White population up 112 percent, black up 2.5 percent, Hispanic up 55 percent, Asian up 394 percent, total growth of 36.5 percent.

The Asian growth spurt is primarily Vietnamese who have colonized a section of Midtown.

Fourth Ward's white population was up 267 percent, black down 55 percent, Hispanic up 17 percent, Asians up 26 percent, overall growth up 200 percent. Here especially the issue of gentrification is in the forefront as many shotgun rentals are being pulled down to make way for the new projects. Says Stephen Fox, an architectural historian at Rice University, "Revitalization has become a code word in Houston for mass destruction of low-income housing and mass displacement of low-income families." He could well be speaking of the Fourth Ward.[43]

The two census tracts here, which cover Midtown pretty completely, give us a lower total population than the redevelopment authority estimates, namely 4,710 (versus 7,500). This could be a difference in territory or it could also reflect growth since the census. The profile is confirming about who is attracted here: The median age in tract 4106 to the west of Main Street is 30.8 years and in tract 3125 on the east, 32.9 years. The western section is 71 percent white, predominately single and male. The eastern half is even more heavily male (79.4 percent) and is likewise mostly a rental population.

Intown Living

What the Midtown/Fourth Ward phenomenon reflects, similar to downtown and the other nearby housing projects mentioned previously, is a shift by a segment of the population to the center. We're concentrating on the absolute center, but were we to cast the net over the entire "center city" that lies inside The Loop, we would have much larger numbers. Still small compared to what continues to happen outside Highway 8, but a clear reversal of the white flight of the past decades.

Documenting this is a survey conducted for the Houston Downtown Management District by CDS Market Research, an update on a similar survey done five years earlier that established the existence of interest in downtown living. The 1998 survey of 761 households in Harris County (incomes above $30,000 and living inside Highway 6) found 30 percent with "some interest" in living downtown or in Midtown and 13 percent with a "high level of interest" and very likely to make the move if the price was right. The survey's "conservative" estimate is that 137,400 households in Harris County have a strong interest in living in downtown or Midtown, nearly half of whom work in these areas or nearby. The survey found that those interested in Intown Living had more college training than the average population, were predominately young (25 to 44), nearly 60 percent white, and with median incomes of $55,600.[44]

If expansive growth continues in Midtown, over time the area could grow southward along the Main Street spine to connect with the handsome

Museum District to the south, effectively blending the two areas together. High-rise condominiums have begun in the Museum District area, like Museum Towers. What higher land prices will mean in Midtown is that more four-to-eight-story buildings, or higher, will be built in the future, a neighborhood association representative predicted, in character more like the Museum District than is present today.

With a healthy dose of optimism, one can envision an entirely new look and feel for intown Houston in the future, with a network of lively, pedestrian-oriented streets, urbane neighborhoods, a handsome greensward through its middle along Buffalo Bayou, and with a good transit system in place used by an Intown Living population concentrated in the downtown historic area and a growing Midtown.

Quite a different portrait from today's downtown with its unfriendly trophy towers, empty lots, scores of parking garages, and grim streetscape—albeit with a historic area and its potential as a real, vibrant urban neighborhood.

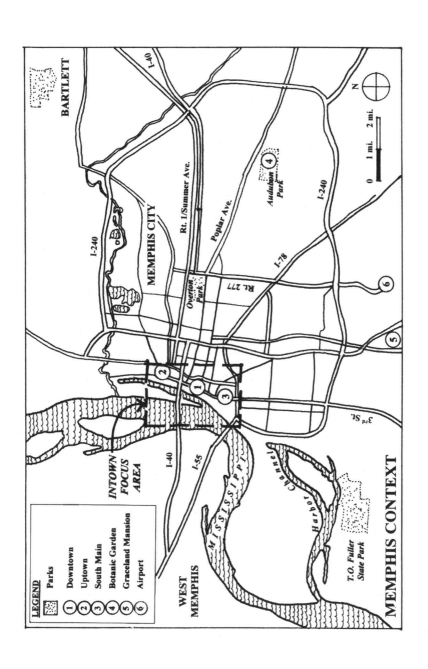

LEGEND

Parks

1 Downtown
2 Uptown
3 South Main
4 Botanic Garden
5 Graceland Mansion
6 Airport

BARTLETT

I-40

MEMPHIS CITY

Rt. 1/Summer Ave.

Poplar Ave.

Audubon Park (4)

I-240

I-240

Overton Park

Rt. 277

I-78

6

5

3rd St.

INTOWN FOCUS AREA

2

1

3

I-40

I-55

WEST MEMPHIS

MISSISSIPPI

Harbor Channel

T.O. Fuller State Park

MEMPHIS CONTEXT

N

0   1 mi.   2 mi.

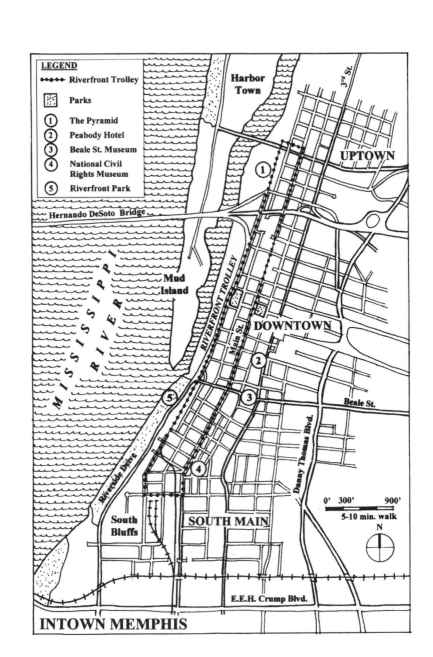

LEGEND
- ••••• Riverfront Trolley
- Parks
- ① The Pyramid
- ② Peabody Hotel
- ③ Beale St. Museum
- ④ National Civil Rights Museum
- ⑤ Riverfront Park

Harbor Town

3rd St.

UPTOWN

Hernando DeSoto Bridge

MISSISSIPPI RIVER

Mud Island

RIVERFRONT TROLLEY

Main St.

DOWNTOWN

Beale St.

Danny Thomas Blvd.

0' 300'   900'
5-10 min. walk

N

Riverside Drive

South Bluffs

SOUTH MAIN

E.E.H. Crump Blvd.

INTOWN MEMPHIS

6

Memphis

> "Have you ever been to Memphis?," he asked.
> "Once when I was a little girl. Some kind of convention for the church. All I remember is the river."
>
> —*John Grisham,* The Firm

Driving through downtown Memphis in 2003 you would take in, as we did, the venerable and handsomely restored Peabody Hotel with a new retail complex adjoining it, the Main Street trolleys, historic Beale Street, views of the Mississippi river, the enormous Pyramid arena, and new museums and stadiums, but you would also have been aware of lots of vacancy, spotty street retail, and deteriorated buildings and lots. You might easily miss the growing presence of middle-class housing in and near downtown Memphis, yet it collectively is perhaps the most dramatic instance of Intown Living in our eight case cities, considering how far it has come.

Memphis, known as "the city on the bluff" overlooking the Mississippi, was nearly destroyed by yellow fever in the 1870s. It later enjoyed a reputation as a notoriously bawdy town, host to gamblers and prostitutes with all manner of dives, with the dubious distinction as "murder capital of the nation." It has survived all that and more.

In more recent times, the city suffered riots and fires following the assassination of Dr. Martin Luther King Jr. in 1968 at the Lorraine Motel here, now the National Civil Rights Museum. Memphis emptied out as whites, who had already begun to desert the downtown, left in droves for the suburbs.

The predominately black neighborhoods of South Memphis likewise were abandoned. In the 1970s, downtown had all but died. Large areas fell to neglect. There were vacant buildings in every block. Once-lively Beale Street was boarded up by the city. The grand old Peabody Hotel was closed.[1] Holdovers from this period, particularly boarded-up and vacant stretches of Main Street in the middle of the city, were still present in 2003.

Center City Commission President Jeff Sanford, in an interview published in 2002, recalled that even in the 1980s, downtown was dead. "I used to ride my bike a lot back in the '80s," he said, "and I can guarantee you that I was in no danger of being hit by anybody. The streets were empty on weekends." Likewise, he reported, he had Tom Lee Park on the Mississippi to himself, as there would be nobody else there.

DOWNTOWN DESERTED

Sanford moved into downtown in 1986.

"Not many people around. So yes, of course, it was empty. There were a couple of night spots, and a few brave patrons, but there was really very little to do before the Orpheum (a theater) and The Peabody were renovated." He goes on to note that the exodus was so swift that a rich stock of architecture was left. "Back in the '60s and '70s, people seemed to have been in such a hurry to leave that they left some of the best behind. Like The Peabody, like all the buildings on South Main, like the buildings right outside our block of Main."[2]

A downtown developer we interviewed noted that Memphis was lucky in one sense: Its market was so poor in those years, it made no sense to tear down old buildings because there was nothing coming along to take their place, saving demolition costs.

Another developer we interviewed recalled coming to Memphis in the 1970s. There was no downtown hotel whatever, and he had to stay in the outskirts. A barbecue place was the only downtown restaurant open at night. During this period of decline, Memphis lost office tenants both to the suburbs and to other cities.

Here's a description of downtown Memphis from 1974:

On every side of the tattered old vaudeville hall, buildings fell to bulldozers. The theater (the Orpheum) stood alone on its downtown block, surrounded by muddy lots. Beale Street's historic clubs and theaters were vacant and crumbling, the landmark Peabody Hotel was closed and Mud Island was, well, mud and tangled trees.

Eight years after the murder of Dr. Martin Luther King Jr. at Memphis's Lorraine Motel, urban renewal had leveled neighborhoods from Front Street to Manassas (about six blocks). Downtown was being dismantled. The venerable Orpheum theater, ornate host to the greats of stage and screen since 1928, was edging into disrepair and could be the next to fall.[3]

Rallying around the slogan, "Orpheum or Asphalt?" a young nonprofit called the Memphis Development Foundation bought the building, then a movie theater, for $285,000 in 1976, after the city refused. It pumped $20 million into its restoration, finally completed in 1997. Foundation leader Bill Matthews recruited a roster of community leaders to help raise the funds needed, which included state and city assistance. While the Orpheum has been enormously successful (a Norah Jones concert in July 2003 sold out in a matter of minutes) and over 300,000 attend events there now in a given year, attempts to redevelop the rest of the block as Beale Street Landing at the key intersection of Beale Street and Riverfront Drive haven't fared as well, a successful developer in Memphis noted.

But the Orpheum was the first big success in this, the southern part of downtown, and it helped to trigger the eventual comeback of South Main, a section very much in play in 2003. During the late 1970s and early 1980s a number of other initiatives and events occurred that helped to spawn the rebirth of Memphis.

EARLY EFFORTS

In 1976, in what was an initial city effort, a pedestrian mall was put in place down Main Street in a formulaic solution that was popular in the 1960s and '70s for downtowns trying to compete with suburban malls. Most of these pedestrian malls have failed and have since been returned to handling vehicles, most famously Chicago's State Street. One restaurateur recalled, however,

"Downtown was really booming and hustling then," he says of the first few years in the late '80s. "You couldn't walk up and down the mall. At lunchtime we had a line out the door." He is now said to be starving for customers.[4]

The mall renamed itself Main Street and had a shot in the arm in the mid-1990s when historic streetcars were re-introduced in lieu of buses and the streetscape was improved with handsome bricks. The switch, we were told, came about when an expressway that was proposed to run through Overton Park was defeated by citizens in a case that went to the Supreme Court. The freed-up funds were applied to the rail project, an activist told us, undertaken by the Memphis Area Transit Authority (MATA). The initial line ran for 2.5 miles, connecting the government center and convention hall on the north with the south end of downtown. A later extension proceeds along the riverfront and extends farther south into a redeveloping area and the expanded National Civil Rights Museum. The cars themselves are splendid; in downtown a good deal of what is seen from them today, however, is vacancy and abandonment along Main. Another extension will link downtown to the Medical District 2.2 miles to the east, costing $74 million and to be completed in 2004.

In 1977, Lyman Baldrich succeeded in starting a great Memphis tradition: The Memphis in May International Festival. This month-long event features a citywide series of concerts, art shows, a Beale Street Music Festival, "World Famous Barbecue Cooking Contest," and a Sunset Symphony, among other activities. One author noted that "May is the month when everyone goes downtown."[5] This annual infusion of people and energy onto the downtown riverfront no doubt is why Memphis in May was cited as one of the catalytic events for downtown Memphis by a leading developer.

Also in 1977, one of the country's early downtown redevelopment agencies was established, namely the Center City Commission, an agency very much in the picture today. It began with a focus on the downtown and has kept it through the present. The agency's funding comes from a special levy on commercial properties, in keeping with like entities in other cities, of 65 cents per $100 of the property's valuation (which is 40 percent of appraised value), with the first $25,000 exempted. This tax generates about $2.8 million annually, according to a 2002 report by the commission.

There are a variety of incentives available from the Center City Commission and affiliated boards, outlined in a CCC report entitled, "Strategic Plan Update 2002–2006," which built on an earlier vision statement of 1999. The stated rationale for the commission's assistance programs is that downtown projects are more costly and complex due to high land costs plus hidden costs that can be associated with infrastructure or environmental issues. They run from the "PILOT Program" (payment-in-lieu of taxes), which freezes taxes at a predevelopment level in exchange for a lump payment up front (we will cite a specific example later), to development loans for renovations and a Main Street tenant loan program of up to 90 percent to encourage retail uses on this key street. Real estate brokers get a bonus for signing tenants in certain downtown properties, and there are bonds for both public projects (tax-exempt) and private undertakings with a public purpose. There's minority-owned business assistance as well.

Along a particularly bleak block of Main Street, the commission hopes its incentives will work to the extent that it has put up large, good-looking signs announcing what projects it plans for many of the buildings. The danger, of course, is that if the developments don't proceed, even with the significant incentives the commission makes available to developers, it will lead to discouragement and make future redevelopment that much harder. One private developer predicted that only half of the announced projects would actually get built.

Also in the public/private partnership are affiliates that help developers with planning, financing, tax abatements, land acquisition, promotions, design review, tenant recruitment, and parking. The Center City Development Corporation offers low-interest loans (such as for the Center for Southern Folklife, mentioned later). The Center City Revenue Finance Corporation issues the tax freezes and offers bonds to help finance projects.

There's a Design Review Board that reviews the design of all projects receiving CCC help. There is also a Downtown Parking Authority that plans and builds parking facilities downtown.

CCC was to begin work on its Streetscape Master Plan in fall 2003, which was to include, on selected streets and sidewalks, cobblestone paving, improved drainage, and tree plantings, a June 2003 CCC bulletin announced.

The agency is operated by a twenty-person board of directors evenly divided between private sector representatives appointed by the city and county mayors and public representatives. As with similar entities in other cities, it operates a uniformed patrol service that helps visitors and works to get homeless people into help programs.

ECONOMIC PICTURE

While the downtown residential market is strong, as we will document, the retail and commercial sectors were soft as of 2003. Center City Commission vice president for planning and development Myron Hughes noted that recruiting retail for downtown is "kind of tough."[6] What has happened to depress the nonresidential market is the continued loss of major downtown anchors like Union Planters Bank, Goldsmith's (a department store), and cotton operations along Front Street. A recent example: Clear Channel radio announced in July 2003 that it was leaving its Beale and Union Street offices for the suburbs, citing parking difficulties, infrastructure problems, and accessibility. "We have 150 employees and our old location favored only about 15 percent of us," said regional vice president Bruce Demps. Also cited was out-of-date wiring.[7]

While there are bright spots, the overall economy in the Memphis area continues to fall behind peers such as Nashville and Atlanta in net migration and net change in income, the Regional Chamber of Commerce reported for the years 1995 to 2000. The area did gain population, but at a slower rate than eight other comparable places, and it had a negative change in total income of $89.7 million. That's because the people moving in made less than those leaving, the chamber's administrative officer reported. The chamber has established a Talent Magnet Collaborative to make Memphis attractive to bright, young professionals (The Creative Class phenomenon again). There's also to be a Memphis Regional Lifestyle Web site.[8]

Another account, from *Southern Business and Development*, a publication from Birmingham, had a more positive take, saying Memphis in 2002 was the "most successful city of its size in attracting capital investment and jobs," ahead of Jacksonville and Orlando, for instance.[9] Perhaps accounting for the difference in these two views of the overall economy is that Memphis was compared to a different set of cities in the two surveys.

The most dynamic sector of the economy from what we could discern is the major medical facilities in and next to downtown Memphis. There is the

Medical Center complex on the east of downtown that goes by that name, and the St. Jude Children's Research Hospital in the Uptown neighborhood to the north of downtown, whose planned redevelopment we outline later. St. Jude had under construction in 2003 a $500 million expansion program involving five new buildings, which was to include 500,000 square feet of patient care facilities plus research labs.[10] The Memphis Biotech Foundation plans a major, $160 million facility, there's a University of Tennessee Cancer Institute for which funds have been committed, and an expansion of the Southern College of Optometry has been completed.

Other assets include the Hartwell Center for Bioinformatics and Biotechnology, GTX INC. The Eye Center, Genome Explorations, Viral Antigens, Molecular Design, and others. The medical device sector of the local economy is said to be growing.[11]

PEABODY RENEWAL

Let us turn now to a really bright spot, The Peabody Hotel, located in the middle of downtown on Union Street between Second and Third. It was bought in 1975 for $75,000 by a major developer, Jack Belz, whose far-flung enterprises today employ 1,110 people. Belz spent $24 million in rehabilitating The Peabody, restoring it to its former grandeur. The reopening in 1981, with a week's worth of parties, we were told, in what seems very true to the Memphis style, was cited by nearly everyone as *the* catalytic event for downtown because of its symbolism as the onetime social center for the city. You have to like a place that ushers five ducks every morning out of an elevator onto a red carpet and parades them ceremoniously into a marble fountain in the middle of the elegant, spacious lobby where they spend the day, returning with equal pomp to their rooftop home at 5:00 P.M.

The success of the hotel then led Belz Enterprises Inc. to acquire the adjoining eight blocks to create a huge mixed-use project called Peabody Place. It includes an apartment building, an office tower, and a historic restoration on Main Street with a museum and grocery market. The Peabody Place Museum here houses the Oriental art and artifact collection of Marilyn and Jack Belz. It is underneath the grocery store that is part of the restored former Goldsmith's Department Store, now called Pembroke Square. There are jade sculptures and ivory carvings in a collection that dates to the 1960s. In July 2003, Belz Enterprises secured a development loan to add another cultural component to Main Street, the money to be used to relocate the Center for Southern Folklore from an interior location to a storefront directly on the street, which will add to the diversity of the 100 block of South Main.

Opening in 2001 was another major part of the complex, an "entertainment and retail center," basically an urban mall. The rationale apparently was that to lure people from the suburbs, they were going to have to be made to feel safe and be given familiar-looking territory—the Faneuil Hall syndrome from Boston, which made suburbanites feel safe downtown. The anchor here is not a department store, which had been the plan until Goldsmith's folded, but a twenty-two-screen movie theater that appeared to be packing in customers. There were a number of subsidies involved, a representative of the project told us, including a loan from the U.S. Department of Housing and Urban Development, Community Development Block Grant funds from same, help from the Economic Development Administration, plus state and county assistance on the parking. The project successfully carried its way through a succession of four city administrations and four county mayors.

The retail side here is familiar to all: Tower Records, Ann Taylor Loft, Gap, Victoria's Secret, etc. We asked an official at the Center City Commission if Peabody Place had drained retail from the downtown streets. His answer was no, it wasn't there to drain. The Peabody entertainment and retail center contains fourteen restaurants, a number of which are at the street level, offsetting in part the inward orientation of the retail component. These include the Dan McGuinness Pub, Fat Tuesday, and Jillian's, which, it should be noted, are just steps away from an alive-again Beale Street with its clubs and bars in a historic setting. A giant parking garage for 1,600 cars adjoins.

Beale Street's recovery began in 1983 when the first club reopened. This was after the City of Memphis acquired most of the properties along the core four blocks in the late 1970s to shut down what was felt to be a decayed, not to say dangerous, area. Gradually businesses opened up and the blocks came to life. A cousin of New Orlean's Bourbon Street, it is a boast of Memphis that Beale Street is Tennessee's number one tourist attraction. There's a club named for famed bluesman B. B. King, Alfred's with a deck and patio, the Blues City Cafe, a bazaar with live music and open-air market on weekends, and, just one block to the south, the Smithsonian's Memphis Rock 'n' Soul Museum in the Gibson Guitar Building, which offers tours of the factory.

Opening in 2002 in another plus for downtown was the boutique, luxury hotel The Madison, with 110 suites. The renovation of the Tennessee Trust Building and adjacent structures was done by Wall Street Hotel LLC at an estimated cost of $13 million. There's a very trendy-looking lobby, a sleek small bar, and a restaurant. Adding still more to the picture of the downtown as the context for Intown Living are four special venues worth mentioning.

FOUR VENUES

First, AutoZone Park (named for the company whose headquarters is downtown facing the river, employing over nine hundred). It is the baseball stadium for the Memphis Redbirds, the AAA affiliate of the St. Louis Cardinals, setting attendance records since opening in 2000; in 2003 it had the second-highest attendance in minor league baseball. It is located on what apparently was a derelict site immediately catty-corner from The Peabody. Built of brick, the stadium presents a friendly face to the street and also has a walkway around the park. Because of the Peabody Place parking and other garages nearby, the stadium is not surrounded by a sea of macadam as is often the case, and it had to build only a relatively small parking garage. Directly behind the park is a new residential project, Echelon at Ballpark, with 375 market-rate apartments built at a cost of $32.5 million.[12]

Under construction, with roof girders being put in place in July 2003, was the FedExForum, a basketball stadium for the National Basketball Association Memphis Grizzlies, transplants from Vancouver. It seats 18,400 for basketball and was to open for the fall 2004 season. The building will also handle ice shows, concerts, rodeos, and the like. Its location is just one half block from Beale Street. This is a combination city/county and private project costing $250 million.[13]

The Grizzlies were playing in The Pyramid, a 22,000-seat arena on the north of downtown near the river. The thirty-two-story pyramid is a gleaming, if not glaring, landmark—its reflective glass can be blinding in the sun. This will still be the venue apparently for rock concerts, wrestling, and other shows, although the newer FedExForum may lure some events away. It opened in 1991 and is surrounded by seemingly endless surface parking areas.

Lastly, an expansion of the convention center on downtown's north side included the addition of a new 2,100-seat Cannon Center for the Performing Arts. Now that sports facilities are in place, the next push by the Memphis establishment is to augment the city's cultural offerings. Led by Steve Odland, chief executive officer of AutoZone, there is to be a campaign to generate $25 million for the Greater Memphis Arts Council. Says Odland: "(Memphis businesses) have really done a great job promoting sports. But having a strong arts community is just as important in attracting new businesses and talented workers to Memphis." In announcing the drive, Odland reported that $17 million had already been raised in pledges during the "silent phase" of the campaign among the area's wealthiest corporations (FedEx headquarters is here, for example).[14]

THE RIVER

We would be remiss not to mention the Mississippi River and its importance to Memphis. Historically the riverfront was the transportation hub that made Memphis one of the key cotton ports of its time. The Mississippi, wide and powerful on this reach of the river, passes by and below the downtown. It serves as an element linking the varied residential developments along it, all of which emphasize their ties to the river, physical and/or visual. The setting here is such that the sunsets occur over wide, green, open space on the Arkansas side, with the river in the foreground. The Peabody and the Madison hotel rooftops have lively Thursday sunset parties to capitalize on these views, well attended by a young crowd from the sample we observed. One apartment building promotion touts: "Sunsets are free!"

We were involved in May 1999, helping to organize an early planning activity that preceded the formation of the Riverfront Development Corporation, one of the recommendations that grew out of the public discussion then. A master plan for the core riverfront was drawn up and adopted in 2002, with an overall price tag of $225 million, envisioned as mostly private investments. A first step was to install a proper walkway along Riverside Drive connecting Tom Lee Park on the south with Jefferson Street about seven blocks north. This walkway passes by the historic cobblestones where cotton barges landed, a poignant reminder of the economy that made Memphis the cotton center of the South in the late nineteenth century. These cobblestones are the only such remnant of the steamboat era on the entire Mississippi river, making them all the more historically important. A park expansion downriver was also accomplished in 2003 by the riverfront entity.

The next project scheduled is a taming of Riverside Drive by adding a parkway-type median and major pedestrian crosswalks. Memphis, like Minneapolis and New Orleans, is blessed in that no interstate highway runs along the river (although it does have massive ramps leading onto Interstate 40 at the north end of the downtown) and that Riverside, with four lanes, can be calmed. Two alternative north-south routes (Third Street and Danny Thomas Blvd.) are available nearby, and an interstate is farther to the east.

A component of this plan is for a major boat dock to be built at the foot of Beale Street. A design competition for this feature was to conclude in October 2003. Initial Federal funds for this work were announced in July 2003.

The big scheme for the riverfront is to fill in a portion of the Wolf River between Mud Island from downtown, creating a lake to the north lined with developable property. However the final product turns out, the riverfront is on the city's priority list for enhancement and for improved accessibility, all of which will serve to solidify its importance to the expanding residential stock in and near downtown Memphis.

THE BEGINNING

Against all this background, we turn to the residential scene in Memphis. We wind the clock back to 1981. In the same month that The Peabody reopened, the first significant new downtown residential project came onto the market, The Shrine Building. There was one earlier, small project, the four Timpani condominiums. By one account, as of 1977, there were just 244 units of market-rate housing in the entire downtown.[15] To get way ahead of our story, as of 2000, there were 5,990 people in the three census tracts comprising the traditional downtown core.

A representative of the Shrine—the top floors had originally been the Shriners' headquarters—related that an earlier residential conversion attempt was killed by the 1968 riots, but a market study that had been undertaken had concluded that there was in fact a market for Intown Living, which served to encourage the later Shrine undertaking.

The 1923 Shrine Building was converted to apartments, helped along by historic tax credits because the building is on the National Register. The twelve-story building, which features a splendid entrance lobby, comes with twenty-plus different floor plans, starting with an efficiency of 419 square feet and going up to two-level penthouses, eighty-two units in all, including a beautiful and gracious top floor apartment we were pleased to visit. Small wonder that filmmakers used it in the movie version of John Grisham's novel *The Firm*. With its height and near-river location, the building offers fine views up and down the Mississippi, taking in the sunsets over the river.

We talked with three people from the building. Each spoke with great affection about it, noting that many stayed there fourteen or eighteen years, perhaps moving from one unit to another. Past views and a roof deck, there's a seventy-five-foot-long pool in the basement plus exercise space, eleven-foot ceilings, plaster ornamentation, and a parking arrangement with a next-door garage. One interesting sidelight: About half the residents were thought to be counter-commuters, working out of downtown. This is a project by Henry Turley who, along with Jack Belz, is credited with sparking the residential growth downtown plus the commercial vitality it does possess. As we'll see, they are teaming up with a new undertaking north of downtown.

We visited another apartment project nearby, Number 10 Main, a recently completed conversion of what was the Commerce Title Building. Actually two buildings, a representative told us, one built in 1904, the other half in 1912. It was "modernized" in the 1950s, which involved removing marble columns from the front. Because 20 percent historic tax credits were used, the restoration had to meet preservation standards, one of which states that new additions must look new. This meant that marble replacement, especially if it matched perfectly, was not allowed, so concrete columns were installed in what would seem like an odd, unintended consequence of a sensible enough standard. The city provided a twenty-year tax freeze, which called for a large upfront payment in lieu of taxes—the PILOT program mentioned previously. The extent of such freezes differs for different uses, the representative here told us. The restoration into apartments created 112 units whose rents range from $950 to $1,350 a month.

Living downtown in Number 10 was simply more fun than the suburbs, one resident told us. Downtown to this person feels like a small town. The building itself is friendly, the rooftop with its hot tub and grills serving as an informal community center. Management hosts four parties a year here, furthering the sense of belonging. Morning coffee is served in the elegant, high-ceilinged lobby.

The largest population group in the building is 40-year-olds, including some recent divorcees, we were told. There's at least one couple with children. In summer 2003, a restaurant was eyeing the 6,000 square feet of streetfront space the building offers.

Another person associated with the building told us of raising kids in the area. He lives in the nearby Exchange Building, which has a large percentage of subsidized apartments. He related how his then 14-year-old daughter became an entrepreneur one summer, opening a sweet shop downtown with money borrowed from the father that was paid back early. She made $3,000 that summer. His son likewise became a messenger.

One of the things the children learned, he related further, was tolerance. They came to see the downtown homeless and panhandlers as nonthreatening. Children are the exception to our Intown Living story, to be sure, but we thought these insights worth recording as one of the minor subtrends we observed in our case cities is the introduction of some families to the downtowns or near-downtown locations.

Past The Shrine and Number 10 are seventeen other core downtown residential buildings, both rental and condominium, with a total of 1,675 units, most of which are fully occupied as of June 2003 according to the Center City Commission.[16] The number will be reduced by eighty-nine as an older apartment building is converted to a hotel. This conforms with the 2000 census figure for the center of downtown as having 2,186 residents.

Before leaving downtown, let us describe two other properties to convey a feeling of what's on the market here. It's important to note that Intown Living in Memphis did in fact begin in the core before spreading to adjacent areas, which might run counter to expectations in a city with a history of racial tension.

Barton Flats with nineteen units (not included in the Center City Commission total) is on South Front Street overlooking the river. It comes with balconies and a rooftop deck and is in the open, exposed-brick loft style. Prices started at $120,000 and as of July 2003, only two units were left.

The nineteen-story Exchange Building with 202 apartments is the building with the subsidized units discussed previously. It was the Cotton and Merchant Exchanges Building built in 1910.

Overall, the *Memphis Business Journal* reported in 2002, the downtown condominiums selling best were priced under $170,000, but units priced between $200,000 and $400,000 were also moving. An apartment converted to condominiums raised its prices four times before settling on a range of $84,000 to $210,000 and selling thirty-seven of sixty-two units. Prices in these ranges would clearly seem to be aimed at the younger slice of the market, or perhaps buyers of weekend flats.[17] The census tract for downtown gives the median age as 43.9, while the largest age bracket again is the 25- to 34-year-olds, over 20 percent of the total. Rentals are 86 percent of the total.

TURNING POINTS

Let us now share the perhaps surprising insights of one of the city's major private developers as to what the factors were that contributed to the rebirth of downtown Memphis. They were not the financial incentives that obviously played a part, but rather some happenings that helped provide the necessary atmospherics.

First mentioned was the opening of Automatic Slim's Tonga Club by Karen Blockman Carrier in 1991, where for the first time in Memphis attention was paid to the experiential aspects of serving food: lighting, music, and decor. The restaurant, on South Second Street across from The Peabody, serves Southwestern and Caribbean cuisine in a very funky atmosphere. The effect was to raise the bar and change the dynamic for downtown restaurants. A number of other stylish places have since opened, such as McEwen's on Monroe Street in 1997, which likes to recall that on its first day fully nine people showed up for lunch, whereas reservations are now recommended. It has gone on to gain recognition for its wine list from the *Wine Spectator* magazine. FeliciaSuzanne's is another first-rate restaurant downtown. Memphis's famous barbecue ribs can still be found, of course, but other choices are available.

This developer next cited events that were instrumental in uplifting the spirits of Memphians across the board. One was the big international festival, Memphis in May, mentioned earlier, and the other was the lighting of the Hernando De Soto Bridge in 1986, the latter event attributed to the leadership of Pat Kerr. This became a community-wide event, with school kids engaged in drawing what the lit bridge would look like, the local newspaper featuring it, radio stations collaborating to promote it, and otherwise getting as many people involved in a totally democratic way for what was altogether a joyous occasion and one that occurs every day. Bridge lightings, festivals, and fireworks are the "Oh Wow!" kinds of things that are often symbolic of hope that uplift community spirit and, in this person's analysis, helped set the stage to make Intown Living possible.

HARBOR TOWN

We turn to another residential area north of downtown where there is a large, multifaceted residential project (actually multiple projects) built on Mud Island. The island has the Mississippi River on one side, the Wolf River on the other. In 1982 on the southern tip of the island a project called Mud Island was opened that received a lot of publicity for its Mississippi River Museum, with an open-air, five-block-long scale model of the river complete with running water, and big outdoor amphitheater for events.

In the late 1980s developer Henry Turley and Belz Enterprises purchased a 135-acre portion north of the Mud Island project and built a residential development, Harbor Town, with a wide range of housing types ranging in price from $114,000 to $425,000. A bridge to the island effectively opened it up to development; access to the Mud Island Museum was by tram. An expansion was under way in 2003 on the island by Belz/Turley to include more single-family houses and condominiums, and also to add office and retail space, an inn, and restaurants to create more of an urban community center in this somewhat suburban-feeling locale. Harbor Town Landing, under construction in mid-2003, was listed as costing $150 million.[18]

The Center City Commission lists twelve different residential projects on Mud Island, six single-family, five apartments, and one small condominium. These developments range in size from the 439 homes in the original Harbor Town to 500 apartments in Riverset. Island Park and Harbor Town Square, where an older cluster of retail exists, have 300 apartments. The Estates at River Pointe contain another 400 apartment units. The area also benefits from a long, linear riverfront walk that fronts the Mississippi, a major amenity for residents now so crowded on sunset evenings that an expansion is planned by the riverfront development group. The island is five minutes from and within the official definition of downtown.

Someone involved with Mud Island shared this interesting insight. He recalled being bugged by new residents wanting a grocery store. After the five hundredth such request, he began to realize it wasn't the milk, bread, and eggs they wanted, but the grocery was an important symbol in a new project that meant there was to be a real community, that it stood for both a sense of neighborhood and a sense of permanency and completeness. Thus came into being Miss Cordelia's Grocery. This was not the first time in our case cities when the presence of a grocery was seen as vital.

There are a total of 2,600 housing units on Mud Island, 75 percent of which are apartments, as listed by the Center City Commission.[19] Locally the island is thought to now contain 5,000 people. The census tract, which may cover only parts of the developments, lists 2,394, fully one-third of whom are age 25 to 34. The median age in the census tract here in 2000 was 31, and singles constituted one-half of the population.

UPTOWN NEXT

In a section to the immediate north of downtown, parallel to Harbor Town, is The Uptown project. It was in its infancy at the time of our visit in mid-2003, although some initial units of infill housing were under construction. The project is a $162 million joint effort by Henry Turley Co. and Belz Enterprises known as the Uptown Partnership, a Belz-Turley Community Development Company. In a complex undertaking, the Uptown Development Plan calls for the renovation of public housing units, new housing to include five hundred affordable single-family homes, renovated apartment units and another eighty-eight-unit apartment project. The developers are partnering with the Memphis Housing Authority. Effectively, this project will integrate a predominately black section of approximately one hundred blocks that includes vacancy and dilapidation. It is also the location of the St. Jude Children's Research Hospital complex, on a fifty-three-acre campus, a major employment center with 2,300 workers.

The plan calls for 1,100 new homes, 25 percent to be public housing, 35 percent affordable (both rental and for sale), and the rest market-rate, also a mix of rent and purchase. Involved is the makeover of Lauderdale Courts, the public housing project famous for the Presley family's residence here, where young Elvis began learning the guitar. The plan document states, in answer to what must be an oft-asked question, "No, we do not yet know the ultimate plans for the Presley Family Apartment." A plaque has been installed at Apartment 328 that says, "It was here that Elvis practiced in the basement laundry room." While other apartments are to be enlarged, one suggestion is that the Presley apartment retain its original size and layout.[20]

The public side will be done according to HOPE VI guidelines developed by the U.S. Department of Housing and Urban Development to keep projects from deteriorating as in the past. This includes replacing dilapidated projects with mixed-income communities, reducing concentrations of poverty, providing support services, and insisting on responsible behavior.

Financing is to come from a mix of public and private sources, including a $35 million HUD HOPE VI grant, $18.1 from the City of Memphis, $58.5 in private equity and loans, plus $14.7 million in public and private grants. Historic tax credits will help in the makeover of Lauderdale Courts, along with city/housing authority funds and $17 million in private equity.[21]

SOUTH SIDE

On the south side of downtown, a mile or so from the Peabody, is another major development, South Bluffs, dating from 1993. It is built on an old railroad property; an active rail installation is immediately next door. The location fronts Riverside Drive running below the bluff. An iron pedestrian bridge over the road connects to a small riverfront park and overlook with beautiful views of the Mississippi as it curves past the city. The park connects to a developing riverfront walkway system.

Another of Henry Turley's endeavors, South Bluffs is a $100 million self-contained project of 510 townhomes and apartments, beautifully detailed and landscaped and well maintained. Residents refer to its "park-like setting with fountains, arbors, gliders and swings."[22] Design features include small front yards and parking in the rear. It is an enclave surrounded by a wall with a gate at the entrance, which apparently was considered necessary to make people feel safe as they ventured to live intown. The gate appears to be open now, and there was no guard when we visited.

The housing type breakdown is 265 apartments, 120 townhomes and 125 lofts. The latter range in size from 875 square feet to 2,350 and rent from $875 to $2,350 a month. From appearances and according to staff, South Bluffs attracts a mixture of young professionals in the apartments and lofts, with older people in the townhomes. The census tract for the area showed a population of 890 in 2000, a median age of 36.5 with the 25-to-34 age bracket accounting for 28 percent of the total, and the next bracket, 35-to-44, the second largest. The project has amenities such as two pools and gas fireplaces in many units, but probably the biggest thing going for it is what is happening outside its boundaries, namely the resurgent, eclectic South Main Street area described in the next section.

Another type of offering on the south of downtown that we should mention is the Rivermark Apartments, converted from a Holiday Inn. It has a riverfront setting overlooking Tom Lee Park and has units as low as $549 a month. It advertises tennis courts, lofts, and covered parking.

SOUTH MAIN

If the restored and thriving Orpheum anchors the north end of the reviving South Main district, then Central Station might be thought of as its southern anchor. Although there are only two trains a day, the transit agency undertook the renovation in a conscious effort to help revive South Main. Decline set in during the 1950s, and it became an "eyesore" and "scary," in the words of Judith Johnson, executive director of Memphis Heritage Inc.

MATA bought the building from the Illinois Central in 1994 for $1.1 million and has since spent $23 million to renovate it into a handsome sixty-three-unit apartment building with commercial space on the street, a restored Main Hall, and conference space, plus a station for the trolley system and facilities for the Amtrak trains. Nearly all the apartments were leased before it was completed. Federal assistance of nearly $18 million was secured.

Making it special is that Central Station was the last building designed by the great Daniel Burnham, built in 1914. It reopened to considerable acclaim in December 1999.[23] Across the street is a venerable institution that somehow survived while the area emptied, the Arcade Restaurant, actually a classic diner.

The South Main neighborhood is home to a major historic attraction, the Lorraine Motel National Civil Rights Museum, which has kept intact the room Dr. Martin Luther King Jr. stayed in when he was shot, with the cars he and his group used still parked in front. The very 1950s motel sign is also intact. Across the street and part of the museum now is the room from which he was shot on April 4, 1968. This was incorporated when the museum expanded in 2002 (it was founded in 1991), adding new exhibits and displaying the murder weapon. There is extensive documentation of the case against James Earl Ray, the state's evidence that never was used as Ray pled guilty and avoided trial. The room is authentic to the time he used it.

The original museum has such features as an audio of a slave auctioneer, Ku Klux Klan regalia, and a replica of a bus like the one in which Rosa Parks sparked a bus boycott in Birmingham, Alabama. A tour ends in Room 306 with a recording of King's moving speech in which he seemed to foretell his death.[24]

Terry Woodward is a Realtor who with her husband is a champion of the South Main neighborhood. They were pioneers when in 1995 they came upon the aging, dilapidated commercial buildings that line the street. But they saw its potential and bought a building at a bargain price, thinking that the top floor would be their weekend apartment and that they would rent the mid-level apartment and lease the street-level space to a store. What happened is that the apartment rented quickly and the retail space was a "very hard sell," as she was quoted in an interview. This told them that there was an Intown Living market, and they have since acquired forty units. They knew that retail development would be slower.

Along with new residents came art galleries, in the time-honored pattern of artists and galleries settling in pioneering areas with their low rents. The South Main Arts District flyer lists twelve galleries, including some that double as studios, and there are others in the area as well. A gallery that we were particularly taken with was devoted to the work of Memphis native Jack Robinson, who became a top portrait photographer in New York, working for Diana Vreeland at *Vogue*. The gallery is owned by Dan Oppenheimer, who befriended Robinson when he returned to Memphis from New York a little down and out, and who has inherited his body of work.[25] The walls are covered with a veritable who's who of the entertainment world, principally from the late 1960s and early 1970s, including, for instance, striking images of Lauren Bacall, Warren Beatty, The Who, James Taylor, Cybill Shepherd, and the like.

In an event similar to one in the Pearl District of Portland, Oregon, the galleries stay open on the last Friday of every month, year-round, for "Free

Trolley Tours" that the South Main Arts District sponsors. The Friday openings, from 6:00 to 10:00 P.M., at first drew fifty or so people, Terry Woodward recalls. Now it attracts thousands, including area residents. Here's how Woodward describes what is attracting new residents: She and her husband love the district's "close-knit sense of community. This is a very desirable place to live. It's been said that in five years more people will live here than on Mud Island. And we know why—it's wonderful. It's a great community. And that's the best thing about it—it's a community." In contrast with the suburbs, from where they have relocated, the sidewalk is the front yard where you see everybody—empty nesters, young singles, and couples with kids as well.[26]

In another contemporaneous account of the neighborhood, it is described this way: "The once desolate streets characterized by abandoned warehouses and derelict storefronts now are alive with residential and commercial activity. Old industrial buildings now house chic, sleek loft apartments, and those once-neglected storefronts now showcase the talent of many a Mid-South artist and designer." This particular account says that as many as three to five thousand people show up for Free Trolley Tours and quotes the South Main Arts District marketing director, George Bryant, as saying, "I've never talked to anyone who hasn't said, 'This is the best time I've had in Memphis.' "[27]

In addition to the galleries there are shops, cafes, and bars in architecturally interesting buildings. Among the area's attractions: The Blue Monkey bar, Fratelli's grocery, the Corkscrew wine shop, Ernestine and Hazel's dance club, Corner Cheesecake, Harry's Detour restaurant, a yoga center, and Marmalade's restaurant. Both the downtown and riverfront trolley lines serve the neighborhood. As of mid-2003, the neighborhood still had a decidedly funky, not to say slightly edgy, air about it, making it for us a slightly off-the-track gem of a section in all of the downtown area.

There are at least five residential projects in South Main besides Central Station, including Central Station Loft Condos built just beyond the station, perhaps foretelling a spread further to the south. One, the Paperworks Condominiums, with sixty-two units, is a conversion from apartments, said to have occurred when the five-year requirement for using historic preservation tax credits for commercial properties, such as apartments, expired.

We visited two, The Lofts and the Wm. Farrington. The Lofts is a stunning makeover of the Orgill Brothers Hardware and Saddlery Building. Its promotional material describes it as "the coolest place to live in downtown Memphis" and promotes the idea of a weekend retreat. "It beats driving back to the burbs after a night on the town," reads a Henry Turley Co. brochure.

Half of the structure is of concrete construction, half with a wood frame, and it contains 125 apartments featuring ten-foot windows, exposed pipes, and timber beams. Many industrial artifacts have been retained in the building's public spaces. The units range in size from 861 to 2,429 square feet and feature fast Web access connections. There's a high-tech incubator across the street in another old warehouse. The riverfront streetcar line passes in front of the building, and bars, clubs, and a market are out the front door.

On South Main Street itself is a smaller offering, the Wm. Farrington, a seventeen-unit condominium in an early-1900s mattress factory, a sales representative told us. The building was first converted to apartments in 1986, but when the units were placed for sale, all new kitchens and cabinets were installed and the wooden floors sanded. There's a garage and a roof deck included. In mid-July 2003, having come on the market only in April, eleven units were sold (with one move-in already), with four closings scheduled within two weeks of our visit. Prices were around $200,000, depending on the unit size (668 square feet to 1,349) and floor (three stories), the buyers being young professionals who saw this as the time to move from renting to owning.

Which is a fitting windup to our Memphis Intown Living story: When a building is priced right, the amenities are up-to-date, and the neighborhood is hip, they will line up to buy (or rent).

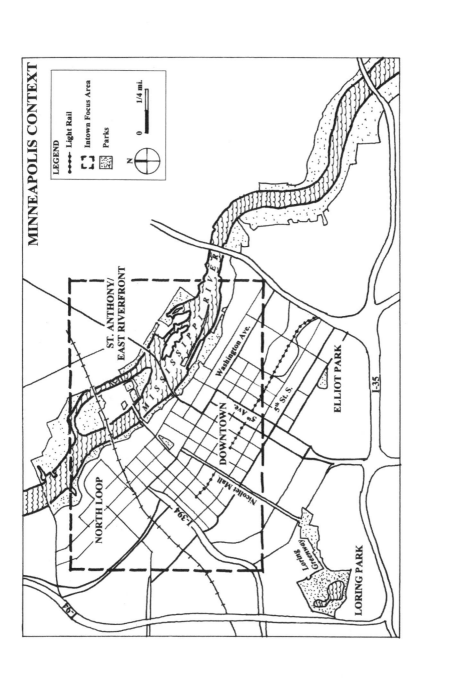

MINNEAPOLIS CONTEXT

LEGEND

•••• Light Rail

[ ] Intown Focus Area

▦ Parks

N

0   1/4 mi.

ST. ANTHONY/
EAST RIVERFRONT

MISSISSIPPI RIVER

NORTH LOOP

DOWNTOWN

Washington Ave.

5th Ave.

5th St. S.

Nicollet Mall

I-394

Loring
Greenway

ELLIOT PARK

I-35

LORING PARK

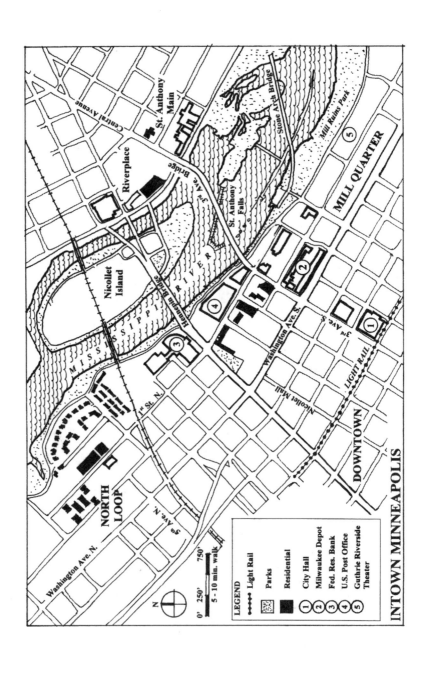

INTOWN MINNEAPOLIS

LEGEND

~~~~ Light Rail

Parks

Residential

① City Hall
② Milwaukee Depot
③ Fed. Res. Bank
④ U.S. Post Office
⑤ Guthrie Riverside Theater

0'   250'   750'

5 - 10 min. walk

N

Minneapolis

Growth will not detract from Minneapolis being a pleasant place to
live. More people will make the city safer and provide markets for
neighborhood commercial activities to which people can walk or bike.
More residents and workers will get involved in local issues . . .
—*The Minneapolis Plan-2000*

It's called the "City of Lakes," but Minneapolis had its origins on the
Mississippi River. The community of St. Anthony was established in 1838
beside the dramatic falls bearing its name. As a book title declares, *The
Falls of St. Anthony: The Waterfall that Built Minneapolis*. The fifteen-foot
drop is the only falls on the entire Mississippi, and its power was harnessed
to drive the flour mills and sawmills that put Minneapolis on the map after
its founding in 1852. Its other name, not coincidentally, is "Mill City."

The city's history of the late nineteenth and early twentieth centuries is
centered on the mills and the innovations in flour processing that originated
here. By 1890 Minneapolis was the largest wheat market in the nation.[1] It
remained a flour milling capital until the 1930s. The Intown Living story in
Minneapolis is in large part a riverfront story, on the river in restored mill
buildings plus new infill construction, in adjacent blocks, and in the warehouses and industrial buildings beside the river to the north of the falls.

Before taking up some of the impressive planning that has gone on, let's
mention a catalytic event on the river. By the account of several we interviewed, the restoration in 1994 of the Stone Arch Bridge just below the

falls was the symbol of the riverfront awakening, the "tipping point" in the phrase of one. It called attention anew to the commercial possibilities on both sides of the river, after some fits and starts in the early 1980s, especially along the St. Anthony side.

The bridge was restored in 1994 for about $3 million. It is visually very striking, featuring arches and a graceful curve of limestone. It was built in 1883 for a railroad, which was closed in 1992. People used it informally after that, but since restoration as a walkway it has borne heavy traffic, apparently in all seasons and regardless of weather conditions. The bridge ties together walkways along both sides of the river, and a trail over the Hennepin Avenue bridge makes possible a walking/biking/blading loop in the heart of the city. This well-used 1.8-mile loop is called the St. Anthony Falls Heritage Trail.

MAJOR PLANNING

Planning here includes a major document, *The Minneapolis Plan,* in four parts. Volume one, the policy statement, has ten chapters. It was adopted by the city council and the mayor in March 2000. The vision statement on page 1.i.1 begins: "Minneapolis is a city that people choose to call home. It offers its residents a progressive tradition of good government, civic participation and a vibrant economy for business and industry." The target audience for its vision is the city's residents, workers, and visitors, in that order, and the vision statement sees the city's future tied to its "livability and quality of life; the character and attractiveness of its neighborhoods; residents' and workers' sense of safety, and the way in which long-time residents welcome new households into the city." Note the residential emphasis because it is a recurring theme, backed up by public dollars as we will describe.

Here are the city's eight plan goals; we'll quote the first and list the others:

"Increase the city's population and tax base by developing and supporting housing choices city-wide through preservation of existing housing and new construction." Goal two is about safety, three about public participation, then commerce, public transportation, natural and historic environments, the marketing of downtown as a place to live, work, play and do business, and lastly, infrastructure investment. Note again the strong emphasis on residential values and neighborhoods.

In elaboration of goal one, the plan talks about infill plus major housing developments with higher density to appeal to newer markets such as seniors and empty nesters. Specific mention is made of riverfront housing. The plan seems to miss the segment of the market that is the young professional, single or dual income, which segment is very much in evidence in the North Loop warehouse area and elsewhere in Minneapolis. The plan projects that the greatest population growth in the city will occur in the central district, which is downtown plus one small neighborhood to the southwest and another on the southeast, projected to be up 38.6 percent by 2020. The next-highest growth rate, on the other side of the river around the University of Minnesota, is projected at 15.4 percent. In numbers, 7,807 new residents by 2020 in central, 4,742 in university.

The significance of these numbers is that growth is projected at all. For the reality of Minneapolis is that from 1950 until now, it was in decline, rather dramatically. Thus the population in the city in 1950 was 521,718, dropping to 482,872 ten years later until hitting bottom in 1990 at 368,383. In the last ten years, the census reported the first increase in six decades, to 382,618. This is the context into which to put the projected growth numbers downtown.

In January 1988, the *Metro 2000 Plan* was published, its third iteration since the first downtown plan of 1959, in cooperation with the Downtown Council, a business organization. At that time, residential development was the number nine priority, with the riverfront seen as the best opportunity for future housing.

Minneapolis Downtown 2010 is the fifth version, adopted in October 1996, with the same public-private sponsorship. It is officially recognized by the previously mentioned *Minneapolis Plan,* which is prepared by the City Planning Department alone without the business group partnership, perhaps accounting for different emphases. Thus the downtown document prepared with the business participation puts priorities on office, retail, entertainment, convention, and education before taking up downtown housing. It does describe downtown as the region's "most unique and prestigious neighborhood," predicting the addition of several thousand residents by 2010 and major new housing areas. The empty-nest market continues to be the focus rather than young professionals. Its definition of "downtown" employs the freeway ring of I-35, I-94, and I-394, which would leave out the burgeoning North Loop area. At the same time, a sketch map on the inside cover of the document appears to include it. Whatever, North Loop is a major part of our Intown Living story.

Minneapolis Downtown 2010, when it does take up downtown living, notes that the population grew while the city as a whole declined, from 1980 to 1990, it was up 2,000 or so to 17,407. It's projected to grow to 23,000 by the year 2010. The report equates residential growth with job expansion, putting it at about 275 units of market-rate housing a year increase since 1985. The emphasis continues to be on the empty nesters and only secondly on what is termed "nontraditional households," namely singles, dual-income couples, and gays. It notes that in Minneapolis, while residents like the urbanity of downtown, they want to live in a "residential area." It identifies both the riverfront and an area adjoining Loring Park as two areas of growth potential. It sees Loring Park, Elliot Park, and the riverfront as places for "true urban neighborhoods." Consistent with other downtown plans, the area east of the river, St. Anthony, apparently because of its different history, is ignored even though parts of it are closer to the central business district than the far reaches of the official downtown.

In winter and spring 2002, a further revision of the plan (*Downtown 2020*) was under way, to, among other things, assess the impact of the light rail line that the previous plan recommended and which was being installed along Fifth Street through the middle of downtown in 2003. The consultants working on the new version foresee increased residential development around the five light rail stations downtown, plus increased commercial activity.[2]

There is also Minneapolis's pioneering Neighborhood Revitalization Program which, in essence, lets communities decide how to allocate public dollars in their areas, a total of $400 million over twenty years. It began in 1990 and has seen $544,500 allocated in downtown, exclusive of the central riverfront. Analysis of the first ten years suggested a little too much parochialism and control by homeowners and businesses.[3]

DEVELOPMENT AGENCY

The reason to outline the extensive planning done in Minneapolis is that it charts the course for a city agency to act, namely the Minneapolis Community Development Agency (MCDA). Redevelopment in what officially is termed the Minneapolis Riverfront District began in the early 1970s. *Mississippi Minneapolis* was the basic MCDA plan document, dated 1972. A coordination board was set up then among the major government entities, succeeded a decade later by a more informal technical staff mechanism that one representative told us was more effective in avoiding the turf battles of the first entity. Thirteen agencies are involved.

Significant to the story are the tools MCDA has used, including tax increment financing for site acquisition/preparation, improvements, and historic preservation; revenue bonds to underwrite private projects; historic investment tax credits for private efforts; municipal bonds, regional, state, and federal park acquisition/development and public improvements; state and federal cleanup funds; and other sources (such as revenues from its parking lots). Tax increment financing was greatly diminished by 2003, and the historic tax credit has been restricted in its application by Congress. Transportation enhancement funds are newly available. MCDA administers five riverfront redevelopment districts, with considerable power to act over a large central city territory.

The agency has taken sequential steps that made possible riverfront redevelopment in the Mill Quarter (the agency's name for an area larger than the Mill District per se). Could the private sector have tackled the railyard removal, aqueduct and grain elevator teardowns, and subsequent street, sidewalk, and utility improvements? Not likely. Here's a description of what the area was like when MCDA began to act:

Riverfront land in the area within the freeway ring is devoted to railroad use, grain elevators and mills and some small industry. The land is vastly under-used and we recommend that a large portion of it be developed for housing to create two new neighborhoods.

They were to be on both sides of the river. It also called for opening up the central riverfront to the public.[4]

Step one was buying five-and-a-half blocks from the railroad and pulling up the tracks. This was a $2 million acquisition, involving 160 acres, our staff contact said. The Washington Avenue viaduct, a huge barrier between the city and the river, was removed, as were old grain elevators. Streets and sidewalks were built and utilities installed, effectively setting the stage for the private sector.

Along with this were the initiatives powered by the park and recreation board to open up the river, acquiring lands, installing parks and pathways, putting in parkways. For instance, the West River Parkway phase one, completed in 1984, cost $8.3 million.[5] By 2003, substantial parts of the central riverfront park were complete, including the Nicollet Island Pavilion/Amphitheater, Main Street in St. Anthony (cobblestone paving that's harmonious with adjacent historic structures), and Mill Ruins Park, phase one.

MCDA details over $1 billion in investments along the river, completed or under construction as of January 2003, combining public and private dollars. One such investment, at $56.4 million, illustrates the collaborative public/private ventures that MCDA uses. This is the Milwaukee Depot, preserved and reused in block one of the agency's railroad acquisition. The headhouse is now a component of a Marriott Courtyard hotel serving as banquet space plus providing sixteen rooms. Important to the city is the preservation of the railroad's sign and clock tower. New construction in the rest of the block provides 340 hotel rooms, including a Residence Inn, and 566 parking spaces, and includes an ice skating rink. The latter was not in MCDA's plans, but a developer talked them into it. This helped make possible the retention of the railroad station shed, now called The Depot. There's also a small freight house that was rehabilitated. Subsidies amounting to $3.4 million were made in direct outlays, for such things as environmental remediation and rehabilitation, plus $8.6 million in tax increment financing for rehabilitation and $4.2 million for parking.[6] Nearly all the direct outlay money has been paid back, our MCDA contact reported.

URBAN RENEWAL

Before detailing additional riverfront projects, particularly housing, we digress to talk about a governmental action preceding these initiatives that dates to the 1970s, namely one of the nation's largest and most devastating urban renewal efforts. We speak of the Gateway Center. It is said to have destroyed "some of the most notable buildings of 19th Century Minneapolis." Architectural historian Larry Millet described it as "the most inexcusable act of civic vandalism in the history of Minneapolis."[7] The area was home to numerous derelicts and flophouses at a major entry point into the city. It's pertinent because the territory affected is directly north of the Mill District. The scars from this wholesale destruction of a neighborhood remain today, and there is a gap of at least four blocks between sections of the riverfront and the central business district still marred with surface parking.

Among the 180 structures torn down was the beloved Metropolitan Building. Its removal triggered a historic preservation movement ten years later.[8] Along with the buildings went 2,500 residents and 450 businesses, many of which never reopened. This was all done in the name of removing blight, in the orthodoxy of the day, which the business/political leadership here like everywhere else saw as necessary for downtown's survival. The plan dates to 1959, as the city sought to counter the retail drain caused by the Southdale Center in the suburb of Edina, in 1956 the nation's first enclosed mall.

In further conformity with the orthodoxy of the day, what replaced "Hobohemia," as a 1937 study called it,[9] were government or commercial buildings set back from the street on isolated pads. The result has properly been termed uninspired, and in fact two of the buildings erected after the destruction in the 1950s and '60s have already been torn down, namely an IBM office and a Sheraton Hotel. A Federal Reserve Building has since been replaced with a new riverfront installation.

A more positive outcome, perhaps, are the apartments that we turn to now because these are the real pioneer residential projects near the river. These are large towers such as River West Apartments (First Street South, built in 1989 and containing 416 units and 577 parking spaces), Rivergate (between First and Second Streets South), The Crossings (Third Street South at Second Avenue), Churchill Apartments (First and Marquette Avenue), and The Towers (First Street South). We visited The Churchill, built in 1981. It is thirty-three stories and has 360 apartments. Most units are one bedroom, in the 710- to 810-square-foot range, and rent from $965 to $1,300 a month, with higher floors costing more. There are a number of amenities in the building, including a pool. There are 60 two-bedroom units. The range of ages in the building is from twenty-one to eighty-eight, with an emphasis on the younger side. The market was said by a representative in the sales office to be soft at the time of our visit (mid-July 2003), but the building was also said to be 98 percent occupied.

MILL QUARTER

Downriver from these earlier projects are the more recent residential projects. Let's describe the ten-building mill complex here, located on the northeastern edge of downtown. (Minneapolis has a peculiar layout in that its grid does not follow a north-south, east-west axis. Even locals get directions muddled.)

Standing at the river's edge, looking right to left, first is an office building with a historic facade and all-new interior, of handsome yellow stone, is the Crown Roller Building. Next to a tall smokestack is the Hyatt/Whitney Hotel, to have been closed in September 2003 for conversion to condominiums. Built from the Whitney Mill, the complex also contains 220,000 square feet of office space. Behind it is the Ceresota Building, which houses a college.

Across the street is the North Star Blanket Building, a pioneering project begun in 1998, whose large neon sign is a visual landmark of the area; it is now condominiums. Units were purchased before rehabilitation began. Potential buyers looked at dead pigeons and collapsed ceilings, plus it smelled like a sewer, recalls developer Peggy Lucas.[10] Its thirty-six units were snapped up, and, a Realtor living there told us that prices doubled in two-and-a-half years. The North Star, Utility, and Stone Arch Lofts completed in 2003 together have ninety-five units with 191 parking spaces and combine rehabilitation with new construction, costing $55 million with subsidies (principally tax increment financing) totaling $7.4 million.[11]

A series of condos is next, mixing historic buildings with new construction, and all high-end. We visited a 4,000-square-foot unit in a restored mill, a beautifully crafted space with a stunning view of St. Anthony Falls. Prices here are in the $1 million range.

Then comes the Washburn A Mill Building ruins, the building almost totally wiped out in a fire in 1991, reborn in 2003 into a museum plus mixed-use. The Washburn Mill is where some of the innovative wheat processing techniques occurred. The museum is mostly new construction artfully fitted into the ruins on three levels. Office space occupies the floors above.

We had an advance tour of the museum with one of its architects two months before opening was to have occurred in September 2003. For us as waterfront people, the signal accomplishment is a wide entrance open free to the public that extends out the back into an exterior courtyard through the remaining original limestone walls to the river, where parklands, pathways, and mill ruin excavations await, along with an Army Corps of Engineers lift dock. We think this is both a generous gesture to the public and a good strategy. Once inside, it will be hard not to be intrigued and therefore to want to visit the museum.

The museum proper, a $31 million project of the Minnesota Historic Society, one of the nation's strongest such organizations, has a separate, for-fee entrance. An elevator takes visitors to the top, where what's left of the original machinery is on view, plus an outdoor viewing deck. The museum below contains displays and interpretive materials about the extraordinary feats accomplished by the mill's early owners, and later the General Mills Company.

Next to the Washburn ruins new condominiums were being woven into the remnants of another part of the mill complex in 2003, which contained silos dominated by a huge "GOLD MEDAL" neon sign. Across a to-be-extended Chicago Avenue is where the new Guthrie Theater, the Guthrie Riverside, is to relocate. It is a major cultural venue in the city and in fact is one of the nation's best-known repertory theaters. Its design, by French architect Jean Nouvel, includes one component to be clad in yellow corrugated metal rising nine stories, with smokestacks. A small theater is on top. An adjoining building is to hold another theater, while the main theater will be housed in a structure of corrugated stainless steel over a glass-walled restaurant. The most innovative feature is a glassed-in pedestrian bridge cantilevered over the street below to provide dramatic views of the falls, St. Anthony on the other side, and the Stone Arch Bridge crossing here. While there is much admiration of the design, naturally there are detractors, who say it looks variously like a Lego design or a stapler, or others who find the yellow cladding too bright.[12] The Guthrie is to be completed in 2005, groundbreaking to have occurred in September 2003. The cost is $125 million, with the public funding for land acquisition and help with design and construction totaling $14.6 million.[13]

Additionally, under construction in 2003 was a mixed-use project in the block near the Marriott complex described previously. It will combine a cultural facility (MacPhail Center for the Arts, a dance studio) with office space and twenty-two residential units called the Metropolitan Lofts. There are 411 parking spaces, which a city official told us was what made the deal work for the developer, who anticipates monthly rentals. The parking is in the center of the block and the development wraps around it, something the city is encouraging in order to have more lively street fronts. The local term for this is "lining," which is new to us. An array of subsidies comes to about $5.6 million.[14]

In the next block and scheduled for development by 2005 is a residential project combining rental units (94) with condominiums (166) and 12,000 square feet of commercial space plus 899 parking spaces, a $60 million investment by Brighton Development Co., one of the major players along the riverfront. The official status of Park Lane Lofts, as it was called in mid-2003, was "approved and pending." Proposed for another of the rail-yard blocks is still another residential project, Mill Place and River Trails Apartments, with 254 units.

We note in passing that these and other new developments will soon take over some of the vast sea of surface parking lots here that serve the Humphrey Metrodome. While helping to restore some of the city's lost urban fabric, the developments will upset those who now congregate before the Minnesota Viking football games in what has to be one of the country's larger tailgate party areas. These are elaborate affairs with barbecues, a few beverages, costumes, and a form of community happening. The top of a parking garage will not be the same.

All of the developments build on previous work along the river, including Mill Ruins Park and the great River Road that runs in front, near the falls. In this historically important section of Minneapolis, then, a large amount of public and private investment and a major planning effort have gone into this area's impending ascendancy. This includes major initiatives by the independent (very) Minneapolis Park and Recreation Board, responsible for the linear park that runs on both sides of the river in the center of the city, the green background, and active recreational area for the investments just described and others to be discussed.

For us, the significant thing is that in mid-2003 the Mill Quarter was already laced with housing with other, major residential projects under construction or in the active planning stages. It is a combination of uses and handsome structures both old and new beside a dramatic stretch of river that few cities can match.

In our view, the new Mill City Museum and the Guthrie Riverside should cement the status of the Mill Quarter on the downtown side of the river as a (perhaps *the*) signature of Minneapolis.

Taken together, the apartments from the urban renewal days, the conversions and new construction infill among the old mills, and the other new construction under way and planned in the adjoining blocks add up to a sizable Intown Living presence on the south riverfront. Enough to have encouraged a small amount of commercial and other services in the area already, such as two coffee shops, two liquor stores, a video rental, a dry cleaner, a deli, and a day care center, plus a chain drug store nearby. There are some restaurants within reach, but their concentration is in mid-downtown's mall and nearby Warehouse District, a bit of a stretch on foot. As relatively thin as this amount of commerce is, it is more than exists in the just-developing North Loop section, where we now turn our attention.

DOWNTOWN'S AMBIANCE

Before we go north along the river, we mention two phenomena about downtown Minneapolis that apply to both segments along the river and the downtown core that have a major effect on the feel of the city. We call Minneapolis the un-Portland because where the latter has narrow streets and small blocks and a lively street scene, including major retail,

Minneapolis by contrast has uniformly wide streets (80 feet) and large blocks (330 by 330 feet) and past its 1960s pedestrian mall, thin commercial development.

This alone makes for a difficult pedestrian experience. Compounding this are three other factors: A cluster of modern office towers, meaning most of them have blank walls on the street, a system of "skywalks" or overhead pedestrian walkways connecting buildings, and a sea of surface parking lots.

The skyline downtown is punctuated with the work of some of America's top modern architectural practices. It is a virtual showcase of this style, featuring towers generally built in the 1980s. What they lack by and large is a welcoming street presence.

The real killer, however, is the skyway network, if you believe with us and most urban commentators that the key to a city's vitality is its street life. Begun in 1962 (we have to recall this was a time when downtowns were feeling the impact of the suburban shopping mall) it was a conscious effort to counter the safety and cleanliness the malls provided. The downtown business community still (at least as recently as 1996 in the *Minneapolis Downtown 2010* plan it participated in preparing) thinks the system is a positive. Currently connecting sixty-five blocks, the skyway "enables downtown to compete successfully with suburban office parks and shopping malls by providing climate-controlled pedestrian circulation." The Minneapolis system, "the finest and most extensive skyway system in the world," is privately owned except when connecting to public buildings, which means, of course, that control over who uses it can be exercised. It is like the underground walkways in Houston and Dallas in this regard.

What it means, as in those two Texas cities, is that shops, cafes, and other services that would ordinarily belong on the street are one level above. That the system can be a little hard to comprehend was brought home to us when we entered it to find a city map shop. We asked an office worker who had been in the building three years. Never heard of it. Looked it up on the lobby screen to no avail. We started exploring and found it, facing away from the intersection where we met our occupant who tried to help us—he had never turned down this particular corridor.

In the same plan document extolling the skyway—incidentally, the newspaper of the downtown community is the *Skyway NEWS*—is a section on the importance of street-level activity. "Streets serve as the primary pedestrian network and are downtown Minneapolis's greatest opportunity for improving the public realm. Streets designed for pedestrian use contribute to downtown's public nature, vibrant image and synergy by encouraging pedestrian circulation and activities, and by integrating downtown's various activities." The document notes that Minneapolis lacks the scale of walkable cities, but still expresses the belief that it has the potential to become "very walkable." It calls for having buildings include features of interest at street level, including retailing, and asks for improvements to the public right of way.[15]

We can attest that downtown Minneapolis in 2003 was—with some few exceptions such as the riverfront walkways and parks—not pedestrian-friendly. Too much potential vitality, in our opinion, is overhead in what are in fact very sterile passageways. In fairness, during the severe winters people no doubt really appreciate them—as we could attest during a visit when the temperature was zero.

Into this picture is coming Minneapolis's first light rail line. In downtown it will traverse Fifth Street South at the eastern edge of the central business district. What impact it will have is conjectural. We heard objections that it did not link suburban residential neighborhoods with downtown in that it was placed along an unused highway right-of-way to lower land acquisition costs. The consequence is that the line won't serve major existing population clusters. It will tie to the Minneapolis/St. Paul airport and, perhaps ominously for the future of downtown retail, it will go to the giant Mall of America, American's largest at 520 stores, sixty restaurants and clubs, fourteen movie theaters, and other features, including a trade school.[16]

NORTH RIVERFRONT

Let's now look at the riverfront north of Hennepin Avenue, the north-south boundary. Here is where conversions and new residential construction are booming. It's where a suburban-style townhouse development, The Landings, was a pacesetter, encouraging people used to the cul-de-sac and the individual lot to settle in an urban location. Built in stages beginning in 1995, the fifty-eight condominium townhomes began selling, a city planner told us, for $300,000 but now command prices in the millions. It was built on railroad property that MCDA bought in the 1980s, which it later spent $1.6 million cleaning up. The Landings is criticized for its gated feeling, but people in the residential business give the developer, George Sherman, credit for having the vision and for being a pioneer in this part of the city. One person we interviewed reflected that "Sherman made the area palatable to the pioneers." The project cost was $25 million and included $4.8 million in subsidies, for land acquisition and soil cleanup.[17]

A similar but somewhat more urban townhome project has been added on the adjoining site, Renaissance on the River, with eighty-four townhomes of between 1,271 and 1,807 square feet, priced as low as $290,000 in 2000. What helps make both of these projects work is that they are beside a graceful parkway that runs along here, next to which is maintained pathways and green space adjoining the river. A 2001 magazine article described new residents to this area as forgoing an eighty-mile round-trip commute to settle in the only city neighborhood that fit their criteria: convenience and new housing. They purchased a $350,000, three-bedroom, three-bathroom residence containing 2,000 square feet. They bike to work, sold one car and liked the fact that the area "feels like a neighborhood."[18]

The forerunner of the North Loop housing was, by several local accounts, the development of the nearby Warehouse District as a nightclub/restaurant/entertainment area. It seems to have an elastic definition, but is generally centered between Third and Sixth Streets North between Hennepin Avenue and Second Avenue North. In the early 1990s, the approximately eight-block district was described this way:

"Ten years ago you could barely walk . . . through the Minneapolis Warehouse District without stepping over an empty whiskey bottle or passing a boarded-up storefront." Prior to its reincarnation as an entertainment area, the once-seedy Warehouse District was populated in the 1980s by artists looking for inexpensive space. As they improved the area, the spaces became trendy stores, townhomes, and condominiums, in a time-honored pattern in which the pioneering artists are priced out. Artists across the river in Northeast Minneapolis fear what happened in the Warehouse District will happen to them. "People don't want a repeat of what happened in the Warehouse District," said Lauri Svedberg, an artist who owns a home and studio in Northeast. "Then, business becomes an enemy rather than an ally."[19]

The best way to convey what is happening in the North Loop, as it is called, or north riverfront in our terminology, is to describe what is taking place along First Street North between First Avenue North and Eighth Avenue.

(Potential confusion comes from Minneapolis's street naming, where you can be at the intersection of Fifth and Fifth. If you mistake "street" for "avenue" you're sunk. A planner with the city has issued a one-page attempt to clarify wayfinding here, noting that downtown Minneapolis has five intersecting street grids, and the street names don't correspond to the cardinal or ordinal directions for which they're named. Thus, avenues designated "north" are actually on the west side of downtown.)

Proceeding from the north, more or less, where the *Star-Tribune* has a plant and a clock tower that serves as a street-end focal point, we have a row of historic structures on the east or river side, generally brick and six stories, with a full-block surface parking lot across the street. Among the historic buildings is the Itasca building, a first residential conversion in this area in 1984 with seventy-one units and commercial space that includes a saloon and a comedy club. It was an $18 million project, with tax increment financing of $4.6 million, including a revenue bond.

In the next block is the Guthrie Lab, a relatively small building rehabilitated for $650,000 as a theater. Adjoining is an office building and the Gaar Scott Lofts, a six-story historic structure, with thirty garden apartments, nine of which are set aside for affordable housing (for persons with income at half the city's median) and seventy condominiums. In the next block are the Creamette Historic Lofts, a new, plain-looking three-story building plus the beautiful, traditional Creamette Company headquarters, combining for a total of 100 rental units. Next is Lindsay Lofts, a new construct of seven stories with a handsome brick facade matching its historic namesake, a six-story building at the corner of Fourth Avenue North being converted to River Walk apartments, townhomes, and flats. An agent marketing Lindsay Lofts said it was appealing successfully to young professionals even with prices at $495,000 (for a 1,908-square-foot unit with river views).

Across from these developments are the RiverStation townhomes, four-story units scattered over two full blocks, with a somewhat privatized feeling conveyed by one street through the middle marked "private" and high gates along the sidewalk. The complex contains 348 condominiums and is said by MCDA to be the largest for-sale housing project in the history of the city. There are 447 parking spaces, many of which are below ground. RiverStation cost $48 million ($3.6 million in tax increment financing was made available to help with land acquisition, soil remediation and public improvements).[20]

Heritage Landing, which was leasing when we saw it in 2003, fills out the remainder of this side of First Street North to Fourth Avenue, offering 229 units, 5,500 square feet of commercial space, and 380 parking spaces, price tag $28.1 million (again, tax increment financing was used to make possible affordable housing and parking, $6.2 million). Twenty percent of the units are for persons with 50 percent of median income; otherwise, it is for market-rate to high-end renters. Units range in size from 761 to 2,562 square feet, with monthly rents from $583 to $2,560 as of May 2002, according to MCDA.

The next two corners were under construction when we visited in July 2003. One, Rock Island Lofts (named for the rail line running beside it), containing sixty-nine units, was said by a Realtor to be one-third sold already. Across First Street, also under construction, is to be an eight-story project called The Reserve with 108 units, which will also have some street-level commercial space. As one of the newer developments, it and the Rock Island development have no public help because tax increment financing has been curtailed by the state legislature.

One of our Realtor contacts in this area said the market was for professionals moving into Minneapolis as well as some empty nesters. She also told us that Realtors themselves were buying units because they know they will appreciate. She reported making $50,000 by handling a sale for someone who bought into a building and then, within a year, decided not to move in.

Past the railroad tracks, we encounter surface parking and then scattered low-rise commercial buildings, containing variously a furrier, office space, bar, design center, antiques, and a funky gift shop. Anchoring this section is Theatre de la Jeune Lune, a five-hundred-seat theater in a rehabilitated warehouse at the corner of First and First that also contains office space. It was helped with a development loan from MCDA. The building was the Minneapolis Van and Warehouse Company, built around the turn of the twentieth century. The territory behind these blocks, between First and Second, had considerable dereliction.

Striking to us, along this entire stretch there were no street trees. The only landscaping was provided by developers inside the sidewalk, as at RiverStation. When we inquired, a city official told us that historic preservationists insisted that since the area was industrial and had no trees in the past, it therefore was not in keeping with this character to add them now. We would hold that since the uses today are totally different, this paean to authenticity is misplaced, that street trees contribute to making urban neighborhood sidewalks attractive and inviting, not to mention providing shade. On hot July days we found ourselves seeking shade like one would try to find cover in a rainfall.

SPREADING WEST

We featured First Street North to convey a sense of the mix, the extent, and the still-evolving nature of the housing boom that is going on here. Already development is spreading. One example is the Washington Lofts on the avenue so named (one block over from Second Street North), containing sixty-two units, including some at affordable rates, on three floors. A resident told us that two-thirds were sold in three months and that the profile of the building was, approximately, 20 percent empty nesters, one-third 30-to-40-year-old single professionals working downtown, and the remainder young people whose parents perhaps were helping with their first property. He further estimated that one-third of the building was gay/lesbian. An interesting design feature of the rehabilitation, which left wooden beams exposed, was to put a central corridor at a five-degree cant, opening up the backsides of all units to a galleria-like skylight. The angled corridor mixes things up visually and encourages a sense of neighborliness along the three-level interior "street" where activities could (and do) take place. Trees and greenery were to be added to give it even more atmosphere. This interior space is also a thoughtful nod to the severe winters.

On Second between Fifth and Seventh Avenues North is a four-story new construction containing a variety of spaces, such as a 146-room extended stay hotel (a Marriott), plus forty units of affordable rental housing and 108 underground parking spaces. The apartments are for those with both 80 percent of median income and 50 percent. This was completed in 2000 at a cost of $15 million, with MCDA investing $2.3 million in tax increment financing, according to its records. A spokesperson for the developer, CSM Corporation, said "the area's residential feel makes it ideal for somebody working downtown for two or three weeks."[21]

A developer driving us around this section pointed to a large old International Harvester plant of multiple stories that is slated to be turned into artists' live/work space. Numerous other industrial buildings in this part of the city are destined for conversion to housing, as long as the market stays as strong as it was in 2003. New construction is also proposed, such as that on Fourth Street at Seventh Avenue North, two blocks south of Washington Avenue North, to be lofts, but with a difference—reduced parking and perhaps a shared car program. With fewer parking spaces, unit prices could be brought in at $300,000 or lower, which this particular developer sees as the core market. This would be a five-story, seventy-unit building whose developer, Kit Richardson, was inspired by the Pearl District in Portland, Oregon. He was quoted as noting: " 'In Portland, they require that all street fronts be active. They have streets that are so much more pedestrian-friendly,' he said. 'Portland has a true streetcar system as well as light rail. When we landed in Portland, we didn't have to rent a car. It's frustrating to come back after seeing such a logical system.' "[22]

Can restaurants be far behind? Opening in early 2003 was New Century Buffet, followed shortly by Sapor, a cafe/wine bar on the still-industrial Washington Avenue North. Taking an expansive view of what the "Warehouse District" constitutes, effectively including the North Loop, a listing in *Skyway NEWS* for July 2002 contained no fewer than forty-six food establishments, running the full range from a comedy club to a deli to bars such as Cuzzy's.[23] The area still has a little of an X-rated flavor as well, including Sex World on Washington Avenue North at Second Avenue.

The Minneapolis Planning Department in a report dated August 2001 using census data, reported that the North Loop population grew from 647 in 1990 to 1,515 in 2000, a 134 percent jump. The predominant age group by far is between 25 and 34, one-third of the total. Next largest was the 35-to-44 group, 18 percent, with a median age of 36. The area is 60 percent white, with renters predominating.

EAST RIVERFRONT

Across the river, on the eastern side of the Mississippi, there is also housing activity. One developer alone, Brighton Development Corporation, which specializes in historic buildings, lists five projects within five blocks of the river, between Hennepin Avenue East and I-35. Closest to the river is Lourdes Square Townhomes (forty units) where the Third Avenue Bridge crosses (Our Lady of Lourdes Church is here). It and nearby Marquette Townhomes and Marquette Historical Buildings are said to have helped spur a commercial revival in the area, along Central

Avenue notably, which features a variety of ethnic restaurants and shops plus art galleries and clothing shops.

Two older projects are worth mentioning. One, RiverPlace, contains 370 units of housing. It was preceded by the St. Anthony Main project of (the late) Benjamin and Jane Thompson (he was a native of St. Paul), one of the first festival marketplaces when it was constructed between 1978 and 1981 (Faneuil Hall in Boston, thought by most to be the mother of festival marketplaces, also by the Thompsons, opened in 1976. It actually was preceded a decade earlier by Ghirardelli Square in San Francisco). It is a cluster of older buildings that was converted into a rabbit warren of shops and restaurants. When the $100 million RiverPlace opened next door in the mid-1980s with a major amount of somewhat similar commercial space, it oversaturated the market and hurt both projects. St. Anthony Main and RiverPlace have been through difficult times, but today St. Anthony survives with the rents from architectural firms and software companies, the addition of a major movie theater, and the attraction of bars and restaurants, some with outdoor seating along an attractive cobblestone street overlooking lush and tree-canopied parkland, the river, and its falls.

Under construction when we visited, and offering forty different apartment floor plans, was Stone Arch Apartments, with 273 units and 253 parking spaces. It is fairly near the University of Minnesota campus and perhaps will serve that market. The project's cost is $33.5 million, and it got started soon enough to receive subsidies, including tax increment financing to make possible affordable housing plus help with environmental remediation, a total of nearly $3 million.[24]

There is other housing here, such as the Village at St. Anthony Falls with thirty rental units, ninety-six condominiums, and forty-eight townhomes, plus commercial spaces and parking for 215. On Nicollet Island, there are twenty-two rehabilitated homes in a single project, plus scattered private houses.

The riverfront is, to our minds, the big Intown Living story in Minneapolis as of 2003, but there are two other areas that are a major part of the picture as well, all within the downtown formed by expressways.

LORING PARK NEIGHBORHOOD

The first area is the southwestern end of Nicollet Mall, past 12th Street South, called Loring Park. At its downtown end, there is a cluster of apartment towers and townhomes, most of which appear to date to the 1980s. We visited one, Marquette Place, a thirty-five-story apartment built in 1987. It is a project of Fine Associates, which erected a number of buildings in the area in this time frame, and which sponsored the Loring Greenway that we will discuss.

Marquette Place contains 240 units, some as small as 753 square feet, with others reaching 1,286 square feet. Rents run $1,215 to $2,300 a month, with apartments on the top floors commanding the higher prices. There are major amenities here, including a twenty-four-hour desk, a free continental breakfast provided every morning (the only such we encountered in the research), balconies, great views of downtown from many units, exercise and entertainment rooms, and a pool. There were vacant units when we visited, and incentives were being offered.

What this building and others in the vicinity have going for them is proximity. Out the door is Nicollet Mall—known locally as "eat street"—which also, in fact, has an active retail scene (Marshall Fields is here). While some restaurants are chains, there are also local institutions such as Vincent that is no more than three blocks away. If you desire, you could plug into the skywalk network. Nearby is Orchestra Hall, churches, the University of St. Thomas, the convention center, and downtown office towers. Groceries are available from "Simon Delivers." In the other direction is Loring Park itself, a lovely green space around Loring Lake. Past this is the Walker Art Center and Minneapolis Sculpture Garden/Cowles Conservatory. The present Guthrie Theater is also here, connected to the Walker, all accessible by a pedestrian bridge over I-94 directly from the park, a design by public artist Siah Armajani. In another direction is the handsome Basilica of St. Mary.

Other residential projects here include 1200 on the Mall, 1225 LaSalle, Loring Green, Loring Towers, and 1350 on the Mall, as well as townhomes and clusters of residential building along Hennepin Avenue, two blocks over from Nicollet. There's a project here on Grant Street containing 208 units of low-rent efficiencies and one-bedroom units for the elderly.[25] Further to the south are townhomes in leafy streets, albeit butting up to I-94, but virtually no single-family residences.

Tying together the varied areas of the Loring Park neighborhood is the Loring Greenway. What is striking, in addition to the private sponsorship of a major public amenity, is how it contrasts with the hard-edged pedestrian mall along Nicollet and the general absence of trees mentioned earlier. The greenway has a significant tree canopy, no vehicles, play and picnic areas, flower gardens, water features, and quiet. The contrast with the buses and taxis that run the mall is dramatic. About four blocks long, the greenway begins on Nicollet Mall, seamlessly bridges over a busy Spruce Place roadway, and ends with the focal point Berger Fountain in the park, with its centerpiece lake. Loring Park is a miniature version of New York's Central Park, surrounded as it is by housing.

Here's a description of the lake:

Though I grew up on the Jersey Shore, the roar of the ocean tide never impressed me as much as the soothing calm of a Minnesota lake. Though the pond in Loring

Park is not big, there is something about sitting beside it that is both conducive to reflection and refreshing. On a windless day, ducks and geese float effortlessly upon its surface as if it were a pane of glass.[26]

Loring Park was once home to mansions, which later were made into rooming houses. It went into a period of decline along with most of Minneapolis, with its population dropping drastically from 12,796 in 1960 to 6,472 in 1990, according to city planning documents. Citizens for a Loring Park Community (CLPC) puts the current population at 7,502, an increase of 14 percent since 1990. The median age is said to be 36.3, mostly white and with few children.[27]

CLPC, incidentally, is an active citizen's organization, judging from its September 2003 newsletter. It has task forces and committees meeting monthly on such subjects as Nicollet Mall, livability, and land use. The group is working with developers to add more affordable housing, to make the convention center expansion a better neighbor, and to encourage the expansion of a housing project for single mothers, Jeremiah. It also funded new signs for the neighborhood put up by the Loring Business Association that depict the area.

There was new construction here in 2003, such as 301 Clifton, a four-story condominium advertising its opening in mid-2004. It has forty-four units with prices starting in the mid-$200,000 range. Features include tall ceilings (twenty feet in some units), rooftop entertainment space, balconies, underground parking, and a business center.

ELLIOT PARK

Our other Intown Living area is the nearby Elliot Park, also within the downtown. During the late nineteenth and early twentieth centuries, this was the city's first intown residential neighborhood. It experienced a spurt of apartment development in the 1920s and still had some upper-income sections. Decline began at around this time, though, and as multifamily properties began to dominate, higher-income residents started moving out, and the overall neighborhood then declined.

Further decline took place after the 1950s when both Elliot Park and Loring Park lost approximately 25 percent of their populations in ten years. Further damaging the neighborhood was the construction of I-94 through its southern boundary, leading to additional population loss in the early 1960s despite some new and converted development. By 1965, Elliot Park was 95 percent a rental neighborhood with "severe problems," including juvenile delinquency and drugs.[28] Another aspect of the neighborhood's change is that as its attractiveness as a residential area declined, commercial and industrial uses moved in, as did some institutions. The population dropped from 9,175 in 1960 to 5,156 in 1990. The census tracts covering a good part of the neighborhood have 6,476 persons living here in 2000. One tract had a striking median age of 25. Nonfamily households were 85 percent of the total, and singles were 70 percent.

Still, Elliot Park had proximity to downtown in its favor and ready interstate access, leading to a gradual comeback in the 1990s as the previous numbers suggest. At the edge of the neighborhood in 2003 was rising the twenty-three-story condominium, Grant Park, known locally as "the fastest-selling large urban development in the country."[29] It will contain 288 condominiums, fifteen flats, and fifteen townhomes, complete with roof deck. There will be a major number of amenities (health club, pool, guest suites). Units will run from 853 square feet to a large 2,800 square feet, priced from $224,000 to over $1 million. An ad in summer 2003, said the building was 75 percent sold, with townhome occupancy in fall 2003, and tower occupancy in summer 2004. Only three of the million-dollar penthouses were said to remain. At the time of our visit a gateway over 10th Street was being constructed that will create a sense of entrance into the neighborhood, and which will serve to dress up the area, especially if accompanied by handsome streetscape treatment.

At the other end of the spectrum in Elliot Park is the three-block-long historic Ninth Street South district. Here remain turn-of-the-century brick structures from when it was the city's first urban neighborhood. A plaque on the rehabilitated "Rapahanock," which has five sections of seven apartments each, notes that it was one of the first residences next to the core of Minneapolis, "an urban city on the frontier."

On the next corner was announced "Historic Lenox Flats," to contain twenty-four two-bedroom condominiums, a project of the Central Community Housing Trust. Across the street were more modest apartments, some in obvious need of repair, which appeared to speak to the area's days in decline.

On the edge of downtown in full view from Ninth Street South was a rather bizarre project, Centre Village, which consisted of eight levels of parking, six levels of an Embassy Suites hotel, and twelve stories on top containing residential units.

PLUS/MINUS

Two factors that affect the city's general ambiance should be discussed. One is the safety/crime issue and the other is public art.

In a survey in 2002 of 1,200 randomly selected citizens about their perceptions of downtown, 63 percent said they visited it at least once a month and 34 percent once a week. Nearly three-quarters felt it was safe. Only 13 percent found downtown dirty, while 56 percent voted it "somewhat clean." People living in and near downtown felt safer than the others in the poll, 87 percent to 73.[30]

The fatal shooting of a university football player in September 2002 cast a bit of a pall on the burgeoning night scene in the downtown. City officials noted that violent crime was down 7 percent from 2001, and nightclub crowds were observed just a week after the incident.

Downtown Council President Sam Grabarski sees nuisance crimes, such as theft and public urination, as the real threat. "Nothing steals the spirit, the vitality, and the commerce of a neighborhood more than nuisance crimes. They go very much to the core sense of well-being that everyone needs," he said. A suburbanite was quoted saying she thought the daytime panhandlers were scary enough and didn't think she'd come after dark. Police complain that they arrest repeat offenders and nothing of consequence happens to them. The bar closing hour is a particularly dicey time when hundreds of people pile out into the street. Police try to break up shoving matches immediately.

A weekly crime report in the downtown newspaper for the first week of July 2003 listed fifteen incidents. They included eleven thefts, three robberies, and one burglary in the downtown running along Hennepin and Nicollet Avenues.[31]

There is a homeless population put at 500, many of whom took to spending the night under highway bridges because shelters were full and the overheads kept them dry. City and state officials have taken to installing "transient barriers" under the bridges, triangular-shaped metal barriers over former sleeping areas. The treatment has been applied to some thirty bridges for $12,000, at a time when state aid for the homeless was being cut, which shelter operators are quick to point out.[32]

In sum, yes there's a "crime problem" of the nuisance, panhandling variety. But it's concentrated downtown and was nowhere in evidence in any of the riverfront neighborhoods we visited or in Elliot or Loring Parks that we saw.

Another, more positive, aspect about Minneapolis in general is its strong public arts program. This is one of those quality-of-life features that people are at least vaguely aware of as contributing to the ambiance of a place. There's the formal kind, such as the sculpture garden next to Walker Art Center, whose centerpiece is a huge spoon with a cherry by Claes Oldenburg and Coosje van Bruggen. There are over fifty artworks in the two-part garden.

Minneapolis has an impressive Art in Public Places Program. Beyond that there are public art pieces commissioned privately. The Art in Public Places agency published a map in 2002 showing fifty-two individual art pieces scattered about the central downtown, including in our residential neighborhoods. We've already mentioned the pedestrian bridge from Loring Park to the Walker Center and the Berger Fountain, the latter one of the city's most recognizable landmarks, the map declares, and the new gateway to Elliot Park.

Other works include a mural about Elliot Park; a water wall sculpture by Maya Lin (at the American Express Center) on Third Avenue South; a fantasy bench serving bus passengers on Hennepin Avenue; art deco elevator doors at Foshay Tower, done in 1929; manhole covers done by various artists; Rockman, a playful sculpture exploring the city's most interesting plaza; Drumlins, which are earth mounds placed in front of the U.S. Courthouse; the restored Grain Belt Beer neon sign at Nicollet Island; a ceramic wall relief entitled River Goddess and a neon work entitled Riverboat in the skyway over Hennepin Avenue East. The program began in 1988 and contributes to the richness of the experience of Minneapolis.

YOUNG POPULATION

So who is moving into the Intown neighborhoods we have described? One barometer is Shane Breault, a 33-year-old advertising copy writer living in the North Loop, who was looking for an "urban vibe." Young professionals such as Breault "are the (loft) trend's lifeblood," a newspaper report declared.[33] At the higher end of the market, median price $500,000, it is more the empty-nester from the suburbs, a developer told us.

But the real action is in the lower price ranges of $200,000 to $400,000. When units at these prices are put on the market, people line up hours in advance with their checkbooks. "Demand for downtown condos and townhomes in the $200,000 to $400,000 range seems insatiable. Some developers are even reconfiguring floor plans to appeal to more price-conscious buyers." Thus an apartment building that failed to sell as condominiums in the 1980s is being reconverted, at prices from under $100,000 to $224,000. In another sign of the times, a building conceived as a fifteen-unit project priced over $400,000 is being reconfigured into thirty smaller units, most of which will range from $200,000 up to $400,000. Within one week, nineteen people made reservations. Demand for downtown condos is driven by people relocating from cities such as Chicago, Atlanta, and Denver, where pricing is similar. "In fact, a higher percentage of people relocating are choosing downtown over the suburbs. About 30 to 40 percent of all downtown buyers are from other cities, compared with 20 to 25 percent of buyers in the suburbs."[34] This was confirmed by a developer we interviewed, who stated that the price point for the downtown condo market appealing to professionals working there was $200,000 to $300,000—the low interest rates of 2003 made this price level very competitive with renting.

Another young person making the move downtown, Matt Clark, 24, walks to work at Wells Fargo and doesn't own a car. "I'd seen my mom and dad spend so much time commuting that I knew I didn't want to do that," he said. His priorities for the North Loop (he's on the association board after serving as student president at the University of Minnesota): Getting rid of surface parking lots, keeping bars open until 2:00 A.M. (from 1:00 A.M.), and making downtown more family-friendly, suggesting free and fun events for families be provided.[35]

And, finally, how many people actually live downtown? A city analysis of the census found 20,000 in the area west (roughly) of the river.[36] With the St. Anthony and Marcy-Holmes neighborhoods east and along the river included, another 6,655 can be added, who are not usually included in discussions of "downtown."

The downtown council commissioned a study of the population, by Maxfield Research, at the opening of the decade. The group stated that as of December 31, 2000, there were 26,200 living in downtown Minneapolis.[37] We're usually skeptical of business association figures, but this one feels about right.

We can attest that the burgeoning residential population that we discuss is truly amazing from when we visited here twenty years ago. We were taken to the area of the mills, for example, which were then in major disarray. One pioneering restaurant was on the Minneapolis side of the river and little else. Twenty years from now, building on what's present in 2003, there's hope that the blank areas of the downtown will be filled and that the streets will become more welcoming to those living here and traveling by foot.

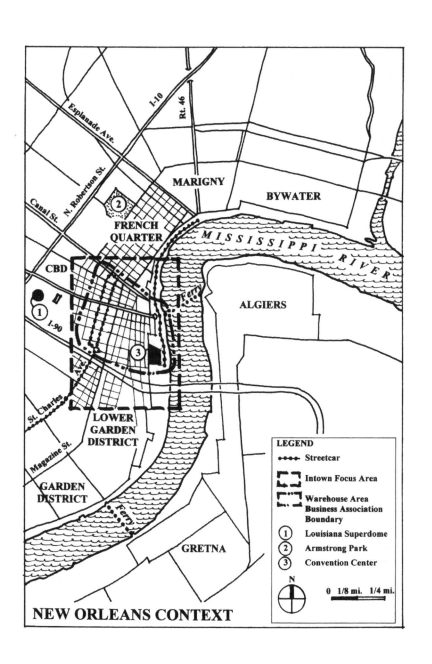

NEW ORLEANS CONTEXT

LEGEND

◆◆◆◆ Streetcar

⌐ ¬ Intown Focus Area
⌐_¬

⌐ ¬ Warehouse Area
¦_¦ Business Association
    Boundary

① Louisiana Superdome

② Armstrong Park

③ Convention Center

N

0   1/8 mi.   1/4 mi.

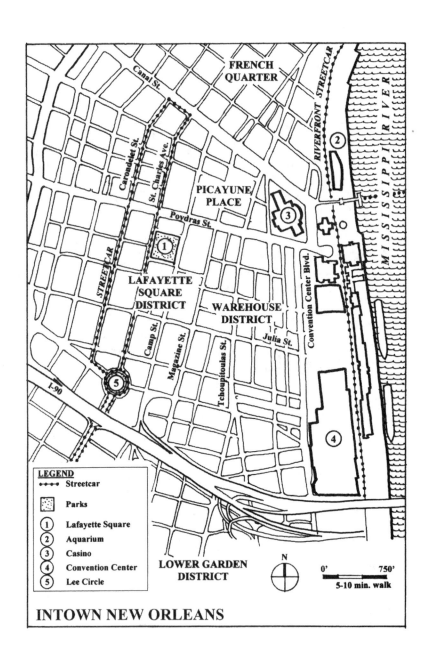

FRENCH
QUARTER

Canal St.

RIVERFRONT STREETCAR

MISSISSIPPI RIVER

Carondelet St.

St. Charles Ave.

PICAYUNE
PLACE

②

Poydras St.

③

①

Convention Center Blvd.

LAFAYETTE
SQUARE
DISTRICT

WAREHOUSE
DISTRICT

STREETCAR

Camp St.

Magazine St.

Tchoupitoulas St.

Julia St.

I-90

⑤

④

LEGEND
•••• Streetcar

☐ Parks

① Lafayette Square
② Aquarium
③ Casino
④ Convention Center
⑤ Lee Circle

LOWER GARDEN
DISTRICT

N

0'   750'

5-10 min. walk

INTOWN NEW ORLEANS

8

New Orleans

> No American city resembled it. The river gave it both wealth and
> sinuous mystery. It was an interior city, an impenetrable city, a city of
> fronts. Outsiders lost themselves in its subtleties and intrigues, in a
> maze of shadow and light and wrong turns.
> —*John Barry*, Rising Tide

New Orleans, with its multicultural heritage, its notoriety as a party city, its
Mardis Gras, unrivaled musical heritage, and mouth-watering cuisine, is
the most exotic of America's cities. New Orleans is characterized by distinctive, colorful neighborhoods that arrayed themselves along the Mississippi
River upriver and downriver over the years as the city spread from its
beginning in the Vieux Carre (French Quarter) circa 1718.

People have made New Orleans home for over three hundred years, and
the architecture of the homes here is more varied and distinctive than in
most cities. The Creole cottage, for instance, is a one-story wooden home
with three bays and might date to the late 1700s. These are found mostly
in the French Quarter and neighboring Faubourg (suburb) Marigny and
Bywater. The American townhouse, by contrast, is a usually a three-story
structure, door on one side with two windows, often brick or stuccoed
brick. These were built in the Lafayette District in the early 1800s. There
are also the Creole townhouse of two to four stories, the shotgun house
with a front porch often with Victorian ornamentation, and the double-
gallery house, a two-story structure with ornamented porch across an
asymmetrical front.[1]

Anyone who visits the city knows of the classic French Quarter centered around Jackson Square that has been and remains home to bluebloods and bohemians alike. Most visitors have probably also taken the historic St. Charles Avenue streetcar out to the Garden District with its handsome homes and lush, leafy streets. The more adventurous may have discovered the Lower Garden District, Algiers, Faubourg Marigny, and Bywater. Up until the last ten years or so it is fair to say that with the exception of the Quarter and the Garden District, many New Orleans neighborhoods were plagued with the problems of many older center cities: poverty, crime, rundown or abandoned housing, and vacant land.

The New Orleans Preservation Resource Center (PRC), founded in 1974, has been a pioneer in getting people to realize that the city's neighborhoods must be brought back to life. One of the programs it launched was Operation Comeback, which we discuss further on. The New Orleans Intown Living story is itself an interesting and telling one of comeback.

WAREHOUSE AREA

We're going to take as our focus area the territory covered by the "Warehouse Area Business Association," 350 acres from the riverfront on the east, Ponchartrain Expressway on the south, Loyola Avenue on the west to Poydras down to Camp, and then Canal Street on the north. We place "Warehouse Area Business Association" in quotes because there is a dispute over the nomenclature(s) of this area. Within the WABA boundaries are the Lafayette District Historic District, the Picayune Place Historic District, and the Warehouse Historic District, portions of the Central Business District, and the riverfront. Residents of the Lafayette District resist being lumped under the label "warehouse"—to the extent of one resident displaying a banner reading "You Are Not in the Warehouse District."

To further confuse things, various pieces of marketing and tourist literature label areas without regard to their legal boundaries. There is an active campaign under way, with some political support, to rename these four downtown historic districts "The American Sector," as it was known around 1803, as a compromise in what some refer to as an identity crisis. As the warehouse label has a certain cachet, gained variously by images in the media from the SoHo neighborhood of New York and from the impetus given to New Orleans' Warehouse District from the World's Fair of 1984, our guess is that the designation will stick at least in an informal way.

Whatever the name, the architecture and feel of the subareas are wonderfully different. The Warehouse District began on newly formed land created by deposits from the Mississippi in the early 1800s. To the commercial and industrial buildings here came the railroads after the Civil War, further stimulating industry. The port was located along this stretch of the river, and warehouses were constructed for the agricultural goods being shipped that gives the area its characteristic building form. Today the Warehouse District still has a wide-open industrial feel to it despite nearly twenty years of gradual redevelopment. The pairs of one-way streets seem wider than they actually are. Buildings are generally two to four stories in height, and there's a spacious relationship of structures to street. The Cotton Mill at four stories plus twenty penthouse condominiums is one of the tallest and largest buildings here, with 273 apartments, many of which have commanding views of downtown and the river. We visited a penthouse unit here whose outdoor patio practically doubled the unit's size and provided views in several directions.

In contrast, Picayune Place is a small area of seven blocks next to and relating to the Financial District. Office use still predominates in generally mid-rise structures. Several small conversions to residential use have been undertaken, including six apartments in the 150-year-old Natchez Building, plus the Walle Building and the Medallion Building, once the warehouse for Johns Manville, built in 1914. Its name is etched along the top. We visited a resident in the Medallion, one of fourteen units in a handsome renovation completed in 1995. It has the loft feel with high ceilings and bare interiors plus great views.

In further contrast is the Lafayette Square District. Here are many classic three- and four-story townhouses, built as early as the late 1700s. A major fire in the French Quarter in 1788 was one impetus to its development. The arrival of Americans wanting their own section, distinct from the Creole settlement of the French Quarter, was another. It was for a long time the most prestigious place to reside, but it began a gradual decline in the 1890s as the Garden District arose as the fashionable place to live, a short distance from the city center. In addition to residential there were (and still are today) a mix of commercial and governmental activities. In the 1950s, for instance, a resident recalls, there was a cluster of small service businesses, such as car repair, typewriter service, and furniture shops.

As the Warehouse and Lafayette Districts evolved at different paces, we shall treat them separately, recognizing that this is arbitrary in that events in one affect the other and that there are similarities as well as the differences. Thus, there are warehouse-type structures in the Lafayette District and old residences in the Warehouse District. A signal occurrence took place in 1976 with the opening of the Contemporary Art Center, physically located in Lafayette, but clearly having an impact on the warehouse neighborhood. And vice versa for the impact of the World's Fair of 1984.

Before taking up our individual neighborhood stories, we should mention a critical planning document, namely a Growth Management Plan done in 1975 by Wallace, Roberts and Todd of Philadelphia and elsewhere. In what has to be called a seminal work for this part of New Orleans, it recommended creating the historic districts that now exist for the Warehouse, Lafayette, and Picayune areas (as well as Canal Street), calling for a moratorium on demolitions, building a residential base (through the Historic Faubourg Ste. Mary Corp.— see the discussion that follows), creating a Historic Districts Landmarks Commission, and establishing the Downtown Development District (DDD) as an umbrella improvement organization.

A quick aside about DDD: It is one of the earliest of its kind, receiving funds from a special levy on downtown properties for supplemental services in the areas of security, sanitation, and marketing plus starting a facade improvement program with a low-interest loan from a local bank, which in turn allows DDD to provide funds at a favorable rate. The organization sponsors an eighteen-member special police force. Its major emphasis in 2003 was on reviving the section of Canal Street that runs through the heart of downtown, where some thought is being given to attracting residents above the street-level retail, a staff person told us. It also sponsors a Parking Lot Enhancement Program and Sidewalk Enhancement Program. The annual budget is $5.2 million.[2]

Lafayette Square

Let's pick up our story in the Lafayette Square District. A newcomer to the city in 1975 recalled for us her first streetcar ride down Carondelet Street. She was shocked at its skid row character so close to the central business district. A visual analysis in 1981 done by the Harvard Business School documented that St. Charles Avenue from Lee Circle for five blocks, past Lafayette Square, was "predominately" skid row with flophouses, bars, and soup kitchens. (St. Charles runs parallel to Carondelet.) Likewise, the block of Julia Street between St. Charles and Camp Street and a block along Camp were the same. "Occasional" skid row characteristics were identified down Julia, its parallel streets St. Joseph and Girod, and on Lafayette Street itself.[3] Julia and Camp was the apparent epicenter of dereliction. Several locals related a version of a saying that if you were bad as a child you were told you would end up at Julia and Camp, or be deposited there.

Conditions worsened in the early 1980s, caused in part by a decision to widen Poydras Avenue to make it the principal downtown business artery, which had the effect of removing the homeless from there into the Lafayette area where the grand homes were made over to boardinghouses.

The legacy of the area's skid row days is still present. In a study prepared in July 2001 for the Warehouse Area Business Association, twenty "controversial influences" were delineated. Among them: Temps Today, a labor pool facility on Magazine Street; the Lafayette/Warehouse District border; Ozanam Inn, a homeless shelter on Camp Street; several bars/flophouses still intact if not in operation; and weekend feeding of homeless people in Lafayette Square.[4] Two ordinances early in the redevelopment were enacted to help deal with the issue, namely a clampdown on bars by requiring that food be served with alcohol and an ordinance barring rooming houses.

One of the five principal issues of the Warehouse Area Business Association today is homelessness. There are two homeless shelters in its general area run by churches, and a third not far afield. Efforts to get them to relocate, which have been under way for years, have fallen on deaf ears as the sponsoring churches reply that they have been there before newcomers arrived to open law offices or to move into townhomes and that they serve a social need. The subject figured prominently in a discussion with Mayor Ray Nagin at the warehouse association's annual meeting that we sat in on in March 2003.

A resident who has been in the Lafayette District since 1981, when he bought one of the three-story flophouses, now an elegant live/work space, brings the story closer to today. He recalled for us that as late as 1994 the area was a "war zone," with rival gangs fighting it out. One intersection several blocks away (in an adjoining neighborhood) had eight murders in one year. A crackdown ensued, and in three years from that date, the crime rate in the city had been sharply reduced.

The first turning point in the Lafayette neighborhood, as mentioned previously, was the opening in 1976 of the Contemporary Arts Center (CAC) in a warehouse donated by Sidney Besthoff of the K&B Corporation, a local drugstore chain. The firm built a new headquarters nearby in 1973 as well as an indoor-outdoor art display space. Together these could be taken as the real first steps of transformation.

Prior to the Center's opening, artists producing contemporary work had no venue. Recalls an activist involved in the creation of CAC, its very first show occurred in 1974 at a church in Bywater, three neighborhoods downriver. That planted the seed for what became the four-story, 40,000-square-foot presence of CAC. The opening show was made a welcoming party, and a young crowd turned out in numbers to see motorcycles, a car of Fats Domino, and other displays. Nighttime jazz concerts were then scheduled, and effectively this section gained a new identity. A warehouse businessperson described CAC as attracting a bohemian, countercultural crowd. He further remembered that it was not air-conditioned years after opening, it was unrenovated, and the bathrooms were terrible! Still the young and middle-aged professionals came. The arts center and the K&B plaza were the catalysts for a burgeoning art scene that is today centered near Lee Circle and along Julia Street, as we will describe.

PRC Role

Simultaneous with the birth of the arts center, the Preservation Resource Center opened its office in 1976 in one of thirteen once-elegant townhouses on Julia at Camp. This was a bold gamble for a two-year-old organization to base itself in such a deteriorated neighborhood. The flophouse it acquired was in a general state of disrepair referred to as alarming, with a back wing in danger of collapse. A main emphasis for PRC at this time was to try to halt demolitions of the area's historic structures. At the other end of the block that PRC moved into was, until very recently, the Hummingbird Bar, described in a guidebook as "a seedy dive under a flop-house."[5] It and a neighboring townhouse are to be transformed into a museum and shop, with offices above, of the McIlhenney Co. from Avery Island, Louisiana, famous as makers of Tabasco® sauce.

Recalls Jim Amdal, an urban planning professor at the University of New Orleans and warehouse area activist and analyst, of what it was like in the early 1980s: "I was often as dismayed by the social reality as I was amazed by the architectural inventory. In those years there were no CBD residents. Julia Street was a rough environment, and the PRC was still a lonely pioneer, having completed their renovation in December, 1980. On many visits to the PRC offices in the spring of 1982, I stepped over dere-licts and drunks rather than greeting my neighbors residing on these same streets today."[6]

One of the keys to the area's revival, an activist told us, was the exis-tence of a revolving fund beginning in 1976, funded one-half with private funds, the other from the Downtown Development District. The Historic Faubourg Ste. Mary Corporation (the area's original name) was a non-profit entity with a residential focus that helped buyers with low-interest loans to buy and fix flophouses and other run-down properties. It also was the recipient of facade donations, for which owners pledged to retain the appearance of a building in exchange for tax breaks (and which later put it into competition with the PRC). There were calls in 2003 for DDD to revive this entity.

Directly across from Lafayette Square, catty-corner from the elegantly restored Lafayette Hotel and two doors from historic Gallier Hall, built in the 1850s, rises a new luxury fourteen-story condominium representing an expansion of Intown Living here. The first four stories of 625 St. Charles, as the project is known, are flush to the sidewalk and maintain the street line. The other stories are set back; at the top are two-level penthouses. Retail is to occupy the first level and the mezzanine, a neighborhood objec-tive, while offices are above and rentable function/entertainment space is on the fourth floor. The building is laced with such amenities as a lap pool, fitness area, massage room, catering kitchen that residents of the thirty-five units can reserve, and video conference space. Interior parking is provided. Pricing here begins at the $500,000 level, which a survey done for the developer determined would sell if sufficiently luxurious, and sales were strong as of 2003.

Explains developer Tom Bauer: "The idea in creating 625 St. Charles is that residents are seeking a less complicated life; they like novelty and change, but require quality, a fair price and extraordinary amenities." Bauer was further quoted: "I have seen a lot of other cities try to recreate Main Street. But it seemed to me that what was needed was to find the real thing . . . I felt a need to create a sense of place, of livability. I felt that could happen in a community that mixes housing with commercial use and other activities that are all within walking distance."[7]

As to the nature of the population in the area, one longtime resident we spoke with described them as dedicated, involved, and highly educated, with many of them artistic and creative. He said they were a leadership group with influence in the city greater by a factor of 100 than average suburbanites.

To its advocates, the Lafayette Square District is the classier neighborhood, with a richer history and a tighter-feeling urban grid than the Warehouse District—hence part of the concern over nomenclature. Others see it as behind the Warehouse District in part because of its skid row past, whose partial presence remains today, resulting in relatively fewer restaurants and other attractions. To the outsider, the distinctions will inevitably blur, the more so as the two areas are filled in.

Warehouse District

In the late 1970s, much as there were early signs of life in Lafayette Square, there were early developments in the Warehouse District also. A *Historic Warehouse District Study and Technical Report* by the PRC, issued in 1982, was undertaken in anticipation of the World's Fair coming to the area in 1984. What it accomplished was to document and bring needed attention to the architectural richness of an area few were familiar with, and not incidentally to serve notice that demolition would be inappropriate and actively opposed. Otherwise there might well have been a tendency to pull down old industrial buildings or dilapidated townhouses. Said the report:

The preservation of the Warehouse District has an economic as well as a cultural dimension. The city today uses its vast historic resources to create a major industry— tourism, which is second only to the Port of New Orleans in its economic impact on the city . . . The Historic Warehouse District can add another dimension and resource to the city's tourist appeal.

The report went on to note that much unregulated demolition was occurring. What it did not foresee was the later residential influx, which indeed in 1982 would have been a stretch. In its appeal for preservation, the report stated: "WHILE VIRTUALLY EVERY CITY CAN BUILD A NEW CONVENTION CENTER AND HOTELS TO MATCH, THEY CANNOT BUILD A NEW HISTORIC RESOURCE." (Emphasis in original.)[8]

That PRC's overall preservation campaign for the area was successful can be attested in the preservation awards given by the Historic District Landmarks Commission in 2002 for the work of the previous decade in the neighborhoods of the central business district. Of the fifteen top awards, ten were in the warehouse business association area. Included were converting a vacant commercial building on St. Charles Avenue to a bakery with residences above, taking a 1906 bank building on Camp Street and making it and the building next door a 119-room hotel, and restoring what remained of an 1833 row of three-story buildings on Magazine and Natchez Streets into a hotel. Nine additional honorable mentions were identified in the area.[9]

Anticipation of the 1984 World's Fair—a major event for the city—resulted in speculators buying property in the area. One Realtor we spoke with who was active at this time introduced us to a new precept of land investment: Sell on anticipation. He gave this advice to landowners who instead preferred to wait for the World's Fair to take place. What would have brought $1 million before the fair sold for $450,000 afterward, he told us.

The fair's focus was on the riverfront and an adjoining eighty-plus acres in the Warehouse District. The land was assembled and the fair pumped $25 million into infrastructure improvements in the district, including new sidewalks, trees, and lighting. The area had declined basically because a shift in port technology to containers moved the port's center of gravity upriver, leaving many wharves in the Warehouse District without a function. (While this is true, you can see in 2003 remnants of the earlier days, such as Gulf Marine and Industrial Supplies unloading materials with forklifts on a Saturday morning on St. Joseph Street—next to a Residence Inn.)

A new Hilton Hotel with 1,600 rooms was built right on the river in 1977, one of the first big initiatives in the area. A party thrown in an old riverfront wharf in 1979 as part of the run-up to the fair opened the eyes of the 2,000 attending to the river's beauty, inasmuch as it had been nearly entirely blocked off behind levees and warehouses until the arrival of the Hilton. People had major trouble finding their way to the event, so foreign was the territory.

(Preceding this and making it all possible was a major event in 1969, namely the canceling of a Robert Moses–designed Riverfront Expressway that for the most part would have been elevated [a tunnel was built for the road under Canal Street, so confident were its backers]. Determined and resourceful activists took on the business/political establishment of the city to beat the road, one of the earliest defeats of the highway lobby.)[10]

The World's Fair was held May 12 to November 11, 1984. Just before closing it was forced to file for bankruptcy, $100 million in debt, leaving many contractors and suppliers unpaid or only partially compensated.[11] It may be a bit of an effort to put the best face on an event that drew millions fewer people than projected (raising the question about the value of market projections), but we consistently heard from the people we interviewed that the fair was fun, that those who did go enjoyed it, and that locals were repeat visitors. One we talked with, living nearby, said he went thirty to forty times! There was a major nighttime party scene along Fulton Street just one block from the main venue, where restaurants remain today.

Plus, they say, there were the residuals. The most significant is the transformation of the fair's exhibit hall to the city's current convention center. Two additions have since been built, bringing the total footage for events to 1.1 million square feet, seventh largest in the nation.[12] There are plans on the drawing boards for another expansion, of nearly 500,000 square feet, but with the economic conditions of 2003 and travel cutbacks, this could be delayed or postponed. Also, it's said, the fair served to heighten awareness of the area, a place where few had ventured before. And, for better or worse, another fair building, one of the riverfront warehouses, became a Rouse Company festival marketplace, called Riverwalk. The downside of this building and the convention center is that they hinder public access to the river more than they enhance it.

Two Developers

Two local developers, by everyone's account, took the next step. Pres Kabecoff and partner Ed Boettner were one pioneering pair, Henry Lambert and Carey Bond the other. They proceeded to renovate old warehouses into apartments, flying in the face of studies that said the area wasn't suited to residential use, and going on their instincts.[13]

Kabecoff's first project was the Federal Fibre Mills, an old rope and twine factory. It had been a part of the World's Fair, which paid for some early improvements. Included were hospitality suites where people recall going to watch fireworks, which subtly introduced them to the architectural strength of the property as well as to a display apartment on the third floor. Part of the attraction, said to have drawn two million people into the building during the fair, was a German beer garden.[14] What this project and others nearby undertaken by Lambert had going for them, market studies to the contrary, was a tradition of Intown Living in New Orleans. The French Quarter and Garden District, and the gentrifying Lower Garden District, which began its rebound in the early 1980s, are examples. So while it was a major gamble, and numerous funding sources turned Kabecoff down, in the context of this city it perhaps wasn't such a giant leap. And with the cleanup of the immediate area courtesy of the fair, and with restaurants and bars present, the 140 units were rented.

One of the factors making a project like Federal Fibre Mills and nearby Julia Place (a turn-of-the-century bag factory) work was a 25 percent historic tax credit (since reduced). This reduction comes straight off the bottom line and was a boon to preservation from the time of its enactment in 1976 and expansion in 1981, until it was watered down during the Reagan Administration as part of "tax reform." One person we interviewed recalls being at a party when the existence of this tax credit was mentioned to a group of lawyers. At first disbelieving, they soon found out it was true, bailed out of their Class A rented offices in the downtown and bought historic properties to rehabilitate and occupy. As courts are in the area, including the U.S. Fifth Circuit Court of Appeals at Lafayette Square, this made sense. Many a law office is present in the area today.

Kabecoff is active on the national real estate development front and a promoter of neighborhood restoration. "Today's developments must focus on restoring neighborhoods in all their complexity, because they are the basic building blocks of cities, an idea that has been overlooked in the suburban master-planned communities of recent years. Reviving these old neighborhoods is a way of acknowledging our debt to who we are," he has been quoted.[15]

Helping to sell these projects was the imagery associated with "lofts." Several in New Orleans concurred with others that the *Seinfeld* television show popularizing urban apartment living had a major impact on 30-year-olds.

There were twenty condominium and apartment buildings in the Warehouse Area Business Alliance territory as of 1997.[16] The number of residents in 2003 was generally given as 2,000. One Realtor that we spoke with said he did a building-by-building survey and came up with the figure of 1,900. On the one hand this can be seen as a relatively small number for a resettlement that began nearly twenty years before; on the other it is not insignificant, given that the area began with zero residents except for derelicts and prostitutes. Also, the first six years or so of the period after the World's Fair was held up by an economy hard-hit by a drop in oil prices. The word that several used to characterize the residential influx into the greater warehouse area is "gradual" up to 2001. There's a suggestion that the pace had begun to accelerate as of 2003. An analyst of the neighborhood says that many of the residents are not from New Orleans, they come from elsewhere, including overseas, and are used to urban lifestyles. It gives the neighborhood a very cosmopolitan air.

The first residential units, especially in the transformed factories and warehouses, were large. By using the historic tax credit, developers were required to rent the units for five years, and they at first attracted a young population. After that period, conversion to condominiums began in the early 1990s and a somewhat older group began to arrive (hence a median age in the forties in the census tract here in 2000). One resident told us that a unit purchased for $197,000 in 1996 would sell for $300,000 in 2003, still very affordable by the standards of other cities. The housing is the city's most expensive in dollars per square foot, according to Danny O'Brien, owner of a firm specializing in locating housing for professionals. He puts the annual price increase in the area at 5 to 8 percent in recent years. The New Orleans Metropolitan Association of Realtors Inc. reports that the square-foot price for warehouse

area condominiums rose from \$142.10 per square foot in 1997 to
\$187.37 in 2001, with an average price of \$280,329.

Young Buyers

Another Realtor we interviewed talked about putting a new luxury condominium on the market in July 2002 and selling all but two of fifty-seven
units by April 2003. The secret, he felt, was to offer small units that are
within the reach of younger buyers, namely 600-square-foot, one-bedroom
units (\$139,000) up to something twice as large for as much as \$249,000.
The median age is 33 or 34 in his project, and the profile is of single professionals, many in the medical field because there are major facilities
nearby, plus lawyers and business owners. A few are empty nesters. For
many it is a first home buy. He echoed others in saying that many are from
out of town.

His analysis is that these buyers represent a market not well served now
in the warehouse area with its larger units of, say, 1,800 square feet in size
and more. The buyers he sees are hard working young professionals for
whom the all-night partying atmosphere in the French Quarter makes it
unattractive as a residential neighborhood. The Quarter is nearby when
the mood strikes, he noted, but it makes the Warehouse District an ideal
location, relatively quiet, with its own attractions, next to the country's
largest party district.

This Realtor's sense is that the warehouse area has become a strong
market since 2001 and that it will, unless the economy drops, take off in
the coming years. Several projects were in various stages of preparation in
2003 to add to the mix.

What's it like living in the area?

(Allison Cartwright) loves to people-watch as she walks by the restaurants, art
galleries and hotels in her neighborhood with her dog Ruby. "It's constant
change; you don't see the same things." You get that a lot from the new crowd of
young professionals who have been migrating into the Warehouse District for the
past few years. They like the activity, the hustle-bustle, the transitory nature of a
place that attracts tourists, locals, transplants from other cities, young singles and
empty-nesters . . . It's a hot spot for people who want to live the urban experience in lofts with 12-foot to 16-foot ceilings, huge windows, doormen and
rooftop decks."[17]

The census has only one tract that is wholly within the study area. Running from the river to Magazine Street and Julia to Canal, it covers much
of the Warehouse District and some of Picayune Place. The population
was 510 as of 2000, with 25-to-34-year-olds the largest age group. The
median age is 44, which reflects the rise in prices in the area attracting an
older, more affluent buyer, and the population is 88 percent white in a city

67 percent black. Nearly 60 percent are single, and nearly 70 percent are in nonfamily households.

Meanwhile a significant, not to say startling, hotel boom has occurred in the Warehouse District, situated as it is near the convention center. This includes the conversion of the Lykes Building on Poydras, once a dominant structure on the skyline at twenty-one stories, from offices to a 285-room hotel. A summary prepared by the Downtown Development District (which covers an area larger than the Warehouse Area Business Alliance) lists seventeen hotel projects built, under construction, or planned, with a total of 4,817 rooms as of January 2003. Of these, nine were completed or under construction in March 2003, the others classified as under "active development." The warehouse area had twenty-three hotels and seven more along its boundaries listed in a city guide.[18] Additional facilities, such as the new Ramada from an old warehouse on Tchoupitoulas at Notre Dame, was well along in construction as of March 2003 in a $45 million undertaking. In all, New Orleans had over 34,000 hotel rooms as of 2002 with more in the works, such as the conversion of the Audubon Building on Canal Street announced in fall 2003.[19]

Two residents spoke of their mixed views about the influx of hotels into the warehouse area. On the positive side, they both said, hotels put people on the streets who are going to and from the convention center as well as into the bars and restaurants, which are less frenetic than those in the French Quarter. Plus many of the projects are renovations, meaning historic buildings are being saved and brought back to life. Two downsides are cited: The hotels are gobbling up surface parking spaces as well as putting parking garages into the first levels, creating a deadly street frontage. Plus they cause bus and truck traffic through the heart of the Warehouse District, taking conventioneers to and from their central business district hotels. On a Thursday in March 2003, between 5:30 and 5:50 P.M. we counted nine large buses and one convention tractor-trailer while seated at an outdoor cafe. The buses were loud enough to stop conversation and disturb the sidewalk cafe ambiance we were enjoying.

Arts District

A final but exciting aspect of the overall warehouse area is the well-established and continually emerging art scene. Centered in the Lafayette Square District but extending into the Warehouse District along Julia Street are museums, galleries, art and crafts studios, and a small theater presence.

First, the museums. We mentioned the pioneering Center for Contemporary Arts. Beyond the work of local artists, there are displays of national/international artists, music and dance performances during the year, plus lectures. Its boast is that it has the city's only free cyber cafe. Attendance in 1999: 102,000, reflecting a steady increase over the years.[20]

In another old warehouse is the Children's Museum at 420 Julia Street full of imaginative, interactive things for kids to do, combining fun with education. There's a kid-sized supermarket, a TV newsroom, a cafe, and places to climb, ride, and explore. Attendance in 1999: 179,549, determined to be 75 percent local.[21]

At the other end of the spectrum is the Confederate Museum near Lee Circle, housed in a Romanesque building from 1891, designed to match the nearby former library. Annual attendance: 15,000.[22]

The big new player nearby is the National D-Day Museum, said to attract a thousand visitors a day. It was founded by author Stephen Ambrose and contains a large collection of articles and oral histories from World War II. It opened in June 2000 after fifteen years of preparation and cost $25 million.[23]

Two new facilities, under construction in 2003, are in the vicinity and will add to the cultural luster of this area. The first is the Ogden Museum of Southern Art, part of the University of New Orleans, to be housed in the restored Taylor Library, a Romanesque building by Henry Hobson, and in a five-story new building, connected by a tunnel behind the Confederate Museum. The library will contain eighteenth- and nineteenth-century works, while the new building on Camp Street will have works from the twentieth and twenty-first centuries. The core collection comes from businessman Roger Ogden.

Nearby is to be Louisiana ArtWorks in a combination of restored structures and new buildings, which will contain fifty studios for artists of various types, a store, an events venue, and a cafe. It's the undertaking of the Arts Council of New Orleans, whose offices will relocate here. It is to contain 90,000 square feet and will also have an outdoor work area plus a rooftop space. Located on Carondelet between Howard Avenue and St. Joseph Street, it will effectively serve as a gateway into what is being marketed as the "Arts District" when it opens in late spring 2004.

A number of promotional maps refer to the area as the "Arts District," yet another name for the territory. This designation calls attention to the significant private gallery scene that exists in the greater warehouse area. For instance, a pamphlet prepared by the Downtown Development District for the Arts District Association listed seventeen galleries that range from contemporary crafts to fine arts to a training center for inner-city youth. There is a coordinated opening of the galleries on the first Saturday of each month and several party nights when the galleries are open during the year. Another neighborhood event is a Saturday morning farmer's market.

The third dimension of the arts scene is the presence of craftspeople working in the area. This includes the very visible New Orleans School of Glassworks and Printmaking Studio/Gallery on Magazine Street, said to be the largest glassworking studio in the South.[24] Less visible is the ArtMetal Studio, where imaginative, ornamental metalwork is created. Another studio produces handcrafted art lamps and chandeliers. There is concern that these artisans will soon be forced out by rising land and building prices. In fact, we heard that the lease on one of the studios cited here was soon to expire, not to be renewed. Artists are now locating in the less-expensive Bywater neighborhood, discussed later.

ADDITIONAL NEIGHBORHOODS

We turn now to adjoining neighborhoods where new Intown Living examples are occurring and/or where rehabilitation is taking place. About four blocks away from the Warehouse District, past the Ponchartrain Expressway river bridges, is a huge apartment complex. Built in 2000, the Saulet consists of 703 units placed in what is described as a "no-man's-land" adjacent to the rejuvenating Lower Garden District. It was up for sale in March 2003 at an asking price of $99 million. The developer is the Greystar Capital Partners of Charleston, South Carolina. The company paid $8 million for its thirteen-acre site, and construction costs came to $60 million.

Locals describe it as a totally self-contained, fortresslike facility, whose residents stay within the complex with its own grocery, dry cleaning, and other services. It is said to be 95 percent occupied, with one-bedroom units renting for $890 and two-bedroom units $1,300. The gated project consists of eleven three- and four-story buildings plus parking garages in what would seem to be an altogether suburban-style development. Its importance is that it demonstrates that the Intown Living phenomenon for central New Orleans consists of a market deeper than people seeking historic loft spaces and the like.[25]

In a nearby section called Central City is an area with significant physical deterioration, a poor, largely black population, and a local leadership apparently jealous of its prerogatives and not welcoming new investment. It lies on the other side of the Ponchartrain Expressway from the Lafayette Historic District and immediately next to the reviving Lower Garden District. A volunteer grassroots effort is beginning, house by house, to turn the situation around. The Felicity Street Redevelopment Corp., a nonprofit founded with some initial private funding, is buying run-down properties, fixing them up, and reselling, plowing its profits back into a revolving fund. Its stated aim is to

maintain a vibrant and sustainable neighborhood in the Lower St. Charles Corridor of Central City. We will achieve this goal by building upon the existing assets of this historic neighborhood; by preserving and renovating the remaining 19th Century buildings; by attracting new homeowners and small-scale commercial enterprises to the area; and by working with current residents and property owners to reinforce and improve the residential quality of the neighborhood.[26]

Felicity, started in 2000, got a jump start by picking up seventeen properties that the owner had to unload because of hefty tax arrears. The organization was able to negotiate that indebtedness down and proceed with renovations. In all it has handled forty properties, its leader reports, and had a portfolio of property worth $700,000 in early 2003, giving it borrowing capacity of $500,000 with which to buy more houses.

We looked at one with severe fire damage that workers were clearing. It looked daunting to us, but not to the organization. Felicity has experience acquiring run-down buildings, including a property with as many as twenty-five people living in a basic two-bedroom house. The new buyers are about one-third from out of town, the majority white and often first-time buyers. A federal subsidy is used to enable some current residents to remain. One example of the rejuvenation taking place includes a concentration along Baronne Street, where a four-unit apartment was scaled back to two, allowing someone to buy it for a residence and earn rental income, for example. Likewise an eight-apartment unit will have been brought back to six.

On March 27, 2003, Mayor Nagin picked Central City as one of seven troubled neighborhoods where city and federal assistance was to be concentrated. Using $2.5 million, the city will provide forgivable loans to low- and moderate-income city employees for a first-time house purchase, up to $4,000. Single parents who buy doubles and agree to rent to someone eligible for federal Section 8 housing subsidy may receive loans up to $20,000. About seven thousand city properties will be sold at half their value, and another $5 million is earmarked for such things as grants for home repairs.

One happy sidelight: The Central City house of jazz great Kid Ory was bought by a preservationist in May 2000. The shotgun double on Jackson Avenue is where Ory lived from 1913 to 1915. The purchase by Dr. William Altman of South Carolina was sparked by a new organization, the African-American Heritage Preservation Council, working with Dillard University and the PRC. Ory, a trombonist, led the first black band to make a recording (in 1922) and was the first to hire Louis Armstrong. Others coming out of the neighborhood include Buddy Bolden, Joe Oliver, Jelly Roll Morton, and Johnny and Baby Dodds.[27]

We have personally witnessed the revival of the Lower Garden District, having stayed at a bed-and-breakfast there over twenty years ago when the nearby St. Thomas housing project was at its most dangerous and deterioration was widespread. The Preservation Resource Center launched Operation Comeback in the neighborhood, providing help to homeowners on a variety of levels. Its success is evident here today along a bustling, home-grown commercial street, Magazine, and in residential sections that feature handsome, restored homes, including large mansions, handsome townhomes, and cottages.

Operation Comeback is now an impressive citywide effort of PRC. It includes both the acquisition of properties for fixup and resale (forty-six such purchases were made in 2002, including five in Central City) and a year-long series of workshops to help homebuyers. In 2002, PRC held thirty-three such programs, reaching 2,524 people. These range from a "Historic House Specialist Realtor Training" to a "Shotgun Summit Workshop" and "Fight Blight!" session. It has a first-time homebuyer training program that includes referrals to lenders, advice on renovations, and the option of attending a twelve-hour training program. The organization is experiencing a lack of affordable housing for its clients and reports that the average price for a house in Orleans Parish (county) rose $15,000 in 2001.

Three other intown residential neighborhoods deserve mention. Faubourg Marigny and Bywater adjoin and lie directly east of the French Quarter, along the Mississippi River. Marigny has a spirited club, coffee cafe, theater, and restaurant scene for about four blocks along Frenchman Street. The neighborhood has been dubbed one of the "hippest" sections in the country. It does not appear to have had the desertion that occurred in the Lafayette District or severe dilapidation of Central City, and rather seems instead to be undergoing a kind of low-key gentrification. The Creole Cottage predominates, while warehouses and industry speak to river-related activity dating to the 1800s. It features a classic neighborhood park, Washington Square.

Bywater has long been a section for artisans and today is attracting artists and craftspeople forced to relocate by high prices elsewhere. An agent with Latter & Blum, one of the city's major realty firms, says the two neighborhoods are "full of artists, musicians, a large gay population, and inhabitants looking for an alternative urban lifestyle rather than middle-class suburbia." Prices in Bywater range from $100,000 to $200,000. Moving in are glass artists, sculptors, painters, writers, and musicians seeking housing and studios. In addition to Creole cottages the architecture includes Victorian and plantation-style homes.[28]

The third neighborhood is the French Quarter. This section experienced a steep decline in its residential population, dropping from over 10,000 people in 1940 to just under 4,000 in 1990. The census recorded a slight increase as of the year 2000, up 5 percent to a total of 4,176. Some think the increase is a mirage, just better census counting. Others are disturbed that the character of residential is changing, that more transitory buyers are moving in and relatively fewer full-time residents remain in the neighborhood. There's also a related issue of illegal tourist rentals by some of the buyers (not more than ninety days' rental allowed). The part-time buyers use condominiums for weekends, or they are corporate buyers. Says a long-time resident, "From a day-to-day experience of living there, it just seems like there's less residents than ever."[29] Backing up this was a survey done in 1999 by a researcher at the University of New Orleans. Jane Brooks said they found that of two hundred condominium owners contacted, 38 percent were permanent residents, but that 54 percent said they were part-time.[30]

Overall, our Intown Living story in New Orleans involves the transformation of desolate corners of former skid rows, the rebirth of old factory, industrial, and office buildings, and the restoration of hundreds of old homes in varied corners of the city. True to its quirky self, unusual juxtapositions abound: An upscale condominium around the corner from an active warehouse operation, a car repair garage, or a tin storage shed. Live/work spaces may be close by a homeless shelter. But Intown Living early in the twenty-first century is a heartening comeback story that is far from over.

In closing with this sentiment from Fred Koenig, a sociology professor at Tulane University, we speculate on one reason why:

People were no longer pedestrians, and they no longer interacted or gathered in coffee shops, taverns, laundromats, barber and beauty shops. The suburbs had no sense of neighborhood. So people turned their eyes back to the city, where they had so many fond memories of laughing and living and enjoying others in arts, for entertainment, in dining, shopping and just plain being stimulated by others. There were places, old neighborhoods as it were, where such a diverse population lived that you could pretty much find a group for any type of interest.[31]

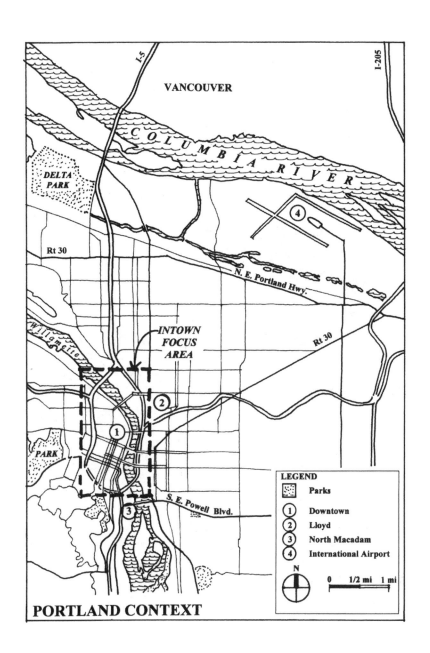

VANCOUVER

C O L U M B I A   R I V E R

I-5

I-205

DELTA
PARK

Rt 30

N. E. Portland Hwy.

Rt 30

Willamette

INTOWN
FOCUS
AREA

①

②

③

④

PARK

S. E. Powell Blvd.

LEGEND

▦ Parks

① Downtown

② Lloyd

③ North Macadam

④ International Airport

N

0   1/2 mi   1 mi

PORTLAND CONTEXT

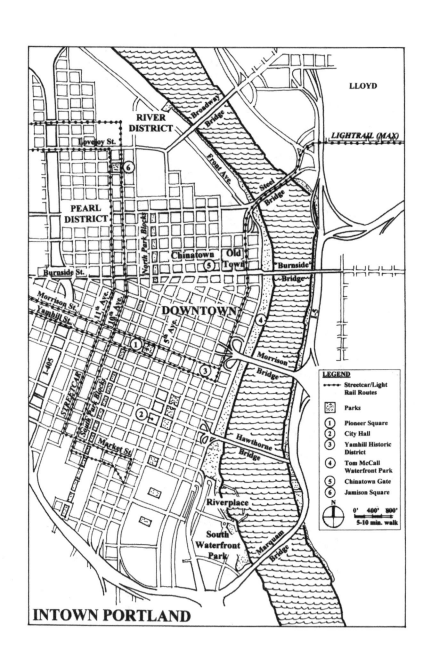

LLOYD

RIVER
DISTRICT

LIGHTRAIL (MAX)

Broadway
Bridge

Front Ave.

Lovejoy St.

6

Steel
Bridge

PEARL
DISTRICT

North Park Blocks

Chinatown Old
Town

5

Burnside St.

Burnside
Bridge

Morrison St.

DOWNTOWN

11th Ave.

10th Ave.

5th Ave.

I-5

Yamhill St.

4

1

Morrison
Bridge

3

I-405

STREETCAR

South Park Blocks

2

Hawthorne
Bridge

Market St.

Riverplace

South
Waterfront
Park

Marquam
Bridge

LEGEND

•••• Streetcar/Light
Rail Routes

Parks

1 Pioneer Square

2 City Hall

3 Yamhill Historic
District

4 Tom McCall
Waterfront Park

5 Chinatown Gate

6 Jamison Square

N

0'   400'   800'

5-10 min. walk

INTOWN PORTLAND

Portland, Oregon

> Rebuilding our cities will be one of the major tasks of the next
> generation . . . in providing for new developments you have the
> opportunity here to do a job of city planning like nowhere else in the
> world.
> —*Lewis Mumford,* Address to the City (Portland) Club

Known for its rain, beautiful gardens, and greenery, a favorite of the
Birkenstock and backpack crowd, Portland is a casual, outdoorsy, low-key
kind of town. The Willamette River runs through it and defines the eastern
edge of the central business district, while the Columbia River runs along
the northern boundary of the city. It is home to the Portland Rose Festival,
the famously huge Powell's Book Store, and one of the first major greenways in the nation. Portland is also something of a poster child for current
urban planning principles, and rightly so in a story that begins thirty-plus
years ago.

Neil Goldschmidt, a onetime poverty lawyer, was elevated from city
council to mayor in 1972 at age 32, which post he held until 1979 when he
went to Washington, D.C., as transportation secretary. From the accounts
of two we interviewed, supported by contemporary histories, his election
was a fundamental turning point in Portland's history, replacing what
apparently had been a business-dominated, conservative city leadership,
one stingy with public investments and wary of government, with a young,
progressive administration. As surprising as it is to read today, given the
level of enlightenment evident now in Portland, up until the 1960s the city

is portrayed as reflecting variously its conservative New England roots as well as its Midwestern origins, as early settlers also came from the Ohio and Missouri valleys. Portland, for all of its looseness, still today has some understated Midwestern characteristics, so much so that it has been likened to river cities like Cincinnati, Kansas City, and Columbus, Ohio.

GENERATIONAL SHIFT

With Goldschmidt came a shift in generations, including a lowering of the average age of city council members by fifteen years, assisted by an active women's group (Politically Organized Women, or POW). The city itself was younger in 1970 than earlier, the proportion of the population in the 15-to-34 age group rising from 22 to 30 percent of the total from the 1950s. The new force in the city was an alliance of the neighborhoods and the business interests with the shared objective of reviving downtown.[1]

Slightly preceding Goldschmidt's election was the progressive administration of Governor Tom McCall, serving 1967 to 1974. They and allies in the business community, especially the City Club, combined forces to rid the downtown of its Harbor Drive in the early 1970s in favor of a park in one of the boldest, most impressive moves any city in North America has made on its waterfront. McCall's legacy is mandated statewide planning and the Urban Growth Boundary program that exists today in Portland and throughout Oregon, and which we describe later, while Goldschmidt's legacy is embodied in the Downtown Plan of 1972 that set in motion policies that help account for today's Pearl/River District resurgence to be discussed in detail in this chapter.[2]

A person with an engineering firm who has followed local politics over the years told us a characteristic of Portland is that basic values are shared, and that the government is relatively clean and held in fairly high regard. This enables it to make things happen on a consensus-type basis. Over the past thirty or more years, there has been a degree of trust-building and less infighting than in other jurisdictions, more collaboration and a willingness to take the long view. Contributing to this is the city's relatively homogeneous population, predominately white and with smaller pockets of poor people than most other cities. (In the 2000 census, the black population in Portland was 6.6 percent, Asian 6.3. Minneapolis, by contrast, had an 18 percent black population.)

Another person we interviewed, in Portland for three years, had this take on the city's characteristic values: One was a spirit of civic-mindedness, including the business leadership; two was a sense of fairness and openness, with deliberative public meetings; three was a closeness to nature; four was a willingness to innovate, to be a little maverick but also pragmatic; and five was a lack of major industry or military to dominate the culture (although Intel and Nike are among the city's major employers).

What we have to remember, our first observer said, is that downtown Portland in the early 1970s was not an attractive picture, nobody was living there (except homeless people), and it was pretty seedy. There was a decline in the middle-class population in the neighborhoods as occurred virtually everywhere. In 1969 the retail and business area was faltering. The city was constantly cited for air pollution, and parking prices downtown were driving people to suburban malls.[3]

MOSES' INFLUENCE

On the south side of downtown, urban renewal had cleared out ethnic neighborhoods in favor of an unattractive auditorium, middle-income apartments and office towers—also bleak—plus parks. This territory of super blocks is today stunningly out of place with the rest of downtown Portland, but it is typical of what business leaders in cities around North America thought was the way to rebuild cities. In Portland, the South Auditorium Urban Renewal program is the direct result of Robert Moses coming to Portland in 1943 and recommending highways, naturally, plus tearing down Union Station and removing the southside neighborhoods. "Freeway City," the plan was titled. The city council endorsed the program a year later.[4] The Moses plan led to the construction of Harbor Drive, which tore down "scores of the handsomest buildings in the city," as a local architect observed, in fact removing what is said to have been the largest collection of cast-iron buildings in the country outside the SoHo district of New York City.[5]

One particularly unfortunate new building in this area, a literally white elephant that is now the Wells Fargo Bank, was so ugly it is said to have been a turning point in public attitudes about what was taking place. Another event that shook people up: Tearing down the old Portland Hotel in the middle of downtown for a parking lot. It's now Pioneer Square, a central, well-used public gathering place.

Today downtown is so vibrant it is hard to picture a down-and-out central Portland as the 1960s ended. Much like people have trouble visualizing a derelict Baltimore Inner Harbor now that it is revitalized.

It was into a bedraggled downtown scene that the younger generation of leaders stepped in the early 1970s. What they effectively did was overturn the Moses-bred direction Portland had been taking since World War II. In its place was developed what was called a "population strategy," which emphasized public transportation, neighborhood revitalization, downtown planning, and the establishment of districts for special housing incentives as its four main precepts. A pedestrian-friendly downtown was the goal, with active retail and attractive employment venues.[6]

The big, symbolic move stemming from this flurry of planning activity in the early '70s was the shift of federal funds from a planned expressway

(think Moses again) to a light rail line. In 1975—after considerable neighborhood opposition, as 1,700 people and 400 homes were to be displaced
in lower middle-class areas on the poorer east side—the Mount Hood
Expressway was scrapped. The road was replaced with MAX (Metropolitan
Area Express), at first a fifteen-mile rail line to the eastern suburb of
Gresham that opened in 1986. An eighteen-mile western line was added
in 1998, winning a 74 percent approval by voters, as well as a spur to the
airport (fare to downtown: $1.25).

Also part of the transportation system is an extensive bus system with
modern equipment, including a fare-free zone downtown and a pair of handsomely paved, one-way streets in center city (Fifth and Sixth Avenues) that
are exclusively for buses. The system works. Reports Metro, the regional
government, TriMet (the bus/rail operator) ridership grew 49 percent from
1990 to 2000 (while the population was up just 24 percent). In the late
1990s Metro reported car travel to downtown on a per capita basis was
beginning to drop.[7]

DOWNTOWN ALIVE

Downtown Portland today is at once lively and somewhat subdued. Due
in part to its heavy investment in transit, downtown streets have very light
traffic. It is possible to cross major streets against the lights even at rush
hour. A New Yorker would find the calm unsettling. The most striking
characteristic of downtown Portland is its walkability. Remarkable for a
Western city, its streets are relatively narrow and its blocks are two hundred feet square, two-thirds or less than standard city blocks, meaning the
city has more corners than usual, giving it the feel of a European city or old
sections in Boston. It's easy to walk from the retail core, say, to the riverfront and then to a restaurant somewhere. The riverfront, not so incidentally, is full of people on a pleasant day. Riverwalks line both sides, and the
numerous bridges over the Willamette permit walkers and joggers to loop
back and forth. A cantilevered/floating walkway along the east side, made
necessary by a roadway pressing against the riverbank, is a remarkable
installation and was instantly popular when it opened in 2001.

Downtown is very green, with many plantings and trees and significant
open space. It is also clean, and there is little graffiti. Overall, the objective
from the Goldschmidt era of creating a lively and walkable downtown has
been achieved, and this is in part why Portland is cited often in urban
planning literature as such a positive example of downtown rebuilding.

Downtown retail from all appearances is healthy, anchored by a
Nordstrom's but also featuring Saks Fifth Avenue and other high-end
shops centered on a Rouse Company indoor mall. (Mayor Goldschmidt is
reported to have told Nordstrom's that it would locate in downtown or
not at all, one of our interviewees told us.)

In addition to a strong retail component, there is a mix of office, hotel, institutions (Portland State University downtown has 36,000 students), cultural, and governmental installations. The workforce downtown numbers 82,000 (as of 2001), the largest portion being between thirty-five and forty-nine years old.[8] There is a significant resident population of 15,198 within the I-5/405 loop that defines center city, 10,430 in the downtown area, and 1,959 in the city's hippest neighborhood: the Pearl District.[9]

In discussing Portland's downtown, we would be remiss if we did not acknowledge the amount and quality of public art that enhances the city's public realm. Whether it's glancing up at the dramatic figure of Portlandia on the City Hall, or drinking water from one of the bronze ornamental water fountains, there are things to delight the eye throughout the city. A focal point and gateway at one end of the riverfront park is Salmon Street Springs. This exuberant and ever-changing fountain encourages people not only to see the magic of water but to play in it! At the other end of the park, one is invited to contemplate the Bill of Rights and the internment of Japanese-Americans during World War II amid Robert Murase's landscape work that includes bas-relief entrance pylons and large stone boulders engraved with poetry. Even a mundane bike rack—like one we discovered in the Pearl—was shaped like a nearby bridge complete with little cars crossing it.

PEARL DISTRICT

The Pearl District, approximately eighty blocks lying to the immediate north of the central business district, in 2003 was booming to such an extent that there was very real concern that escalating real estate values would damage the funky, artist-friendly atmosphere that had been established here. Condominiums in the Pearl are more expensive per square foot than mansions in Lake Oswego, previously the area's most expensive real estate. Prices were at $330 per square foot in 2003, while lakefront properties ranged from $200 to $300 per square foot.[10]

Artists were among the first to discover the abandoned warehouses that dominate the district, starting in the 1980s. A first Pearl District Arts Festival involving seven galleries was held on a Saturday in October 1987. A review noted that part of the atmosphere included "broken streets and dusty steps, cobwebs and concrete stairwells, creaking floors and small talk." Also noted were "giant trucks banging over potholed streets."[11]

Otherwise, one of the first developers to make a move in the Pearl in the 1980s told us, the area was strictly for storage and moving companies. It went dead at 4:00 P.M., there were no lights, and there was no place to get a cup of coffee. Social problems were minor, however, this person told us, with just scattered drug use and occasional transients sleeping on loading docks. The area's eventual recovery didn't have big social issues to contend with. A design firm made a pioneering move into the area in 1984 because space was large and cheap, a harbinger of things to come, a principal of the firm recounted.

Another of the pioneering developers in the Pearl District recalled for us the early days. The people moving here in the late 1980s and early '90s were "urban pioneers—Democrats, sophisticated people a little out of the mainstream," was his perception. He said the early mix was split between the 30-year-olds and the older, baby-boomer generations. They were interested in the gritty character of the neighborhood. Incidentally, this developer predicted the Lloyd District on the east side of the Willamette River, where the convention center and stadium are located, will be a hot new area, offering a significant price differential over the Pearl and nearby areas. This developer confirmed the respect that the private sector has for the local government, declaring city employees to be good and the directors at the top to be high quality—with no prompting by us.

The overall effect today in the Pearl District is of a surging, eclectic area on the move. Despite increasing rents, the Pearl as of 2003 had the city's largest concentration of art galleries. The galleries combine for a First Thursday evening opening, which more than one person described as a large street party. The *City Smart* guidebook, third edition put out in 2000, had this report: "While First Thursdays is a citywide happening, the heart of this event is definitely in the Pearl District and centered at NW 13th and Glisan. If you unknowingly stumbled upon this intersection on a warm Thursday evening at the start of the month, you might not believe you were in Portland."

To the art activity add a high-end retail scene and varied restaurants in a city that does not lack for same. By one listing the Pearl District has seventeen restaurants and six pubs, including the original BridgePort brewpub in an old brick structure. There were forty-two stores of various types in 2003, including a spa, a graphics design shop, fitness centers, Patagonia, Powell's Books, Roche Bobois, Urban Wineworks, and furniture shops such as What the Wind Blew In, as well as twenty-four fine arts galleries. We interviewed three of the developers in the Pearl plus a Realtor who works with a fourth. We will describe a sample of the products they were marketing besides the general ambiance of the neighborhood.

Sample Buildings

Marshall Wells Lofts is a rehabilitation of a Daniel Burnham–designed warehouse, circa 1910, distinguished by large beams running on a diagonal through the building, which are not only retained but exposed. The building is listed on the National Register of Historic Places. The 164 condominiums carved out of the building are true loft spaces, very industrial feeling with high ceilings, large windows, and fine views. In its center is an open atrium, and on the first level is parking, well disguised. Units, mostly sold as of spring 2003, range in size from 633 square feet to nineteen two-story penthouses of over 2,800 square feet. This is a $22.6 million project.[12] The population here is 68 percent single, with an age range from 30 to 60 in a bell curve tilted to the younger side, a representative reported. A tax freeze was an important contribution to making the project work; the building is assessed for tax purposes without reflecting the developer's improvements for fifteen years. Also important was the approval of a zoning change that allowed more height for residential uses, which required state legislature approval.

The developer Robert Ball in 2003 had just acquired the Meier & Frank Warehouse two blocks away, which contained 280,000 square feet that Ball planned to convert to condominiums. Between it and the Marshall Wells Lofts on the same side of 14th Street was a new construction called The Edge, where the REI store was to locate. Under construction in spring 2003, this was to contain 117 condominiums, plus parking.

The Gregory, a personal favorite, is an Art Deco gem, in the middle of the Pearl District on a block straddling the streetcar lines. The decorative detailing on the facades is stunning. It contains ground floor retail, office space on the second, third, and fourth floors, and condominiums above, with penthouses on the 11th and 12th floors (making it one of the area's tallest). The size range here is from 750 square feet to 3,350, with ceilings in the ten-foot range. A person familiar with the Gregory put its residents' average age at about 40 years, slightly older than in other nearby condominiums. The population is professional, two-thirds single and young, predominately male and with a large percentage gay. Low interest rates in 2003 were helping younger buyers, and empty nesters are arriving, some of whom are acquiring second homes intown to pair with houses in the country or on the coast.

Promotional literature for the Chown Pella Lofts, where you step up onto the former loading docks to enter the building, describes the building as "an old brick and heavy timber structure with the original 10-foot-high ceilings of tongue and groove planks supported by massive heavy wood beams. The building is listed on the National Historic Register and has all the nooks, crannies and old Portland ambiance that simply cannot be duplicated today." It's a 100-year-old warehouse (actually two buildings) whose last occupant was the Chown window and door company. The project offers units ranging from 740 to 1,850 square feet in size. "Industrial strength living" is the sales pitch, which like its counterparts makes much of the ambiance of the Pearl.

Here is how the owner of a new construction, the six-story McKenzie Lofts built in 1998, sells its seventy-five units: "What attracts people and businesses here is an uncommon desire for a more active, urban way of living and doing business away from suburban sprawl, commuter traffic and the responsibilities of conventional home ownership. The Pearl District lifestyle is about freedom and creative living—following a path of your choosing, rather than surrender to a conventional suburban lifestyle."

As 2003 began, the Pearl District had the most housing under construction or permitted than at any time previously, in the face of a generally slow real estate market, especially for properties over $500,000. There were 1,600 units, condominiums and apartments, under way, with the latter dominating. Rents are high by Portland standards, $800 to $2,000 a month. Reported Tiffany Sweitzer, managing partner of Hoyt Street Properties: The upper-end market was softening, but smaller units (600 to 800 square feet) were "selling fast."[13] This represents a shift from several years ago, a real estate manager told us, when the higher-end properties were selling faster. One new neighbor is to be former Governor John Kitzhaber.

Government Initiatives

While we must credit the artists and pioneering developers—and the person who observed twenty years ago that the galleries and lofts inside the old industrial warehouses were like pearls in an oyster—a further truth is that the Pearl and adjacent River District development are also the result of the conscious city program to revive downtown dating back to the early 1970s. The mayor in 2003, Vera Katz, in office since 1993, is a product of the progressive movement that took over the city in 1972 and is thus a link to the goals established then.

There were other initiatives as well from the yeasty years in the '70s, like a city office that supported neighborhood associations, but for our story, the pertinent policy is the one promoting Intown Living. This is both governmental, namely through the Portland Development Commission, and from the downtown business community. The Portland Business Alliance has a staff member working full-time on housing. The current emphasis of the Alliance is to develop a program that will provide more workforce and middle-income housing in the city.

The governmental side works with the private sector to accomplish its housing aims. One method is a ten-year property tax exemption for qualified buyers who meet income and purchase price guidelines. Another method is direct investments in needed public facilities.

The largest redevelopment project in the Pearl District (in fact, in the city) is The Brewery Blocks on five sites at the southern edge of the Pearl. It is to have 220,000 square feet of retail (and already has a Whole Foods grocery), 400,000 square feet of office space, 1,200 underground parking spaces, and 123 condominiums. As of early 2003, here is where it stood: Block one was completed and is where Whole Foods and Portland Energy Solutions (a small Enron entity) are housed. Block two, containing the brewhouse, was nearing completion of a ten-story office with street-level retail. Block three, scheduled for 2004, involves converting an 1891 armory to retail and a fifteen-story condominium. Block four is nearing completion for office and retail and will house the Art Institute of Portland. Block five comes later.[14]

In the face of an economic downturn in 2002 and high office vacancy, the Brewery Blocks' developer, Gerding/Edlen, reported it was still having some success in leasing its expanding space. The developer reported block one fully leased, block two at 25 percent (hoping to soon be at 90 percent), and block four at 60 percent. The residential portion hadn't begun in 2002. Said a broker, J. Clayton Hering: "I believe they are doing as well as—if not better than—the marketplace." They had hoped to land outdoor gear provider REI, but it chose another Pearl District site because of a lack of free parking.[15]

An official with the Portland Development Commission (PDC) told us it had invested $8 million in the $250 million undertaking, namely a $6 million loan to help with the underground parking and $2 million in grants for public improvements (streets/sidewalks). The funds come from a tax increment financing fund for which property taxes are capped and increases stemming from investments are pooled and bonds issued. PDC has a $60 million loan from the city (it's paid back $32 million), which it used to purchase forty acres of former railroad land, the disposition of which we'll take up now because it is central to the River District residential story.

PDC bought the land north of the Pearl District to the Willamette River. This is part of the official River District, which PDC declared in 1998 an urban renewal district. This gave the agency the authority to map out goals for the territory, and in the case of the railroad yards, having title meant that it could negotiate with whoever wanted to buy them. The urban renewal designation gives PDC the basis on which to support the Brewery Block project and other initiatives in the Pearl District. It encompasses the Old Town and Chinatown neighborhoods as well.

The buyer of the railyard property was Hoyt Street Properties, LLC (the land runs north from Hoyt Street). The company hammered out an agreement with PDC in 1997, updated two years later. It is fifty-two pages in length plus appendices and spells out the minimum housing densities that will be allowed per block (Blocks A through N, carefully mapped). Further, the documents spell out how many "extremely low-income" units there are to be, how many low-income units there will be, the number of moderate-income units, as well as middle and upper. Further, there is an annual accounting rendered by PDC of its targets, in a report to the city council, which adopted the River District Housing Implementation Strategy in 1994.

By agreeing to these targets, the developer got in return agreement by PDC that it would fund certain public improvements. Hoyt Street Properties knew it needed park spaces, for instance, to help sell condominiums in as green a city as Portland is, especially if there were to be families. And it knew an overhead ramp along Lovejoy Street had to come down because it severed the area from the Pearl District, of which its project is a natural extension. The document has PDC's agreement to do these and related things in a specific timetable.

In the parks agreement, Hoyt Street agreed to turn over the land and some rights-of-way, and the city agreed to build two parks before adjacent buildings were ready for occupancy, pledging to begin by March 8, 2000. With the parks came added density levels in the housing as part of the city/developer trade-offs. There are to be three park spaces in all. Jamison Square was completed in summer 2002. Along one edge of it is the first section of a planned boardwalk that will carry all the way to the Willamette River. On the opposite edge, there is a public art installation consisting of a row of very colorful pylons.

Here's how the exchange works. The initial density for the area was set at 14 units per acre. When the ramp came down, it jumped to 87 units per acre. The first park increased the target to 109 and the streetcar (see later discussion) lifted the target density to 131 units per acre. The agreement runs for fifty years.[16]

The Hoyt Street Property projects are attractive, low-rise buildings marching in a line from the edge of the Pearl District toward the river. Beginning at Irving Street, the buildings front the streetcar line, to one side or the other, effectively extending the Pearl District in feel, appearance, and dominant middle-class ambiance. Its projects extended five blocks as of 2003, about four blocks away from reaching the riverfront.

In its report card on how its River District housing objectives were being met as of fall 2002, PDC reported the following: Since 1994, thirty-five projects built with 3,524 units. It further surveyed the rental housing scene in summer 2002 and found the following: single room occupancy (SRO) comprised 42 percent of the total (occurring primarily in Old Town/Chinatown as opposed to the Pearl), studios comprised 19 percent, one-bedroom units were 27 percent, and two bedrooms just 12 percent, a total of 2,866 rentals.

The report card notes the considerable public investment required to make the housing work. "Recognizing that it will require a variety of amenities and services to attract a diversity of household types to the (River) District, PDC and the River District Steering Committee are working with neighborhood residents and other interested parties to assure a full range of community services," PDC declared.

The report listed the nine projects built, under construction or under design review by Hoyt Street Properties, condominium buildings, generally with 120 to 130 units, plus one rental project, a total of 1,085 units at a density of 144 units per acre, significantly exceeding the early targeted levels. PDC also found that its goals for low-income housing were exceeded; its goal was to have 15 percent available to persons with 0 to 50 percent of median family income, and it had achieved 20 percent. The survey found that a sizable percentage of units were small (under 700 square feet), another of the agreed-upon targets.

In summary, PDC found that since 1999 (as of summer 2002), the River District had seen 2,032 units of new housing built, 21 percent of which was low-income, of a twenty-year target of 3,350 units.[17]

Clustered around Hoyt's buildings are the work of other developers, mostly residential but including such installations as RiverTec, an office rehabilitation (75,000 square feet), the Pacific Northwest College of Art (enrollment 1,400) in an old brick electrical supply warehouse, the "Jean Vollum Natural Capital Center" with 50,000 square feet of office and retail (a group of conservation-minded nonprofits are here along with an organic foods outlet), as well as a Creative Services Center with 80,000 square feet of office. There's also a headquarters for a national advertising firm in an old ice house.

At the northernmost section of the River District is a tract of riverfront land owned by the Port of Portland. In 2000, the port sold fifteen acres to Riverscape LLC, a company owned by Seattle developers, for $7.5 million. Their plan, subject to city approval under PDC's urban renewal designation, calls for 600 condominiums, 170 affordable apartments, and some 175,000 square feet of commercial development. The site has 1,800 linear feet of river frontage that would seem certain to be required to have significant open space and walkway connections.[18]

Streetcar Desired

Not to be overlooked and a key element to the success of the Pearl/River District was its streetcar project ($52 million) that the city committed itself to. Its importance to the Pearl/River neighborhood is that it meant a direct public transit link every fifteen minutes into downtown, and beyond, in fact, to Portland State University. At Pioneer Square it plugs into the MAX east-west rail network, plus numerous bus lines. In exchange for the streetcar, Hoyt Street's developers agreed to increase housing densities by one unit per 2,000 square feet (or twenty-two units per acre) above an earlier standard agreed to.

The streetcar also links to Northwest 23rd Street (in the West Hills area, known locally as "Trendy Third"), running through the Pearl along 10th and 11th Avenues. It is to be extended eastward. West Hills contains the city's densest area, with its own retail cluster. The area is relatively nearby, making the retail surge in the Pearl the more remarkable. In fact, it's said the streetcar enables well-to-do West Hills residents to drop down to sample what the Pearl has to offer.

Streetcar financing came from a combination of sources. Parking revenue contributed $2 million and parking bonds another $28 million. Eight million came from the local improvement district, $7.5 million from tax increment financing, $1 million from the state highway department, and $500,000 from the federal Department of Housing and Urban Development. Another $5 million came from the transit agency, which used a like amount of federal funds elsewhere.

The cars themselves are built in the Czech Republic and are narrow, designed to run on streets with minimum traffic disruption. They are also short, sixty-six feet in length (while the MAX cars that run in tandem are ninety-two feet). The track bed is twelve inches wide versus the standard eighteen inches, and shallow. This latter factor meant that construction was shallow and did not require relocating many utilities.[19]

Service began in summer 2001, and ridership quickly surpassed expectations. By October of that year, the weekday ridership was 2,700 and on Saturdays hit 3,300. Projections had been not to reach 2,500 weekday riders until mid-2002.[20] The stations are now equipped with signs advising how long the wait is for the next car. On the edge of the Pearl Neighborhood, the streetcar enters the downtown fare-free zone.

The Demographics

The most accurate population data we could find is from a housing survey from October 20, 2002 by the Portland Business Alliance. It used a neighborhood definition of the Pearl District that extends to the riverfront, not including the Old Town neighborhood, with Broadway as the north-south boundary between the two. It found 1,600 units of housing with 1,959 people in our core area, with owners nearly double the number of renters. While small, the population represents a huge increase from the beginning days of the 1980s when the area was devoid of residents. In downtown overall, the area along both sides of the Willamette River between Interstate 405 on the west (the boundary of the River District) and Interstate 5 on the east, the survey counted 15,193 people, the majority in the traditional downtown.[21]

Using its larger area River District definition, which includes Old Town/Chinatown, the Portland Development Commission, employing census data, reported 4,302 persons in 2000, up 94 percent from 1990. The city as a whole grew by 21 percent.[22]

The census tract boundaries are not too helpful. Tract 51 goes from the river to 12th Street, splitting the Pearl District. Fully one-third of its population lives in group quarters, reflecting the Old Town area. The adjoining tract, 50, covers the rest of Pearl but spills over the Interstate 405 boundary. Its population of 690 in the year 2000 is interesting in that the median age was 31.7 years, with the 24-to-35 age group comprising 40 percent of the total. The area was nearly all white (96 percent) and nonfamily (84 percent), which is probably reflective of the part of the Pearl included.

The Pearl District feels larger than the numbers suggest. One newspaper account, in fact, put the population at 5,000, but unfortunately had no backup. The Pearl District Development Plan Steering Committee, headed by developer John Carroll and funded by PDC in 2001, stated that from a baseline of 1,300 residents and 9,000 jobs in the year 2000, it projected 12,500 residents and 21,000 jobs with full buildout. A comprehensive and well-done action plan document, it was approved by the city council in October 2001.[23]

With its success in stimulating housing, both in the Pearl neighborhood and in downtown, the Portland Business Alliance sees challenges ahead in making the city accessible to what it calls the workforce population.

Even in hard economic times, the Central City and close-in neighborhoods have become very desirable places to live and work for most income groups . . . Development policy discussions must include a greater range of income diversity, including unit goals for the downtown workforce and growing populations earning moderate and middle incomes (which have limited choices) . . . Achieving the City goal of having residential units in the Central City (Downtown, Old Town and Pearl District as extended) that reflect the income diversity of the City as a whole will involve bold new thinking on the use and effect of public investment in moderate/middle income housing in a development climate where competition for the best residential land will intensify, increasing pressure on costs, rents, and sales prices . . .

The two areas the business group were planning to study further were the lack of housing it sees available for the workforce population, and the critical 24-to-35 age group. This group, the Alliance notes, grew by 45,000 from 1990 to 2000. "Our ability to capture this population is key to sustained economic growth and livability."[24] A familiar business-driven refrain.

Subsidies for middle-income housing is obviously a touchy subject. In fact, a reaction was reported to be setting in for just this kind of support as it is reflected in the Pearl District. In Portland, you can earn up to $46,000 a year and buy a condominium for as much as $175,000 and receive a personal ten-year property tax waiver. A member of the city council in mid-2003 was beginning to raise questions about what had been assumed to be established public policy. Randy Leonard said he was surprised to learn that property tax breaks for developers were available where units rent for as much as $2,000 a month. While the Pearl seems established as of 2003, getting the south waterfront developed will probably need this kind of stimulus (as discussed later).[25]

Meanwhile, the business alliance sponsors a downtown open house tour of available properties. In 2002, hundreds of people went through nineteen properties, centered in the Pearl. Part of the motivation was to show people that the area was not just for singles and the wealthy. Interest was, shall we say, keen. At Streetcar Lofts on Northwest 12th Avenue, there were thirty people waiting in line to get a view of units ranging from $180,000 to $662,000, with a fifteen-minute wait. "It's been nuts since we opened," a worker on site was quoted.[26] The 2003 tour was held on June 1 and included thirty properties.

In Chinatown/Old Town, there is a heavier emphasis on rental units and more institutional developments, such as a Port of Portland headquarters. This is where the Single Room Occupancy (SRO) housing is concentrated. The feel here is markedly different from the Pearl—indeed this was the locale of Portland's Skid Row. There are a number of social service agencies such as the Salvation Army, whose clientele give the area a certain sketchiness, and a Chinatown that appears to have seen better days. Mixed in with the institutions and agencies is a cluster of nightclubs, attracting college students and other young people in an unusual juxtaposition of populations, from down-and-out to prosperous youth. The neighborhood houses the popular Portland Saturday Market. A new Classic Chinese Garden has been added.

OTHER NEIGHBORHOODS

We turn now to other instances of Intown Living in Portland. Coming on the market in 2003 in the downtown's West End was a forty-unit con-dominium, The Mosaic, one of whose outstanding characteristics is that it will have no parking for its residents; it does provide a bike parking area. It is on the streetcar line and near a host of attractions like the Portland Art Museum and a concert hall. "This is about urban living," the devel-oper was quoted. "These aren't family homes." In fact, the units range from 460 to 1,191 square feet and in price from $134,900 to $377,000. If it succeeds (twelve were sold before it was completed), it may portend a trend for the area.[27]

Still another downtown development was taking shape in 2003. Museum Place is a three-block mixed-use undertaking next to the Portland Art Museum. Museum Place South was under construction in January 2003, to house a Safeway store under a residential component with 128 market-rate apartments, 12 townhouses, and a courtyard, underneath which is parking for 225 spaces. About to be completed in early 2003 was The St. Francis, to replace an aging SRO facility. A third component, in the planning stage, was a 231-unit condominium with ground floor retail and parking. An updated YWCA center is also part of the development, with fifty units of transitional housing to have been completed in early 2003.[28]

One of our favorite mixed-use projects is RiverPlace, located on the edge of downtown and beside Tom McCall Waterfront Park, a seventy-three acre park that replaced Harbor Drive. PDC, the site owner, invested in sig-nificant public improvements before putting the area on the market. Included were a marina enclosed by twin breakwaters, a public walkway extension, shore stabilization, and roadways, all costing $6 million.

Cornerstone Columbia Development Company was chosen to build the project in the mid-1980s in a competition. Phase one was 150 condominiums, moderately priced, a boutique hotel with seventy-five rooms, and a promenade lined with shops sited between major restaurants at either end. There's underground parking (433 spaces), some office space, and recreation facilities, all done under the strict design controls of PDC. Public access was a mandate, with privacy maintained by having gated entrances to the housing, which was raised above the commercial area. Interior courtyards add to the sense of privacy. An office/residential building went up nearby also. A popular floating restaurant was added to the marina.

Phase two, immediately adjacent, was a 108-unit apartment complex with retail spaces along the riverfront. The two phases cost $44 million.[29]

Since RiverPlace went up in the 1980s, development has spread southward, including additional housing, eventually to fill in the space to Marquam Bridge in what was a former industrial no-man's-land. PDC reports that there is now a total of 500 residential units in what it calls the South Waterfront Park area.

In front of the newer housing is a beautifully landscaped public park. Unlike the McCall Waterfront Park, which is the site of major public gatherings, the park here is intended primarily for neighborhood use. Included are a formal garden space with terraces and tree groves, ponds, and a knoll that serves as a screen from the nearby bridge. An esplanade runs the length of the park, linking to the rest of the riverfront. The park cost $4.2 million, PDC reports, and was completed in 1999. This area also includes office and commercial space.

Moving forward in 2003 were plans to build out the remaining space between the park and the bridge. Scheduled for development is a mixed-use project consisting of two buildings containing 170 condominiums, one eleven stories, the other eight, to be built over parking. A four-story, one-hundred-room hotel is to be completed in 2005. This project, by Riverplace Partners, sets the stage for a major new project that in spring 2003 was moving from the concept stage to a major development south of Marquam Bridge. Riverplace Partners is headed by Homer Williams, the person who initially led Hoyt Street Properties in the River District.

South Waterfront

We turn now to the inauspiciously named North Macadam project area south of Marquam Bridge. The entire site, about eighty acres, is largely filled land with some remaining marine industry, such as a barge-building operation. The city's plan calls for a total remake, with just a few buildings to remain, into a new and very urban section in the central city's last major undeveloped area.

The ambition, shared by the private sector, is to make North Macadam a key component of a projected bioscience research center. This is to link the existing Oregon Health and Science University, 12,000 persons, located on a hill overlooking Macadam, plus nearby Portland State University. An effort to involve Oregon State University is also being made. The city-developed framework plan looks to locate 10,000 jobs on the site and 3,000 homes, to be developed over the next twenty years. Envisioned are as many as fifty new buildings.

Key parcels in the center are in the hands of Homer Williams, a developer with a long track record in Portland. With approvals, he plans to begin work as early as 2004 on the streets and the first towers, which would rise variously 14, 18, and 19 stories, set back 325 feet from the river. There is to be a two-hundred-foot grid like in downtown, and housing is to range from affordable units to top end, with some units planned to market for $140,000. The deep setback is to accommodate a planned 250-foot-wide greenway along the river. Earlier plans were for only a fifty-foot setback and height limits of ninety-five feet. Obviously the private sector was persuasive in arguing that greater heights in exchange for wider riverfront open space would be beneficial.[30]

Two key transportation links are planned to what is now an isolated area, ringed by roads and crossed by bridges but unconnected to either. The most ambitious is an aerial tram to run from Oregon Health and Science University to the center of the site, near Ross Island Bridge where the first development is foreseen. It's said to be only the second such installation in the U.S. (the first is at Roosevelt Island in New York City), budgeted at $15 million. Nearby residents are opposed. A design competition by Portland Aerial Transportation in 2003 was won by Angelil/Graham/Pfenning/Scholl Architecture of Los Angeles and Zurich. The proposed lower station on the river would be covered in grass in the winning design concept.[31]

The second link is to extend the streetcar past Portland State University where it has a turn-around now into the Macadam site, running through the RiverPlace project. Planning for the extension was under way in 2003, and funds were being pursued.

The agreement being hammered out with two private development firms and the city calls for public investment totalling $274 million and the private share to total $1.6 billion. The agreement is similar to the one put in place for the River District. The final document was to go before the Portland Development Commission in July 2003, and if approved, to the city council.[32] An advisory committee meeting in June voted narrowly, five-to-four, to approve the first segment of the plan, with opposition coming from affordable housing advocates who felt not enough was provided, and from nearby neighbors fearful of traffic impacts.[33]

Eastside Developments

We want to elaborate a bit about the eastside Lloyd District across the river from downtown that was mentioned in one of our interviews as having great potential. At present it is an area with jobs but few amenities to support residential development. Office buildings dot the area.

Nonetheless, new residential is beginning to happen. The first part of a full block project, the Cascadian, was completed in 2003. It is a nine-story building with fifty-nine condominiums and includes ground floor retail and parking. The more ambitious phase two was in the planning stage as of early 2003. It would be a $44 million tower containing 260 market-rate units.

The Cornerstone Apartments, 116 units, were built in 1998. This is a four-story development with rents running from $700 to $1,000 per month as of early 2003. And the Irvington Place Condominiums, also completed in 1998, added fifty units plus seven row houses to the equation. Retail is a component here also. A new Safeway grocery went into the area in 1999, with a 35,000-square-foot store replacing a store about two-thirds its size.[34]

Trammel Crow Residential, one of the largest developers nationally, was projecting a 184-unit apartment on a full city block in the area. It aims to attract renters who have been drawn to the Pearl. As of early 2003 it was in the "on the drawing board" category after having initially been announced to begin in fall 2002.[35]

GROWTH BOUNDARY

The final part of the Portland Intown Living story is the role its Urban Growth Boundary plays in intensifying residential development in the city and in outlying communities targeted for expanded housing. Several people whom we interviewed, including an official with the Metro regional agency that administers the boundary, see that it is now beginning to have an impact, some twenty-five years after being put in place. A first impact was to arrest a decline in density that the area had been experiencing. In 1994 the Portland area built new housing at a rate of five units per acre, and four years later that was increased to eight dwellings an acre. The average lot was also much smaller, 6,200 square feet, down from an average of 12,800 square feet in 1978 before the boundary.[36]

Before tackling a thumbnail sketch of how a growth boundary came into being, restricting as it does private development opportunities, let's describe what it is. The first thing to say about the Portland Urban Growth Boundary is that it is huge: The area is 364 square miles in size and includes 24 independent cities plus urban portions of three counties—a

Dallas-sized dimension. Further, it may be expanded, and in fact there have been two additions since 1979, plus a large increase was voted in June 2003, making room for as many as 38,000 new homes outside the old boundary.[37] The boundary was deliberately made large initially, one person we interviewed said, so as not to appear too restrictive.

How did this come into being? The surprising answer is that the impetus came in the 1970s from the agricultural community. They saw their farms and their way of life threatened by urban expansion. They had to look no farther than California for a foretaste of what awaited them. Oregon was and still is a growth state, and its cities were spreading rapidly onto valuable farmland.

Governor Tom McCall by all accounts was the one who put together a winning coalition of agriculture, environmentalists (the 1970s saw the realization of the environmental movement), and urban interests to hammer out a plan acceptable to the development industry. McCall personalized the movement to make land-use planning a priority, captured in a 1972 speech that everyone considers a landmark (so to speak) moment. He decried "unfettered despoiling of the land," said the state's quality of life was at stake, denounced "coastal condomania, and the ravenous rampage of suburbia in the Willamette Valley," and said the state had to be protected from "grasping wastrels of the land."[38] After a rousing speech, McCall campaigned around the state on behalf of a land-use planning law that the state legislature adopted that year, the nation's first.

What the state law did was require every city and county to develop a long-range plan that met state requirements, which were to include establishing urban growth boundaries, addressing how urban land was to be wisely used, and protecting natural resources. The state can require local entities to make changes to conform to its policies—that is, the program has some teeth. The agency selected by Portland area voters in 1978 to develop the boundary is the Metropolitan Service District, shortened to Metro, which combined a sanitary district entity and a voluntary council of governments. Metro is unique in that its office holders are elected by the 1.3 million people inside the boundary it established.

In 1992, voters approved a home-rule charter for Metro that made growth management its top priority and required the adoption of a framework plan. That led to an intensive analysis, involving thousands of people and many meetings, to hammer out how the growth boundary was to work. This resulted in a report, *Region 2040: Decision for Tomorrow, Concepts for Growth*. Included were the results of a questionnaire returned by 17,000 people. What the report, issued in June 1994, did was to force a decision by the Metro Council on how to accommodate the area's projected growth, giving it three options: Growing out by expanding the boundary, growing up by adding to density, or putting growth into neighboring cities. The prospect is that a half million new jobs and residents will appear by 2017. The council in 1995 adopted its own version, drawing on the three proposals, the 2040 Growth Concept. It allows some expansion of the boundary (14,500 more acres over fifty years) but puts its emphasis on more efficient land use in cities, with business centers on main streets and at transit centers. Other facets cover transportation, natural area protection, neighborhood stabilization, and affordable housing. More multi-family housing would be built as one consequence. The plan calls for sharply increasing densities in central Portland, which as we have seen, is what PDC is pushing in the River District in its agreement with Hoyt Street Properties.[39]

Another consequence of the boundary is to cause buyers to look anew at areas they might have bypassed in the past, as in the Lloyd District discussed previously. Another indication that the boundary is beginning to have impact: Gresham, a town at the eastern end of the MAX service, has shot up from 4,000 people to 90,000 over forty years, and it has rebuilt a traditional downtown after losing it to suburban malls.

Conservatives are attacking the growth boundary (and smart growth initiatives elsewhere) as causing inflated real estate prices by restricting land for development. Portland's reality is that its land price increases in the 1990s were in line with cities of comparable size that were not thinking about boundaries, such as Charlotte, North Carolina.[40]

Portland's combination of natural setting (a huge forest exists within Portland, and hiking trails abound in the area), progressive policies that support compact, walkable urban neighborhoods, a strong public school system (up until 2003, at least), an educated, fairly sophisticated and informed populace, as well as its hipness, add up to a place the Creative Class has discovered. "After losing its young people in the long recession of the 1980s, Portland in the last decade of the century became a hot town for people aged 18 to 35." Recruiting talent from top law firms, for instance, had become easy, author Carl Abbott declared.[41]

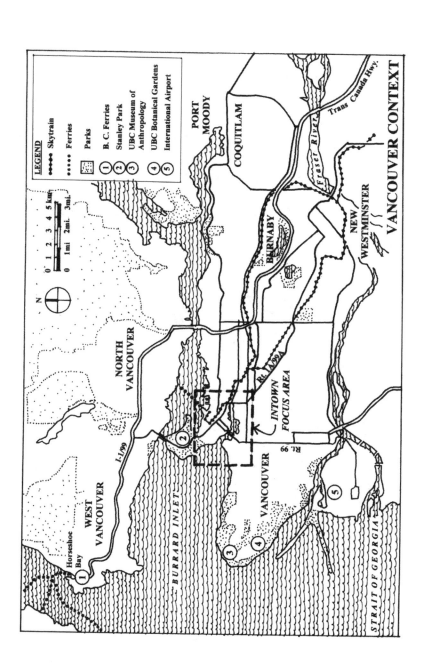

VANCOUVER CONTEXT

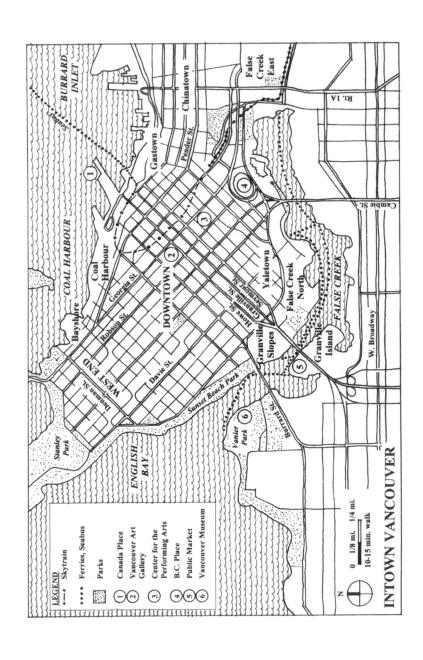

INTOWN VANCOUVER

N

0   1/8 mi.   1/4 mi.
10-15 min. walk

LEGEND

- ·—·— Skytrain
- ·•·• Ferries, Seabus
- (shaded) Parks

- ① Canada Place
- ② Vancouver Art Gallery
- ③ Center for the Performing Arts
- ④ B.C. Place
- ⑤ Public Market
- ⑥ Vancouver Museum

10

Vancouver

> For five millennia our human settlements were built to human scale, to
> the five or ten minute walk, which defined neighborhoods, within
> which all of life's necessities and many of its frivolities could be found.
> —*Robert Davis,* Preservation in Print

If you have not been to Vancouver, British Columbia, for a decade or
more, you are in for a jolt as you approach Burrard Bridge to enter downtown. Where once there was a relatively low-profile city there is now a
dramatic skyline with scores of high-rise towers that tell you downtown
Vancouver is growing rapidly, and upward. You are sure to ask, "Will
I like this change?" We think that if you love cities, most definitely, yes.

Several factors lie behind an incredible expansion of downtown residential development that is occurring in Vancouver. First is the extraordinary
natural beauty of the place, to which has been added strong civic leadership supporting additional housing, including a commitment to quality
urban design and backed by an informed citizenry.

SPLENDID SETTING

The natural setting here is in league with the most stunning urban
waterfronts in the world—Cape Town, South Africa; Hong Kong, China;
Rio de Janeiro, Brazil; San Francisco, California; and Sydney, Australia
come to mind. Plus, Vancouver enjoys a benign climate, albeit a little

wet. While Toronto has a 24 degree Fahrenheit average temperature in January, Vancouver is 35; in July Toronto is 72 degrees Fahrenheit, Vancouver 62.

It is no wonder that Vancouverites identified "access to and enjoyment of the natural setting" as their number one goal in a survey in 1980 of 5,000 residents. Maintaining views of the mountains and water was mentioned next. The importance of natural greenery and landscaping plus parks and waterfront access were also cited. The broad number two goal was "growth management," which is an indication of the sophisticated and progressive nature of the population.[1]

Other reasons can be cited as to why Vancouver ranks high on a number of the livability indexes of the world's cities, making it a magnet for immigrants and young professionals alike. The Swiss Corporate Resources Group surveyed firms that send executives overseas on assignments and asked them to rate the quality of life of 192 cities. Vancouver was number one.[2] Likewise, an Internet posting by Mercer Human Resources Consulting rated fifty cities for best quality of life. Here Vancouver was second to Zurich.

It's a Vancouver conceit that it is the un-Toronto of Canada. "Toronto is establishment. Vancouver is hipper, looser, livelier and more relaxed," is how one comparison put it. Said one who left Toronto: "Out here being a workaholic is not cool. Like Seattle, we have a real appreciation of underground amusements and we like little art galleries and speakeasies. Big things tend to fail more."[3]

Another noteworthy factor that plays a major role in Vancouver's high livability score: There is no expressway anywhere in downtown. A large roadway such as Pacific Boulevard runs through Concord Pacific Place, but no overhead or multilane freeway exists on the peninsula. One was of course proposed, as everywhere else, but the residents of historic Chinatown, who would have borne the brunt of the proposal, fought it successfully. Chinatown is located on the eastern edge of downtown, straddling the Main Street boundary that demarks the central area. Meanwhile, coming into being in the 1980s was the Skytrain rail line from the downtown Waterfront Station, extending about eighteen miles to the burgeoning eastern suburbs.

Downtown is small and compact, just three miles from end to end (only 5.1 percent of the city's total land area), and includes Stanley Park's green space, 6.44 acres, at the tip.[4] Downtown Vancouver is surrounded almost completely by water (a land bridge leads to the east). English Bay is on the west, with mountains in the distance. Coal Harbour and Burrard Inlet are on the north, with a close-in mountain range, often snow-capped, overlooking them. False Creek lies along the southern edge. Given this self-contained geography and a demand for Intown Living, the solution is in density and height.

RAPID GROWTH

Make no mistake, while the increase in the downtown population is dramatic, as we are about to discuss, the sprawl that is everywhere in North America is here as well. Whereas Vancouver was a sleepy city of 29,000 at the turn of the twentieth century, there are now nearly two million people in the greater Vancouver region (2001 census), 545,671 of whom live in the city (27 percent). And of the city population, the downtown peninsula now is home to 70,091 people, up 22,803 (48 percent) in the decade 1991 to 2001. The city notes with some pride that its downtown growth outpaced New York and Chicago in numbers and percentage, with only Seattle among major cities having a higher percent increase.[5]

A further indication of the ethos in Vancouver is the use of the word "urban" frequently; it is seen as positive value. Thus we have "Daycare for Urban Dogs," the "urban beach" and materials for the "urban gardener."

Although hard to quantify, it's clear that there is a large gay population and a tolerance for same. Vancouver is the first city where we've seen gay pride banners along with a neighborhood flag on the light poles (along Davie Street in the West End, center of the gay culture). This area also features open pot-smoking and considerable hanging out, and not a little panhandling. There's also a sizable homeless contingent, given the city's easygoing ways. Here is an insight into just how easygoing Vancouver is: If you're receiving public assistance and have a dog, that's $50 more a month allowance! Many street people have dogs, unsurprisingly.

We turn now to a positive and impressive aspect of downtown Vancouver, and next to its largest evident negative.

ARTS BIG

There is a strong presence of the arts in general, and a significant public art program in particular. Developers contribute 1 percent per leasable foot. This has resulted in, among other things, an array of fifty-seven works around the perimeter of downtown Vancouver, about eight miles in length all told. The attention paid the arts in Vancouver is a sign of its attention to design and reflects the sophistication of the city.

It starts with the dramatic "sails" of the Canada Place pavilion, built for Expo '86 and now the convention center/hotel and world trade office complex. Its perimeter walkway is completely public and is distinguished by well-done interpretive plaques. It is a redevelopment of an old pier.

Here is a sampling of the highlights among other works large and small:

- "Make West, 1997" by Bill Pechet along Coal Harbour Quay is bronze fragments in the paving stones quoting local and regional histories. They are located near the base of two residential towers. The fragments can become a game, one leading to another.

- "Weave, 2002" by Douglas Senft is on the water side of a residential tower, telling Coal Harbour's history. A collection of bronze rings tells about old growth trees; steel benches carry First Nation, Spanish, and English words, and there are aluminum tree grates making reference to aviation history.
- There's a rotating sculpture exhibit in the park on English Bay, the Vancouver International Sculpture Project by the Buschlen Mowatt Gallery with the Vancouver Park Board.
- "George Cunningham Memorial Sundial, 1967" by Gehard Class commemorates three men with the first land claims by nonnatives in what is now the West End. They were labeled "greenhorns" because the land was so far from the city center. It's on Denman Street, the commercial heart of this popular neighborhood.
- "The Swimmer, 1997" by George Norris is an abstract steel sculpture near the aquatic center that suggests the swimming motion.
- "GRANtable, 1998" by Bill Pechet and Stephanie Robb is a large concrete table and chairs (with peep holes) in a small park that can work as a picnic table or chess set.
- A favorite of ours, "Making High Tide and Waiting for Low Tide, 1996" by Don Vaughan, landscape architect, is at the water's edge in Lam Park with an open, inscribed ring construction on columns, into which the tide moves in and out, the other portion being granite boulders.
- "Collection, 1994" by Mark Lewis consists of six bright wedges on pedestals, three of which are time capsules with found objects listed, and the other three trash containers.
- "Brush with Illumination, 1998" by Buster Simpson is a steel shaft in False Creek that moves as its large steel buoys respond to the current and tide, whose movements are transmitted to a Web site: www.brushdelux.com.[6]

Vancouver was named the big-city cultural capital of Canada for 2003, giving the city $500,000 (Cdn.) in federal matching dollars. The money was to have sponsored a gala for aboriginal artists in the fall of 2003 and a multiday festival on False Creek in 2004, and is to create new artists' studios, among other things. The False Creek event was to have decorated boats, illuminated sculptures, fountains, and kinetic floats, plus food and performances. The city also hopes to sponsor more public art pieces. The program is modeled on one in place in Europe since 1989, where cities compete each year to be named the "cultural capital." Vancouver's application bested Ottawa and Trois-Rivieres, Quebec.[7] The city itself allots $7 million for its cultural budget.

DRUG TRADE

As in any city, even in one with so much going for it, a dark side looms. Vancouver is a major center of North American drug trafficking. Its large port, relatively open border with the United States, proximity to Asia, and the presence of assorted criminal gangs on the city's Eastside has spelled trouble. Heroin is the import of choice. Also thought to be a factor: the lack of mandatory jail terms for drug trading that the U.S. has, attracting American dealers here.

One result is a network of pawnshops and all-night stores on the Eastside and soaring crime rates. Between 1990 and 1996, thefts from cars went from 20,000 to 38,000. Overdose deaths are thought to be the highest in North America.[8] Vancouver has the developed world's highest incidence of people infected with HIV. This came about, police say, when people started sharing needles and shot up as many as twenty times a day instead of three. As many as 10,000 addicts are thought to be infected.[9]

Vancouver magazine conducted market research on which things would make readers happiest. The choices included improving traffic, cutting down panhandling, landing the winter Olympics, and curbing the Eastside drug problem. Curbing drug use received over half the responses; dealing with panhandling was next with just a 5 percent vote.[10]

In 1997, then–Mayor Philip Owen formed Vancouver's Coalition for Crime Prevention and Drug Treatment. Over the years the city has been host to a series of conferences on the drug issue as it wrestled with what course to take. In 2003, forty police were assigned to Eastside. In addition to this police crackdown, there was also afoot an initiative where clean needles were to be made publicly available, a controversial initiative, an interviewee told us, that was based on experience in Germany.[11] In fact, a safe-injection site was opened on September 15, 2003, in the Eastside, North America's first.[12]

The crackdown was said to be working better than expected in early 2003. "The numbers (of dealers) are a lot smaller," Inspector Doug LePard, the police officer overseeing the Eastside effort, was quoted. "This has happened a lot quicker than we thought it would," he added. One concern was that drug activity has simply moved westward. A resident living in the West End reflected in an interview that her neighborhood had an active drug scene. But, in Eastside, the police reported favorable responses. Wrote one resident of the area: "I'm an artist in Gastown and since I moved here in 1984, I've been mugged, beaten up, threatened and constantly harassed by dealers. Now I don't have that fear." The police operation began on April 7, 2003, and is said to target dealers rather than users.[13]

The police effort, a three-month trial, is part of a four-pronged approach that Vancouver has settled on, one that includes treatment, prevention, and harm reduction as well as the enforcement push. A doctor at St. Paul's Hospital reported that some addicts are reducing their use and are seeking methadone treatment at the hospital's addiction center as a result of the police work. Others are critical of the police, saying dealers are going underground and violence is increasing.

At least one merchant was pleased with the police presence. Rory Nymark, who manages a Save-on-Meat shop on West Hastings near Main, one of the few businesses along a drug strip, reported he sometimes had to call 911 eight to ten times a day because of cocaine dealing outside his shop. Now, in early May 2003, after one month of stepped-up police, he's spending less time on the phone and more with customers. "We don't usually get the Yaletown crowd coming in, but we're seeing that, too," Nymark said. A legal organization, Picot, was critical of the police, accusing them of illegal searches and brutality. The Human Rights Watch of New York was expected to criticize the police also.[14]

Meanwhile, on another front, the head of the city's tenant assistance program reported that the number of people sleeping on city streets doubled from 2001 to 2003. Judy Graves said the March count in Eastside turned up twice the number of people on the streets as a count the previous year. She also reported an increase of people on the streets of the West End. The number of homeless is somewhere between 600 and 1,200. The increase is attributed to cuts in the country's welfare system.[15]

These negatives are far enough away from the developing residential neighborhoods that they are not deterring the surge of new residents flocking to the towers, townhomes, and conversions that are becoming available on the downtown Vancouver peninsula as of spring 2003. This brings us to the heart of our Intown Living story here.

GOVERNMENT'S ROLE

An important aspect of the Vancouver housing story not readily apparent is the large role played by the city government in general and by its professional staff in particular. This is a place where the city in the mid-1950s decided that it wanted to attract more people to the downtown shopping and commercial district. So it changed zoning to permit high-rise apartment buildings in the West End. As a result, in thirteen years 220 apartments were built.[16]

This set a precedent not only for a major residential population in downtown Vancouver but also for decisive, activist government working with the private sector. A transplant from Austin, Texas, related that the extent to which local government intervenes in the development process would be labeled communism in Texas! For instance, in one of the major new residential areas under construction in 2003, False Creek North, 91 of the site's 204 acres (which includes water areas) are required to be turned over from the developer here for public realm purposes—that's 45 percent. The extraction from the developer does not stop there, but extends to having the firm build roads, a multipurpose community center, parks, day care facilities, and walkways. Both the city and the developer acknowledge that the original purchase price for the land, sold by the province when it was strapped, was relatively low, making these extractions work financially.

There is no such thing as "zoning by right." All projects must seek a permit. The amount of discretion left to planning staff in the project review is without precedent in the U.S. Incentives and guidelines are the approach, and there's a give-and-take across the table between the city and the private interests, under the broad policy standards established by the elected political leadership. The leadership respects its professional staff and accepts that political interventions should be limited.

The amazing thing is that the private side of this equation respects the process. One private developer told us: "The city forces developers to make the right moves." Appeals to court so common in the U.S. are rare, and nearly all city rulings (there's a three-person review committee representing the planning, engineering, and city manager's offices) are final. An issue that can't be resolved by this committee and the private side is taken to the city council for a decision.

Writes Planning Co-Director Larry Beasley:

The result is that, even with the grandest urban development gestures, the rezoning process seldom fails, public hearings are relatively calm, and most citizens seem satisfied with the results. Without the strong political commitment and wide public buy-in of its comprehensive "living first" strategy, Vancouver would be light-years behind where it needs to be to position itself for the future.[17]

It was not always thus. Both a development firm representative and a city official whom we interviewed separately said that the first five years of the relationship between the city and the Concord Pacific Place development firm was rocky, the traditional antagonistic city-developer standoff. New leadership at the firm made a commitment to improving the dialogue, and simultaneously the city recognized it was coming on too aggressively and needed to speak with a single voice. Since these early days in the late 1980s, the relationship has been smoother, to the extent that the developer shares with the city its pro forma documents on projects when seeking approvals. When the market turns down, this helps reinforce the developer's request for less-stringent standards in building materials, for example. And the city for its part has learned development economics, helped by its real estate arm.

In addition to the city review committee there is a public advisory group and a design review panel. The private development side is not getting all it wants. There's a growing clamor to allow greater heights, for instance, piercing the 500-foot ceiling now in place. A tower of 600 feet was to enter the permitting process in 2003. City planning recommended adding four architects with high-rise experience to the design review panel for this and another tower proposal coming up.[18] Service on this peer review panel is voluntary.

Here is an indication of the regard given the city's professional planning staff. In booklets or fact sheets, the staff person assigned to a particular project is listed along with the developer, architect, and so forth. Contrast this with the anonymity under which most planners in the U.S. toil.

WEST END

West End has been a flourishing residential area for a century and sets the precedent for Intown Living in Vancouver. The middle class never really completely left here. It is an important part of the background to the downtown residential story now unfolding. It has been a residential neighborhood since the turn of the twentieth century, when it was the city's upper-income area. Around 1910 a new posh neighborhood, Shaughnessy Heights, came into being that drew people away from the West End. Gradually the mansions in the area were replaced with low-rise boardinghouses, although several remain. So the idea of stimulating more residential development, and at higher density and greater heights, came as less of a bolt from the blue than it might elsewhere.

Today, according to a neighborhood activist we interviewed, it is a first stop for immigrants flocking to Vancouver, largely from Asia and Eastern Europe. Its population remains fairly steady despite the turnover: It contained 37,050 people in 1986, according to the census (done every five years in Canada), and 37,190 in 1991. By 2001 the West End was up to 42,154 people. Our interviewee said there are relatively few single-family residences; they are estimated to number only 183, in fact.

One of the lessons from the West End, a former city councilor told us, was that the public had a negative reaction to the boxy modern apartment architecture of the 1960s there. So when the city undertook its next big housing redevelopment initiative, south of False Creek in the 1970s, the approach was for low-rise, garden apartments, human-scaled and with lots of green. The mistake made here, the city later realized, was that roads were allowed to separate the housing from the waterfront. That becomes very important when we move the story forward to the late 1980s.

It was then that large waterfront parcels became available that are the focus now of the explosive growth in residences. Concord Pacific Place bought one site, former railyards and a manufacturing site that had been cleared for Expo '86 here. Marathon Developments was the real estate arm of Canadian Pacific Ltd., the successor company to the Canadian Pacific Railway, and it fell heir to onetime railyards at Coal Harbour. A third major site, Bayshore, is being developed by Tokyo-based Aoki Company. And still another project, Citygate on the eastern end of False Creek, has been significantly built. All feature generous waterfront accessibility; the first three mentioned are directly on their water bodies, while Citygate is set back and has a light rail track in front if it, but it still has fine water views.

Behind these major single-owner developments was an extraordinary action by the city. With the market for office space soft in the 1980s, the city decided to rezone eight million square feet of commercial space in favor of residential. This came after the city's self-image had received a major uplift from the success of Expo '86. Many we interviewed said Expo was a watershed event for Vancouver, putting it on the international stage and proving to itself its ability to accomplish. The fair drew 21 million people.

CENTRAL PLAN

The basic document that the city works from is the *Central Area Plan,* adopted by the city council on December 3, 1991. It is a model of municipal enlightenment. It is also written in clear English.

Among the broad goals established are creating "an alive downtown" where "public streets are the primary scene of public life," ensuring that the central area is "a place to live and visit for all people," that natural values be reflected, where walking, supplemented by public transit and bicycles, is "the primary means of moving around." The document declares that housing is of "major importance in achieving central area goals. More housing brings vitality and life to downtown and provides customers for shops and services. In particular, housing for a variety of household types brings a diversity of human activity to the downtown."[19] The plan notes that regional policies of the 1980s called for more housing in Vancouver and the city took steps to move in that direction, so that by 1991 housing was called for in North False Creek, Granville Slopes, Coal Harbour (Marathon Development plus Bayshore mentioned previously), East False Creek, and Downtown South.

After dealing with policies for office and housing developments, the plan document then tackles a "Livability Policy" with the goal of affirming the "spirit of place." After noting Vancouver's reputation as a comfortable place to live, with its parks and open space, low volume of traffic, and relative safety, it deals with issues stemming from the plan's higher density allowance, such as privacy, noise, odors, shadowing, and views. Here good design becomes important, but the document says fixed standards are not what is called for but rather qualitative aspects such as tower placement and spacing. These are to be individual decisions specific to sites within broad zoning categories.

Preceding the adoption of the overall *Central Area Plan* were approvals of specific development plans for False Creek North and Coal Harbour, both from 1990. Downtown South Guidelines were approved on July 30, 1991.

The policies needed to be put in place because of the coming together of several powerful factors. Immigration, particularly from Hong Kong in the 1990s when people left in anticipation of the Communist government takeover in 1997, meant that there was money to be invested and a demand for downtown housing.

HUGE PROJECT

This leads us to a discussion of the largest single project, Concord Pacific Place (officially Concord Place Developments Corporation) on False Creek North. Its first building went up in 1993, and now it has thirty-seven residential towers in place, all sold/leased, with others under construction and still others being marketed. When complete there will be a total of sixty-one towers containing 9,100 units of housing. At the planning department figure of 1.5 persons per unit, that's 13,650 people (the company's projection is for a population of 15,000).

A sizable concentration of residential towers may not sound appealing, but what's being built here is. Predominately white with green-tinted windows and matching trim, no more than thirty stories high and with a minimum of eighty feet between buildings, the overall impact is visually pleasing, somewhat airy in feel. Helping this sense are several design factors. One, a number of smaller, sometimes brick townhouses, are interspersed. There is major park space, and a heavily used three-tier walkway system runs along the waterfront. The principal path is a generous thirty-five feet. The traffic was put at 1,500 persons per hour by a resident. He also related that the planners misjudged the ratio of foot traffic to wheels, building a two-thirds/one-third ratio. Newer sections are 50-50 because rollerblading is a huge sport. A greenway system has been in the works since 1992 when the city council adopted the idea in principle and directed a staff study, which led to the council's adopting the *Vancouver Greenways Plan* on July 18, 1995.

HIGH-RISES

There is a public acceptance of high-rises in Vancouver, an architect told us. It's because there is a realization that relatively slender towers means there's light and air between them. The urban design solution to the problem of towers overwhelming a pedestrian is to put low-rise townhomes along the sidewalks. The towers are then set into the interior of the block, a precedent established in one of the first of the new projects, Granville Slope, to be described later. Another major design decision: All parking is underground, which is more costly but means there are no yawning garage facades facing the sidewalk. Even the garage entrances are carefully placed to minimize the intrusion.

Standing at the foot of Davie Street, one of the main arteries leading from the site to the West End, on a traffic circle with major art pieces, you take in the following: with False Creek behind you, to your left are four- and six-story townhomes fronting the generous brick walkway. Behind is a twenty-two-story tower and on the corner, a thirty-story building. To the right is a row of retail with housing on the two levels above, behind which are additional thirty-story towers well spaced apart, with several twelve-story buildings farther to the right.

The art pieces inform you that on this site there were sawmills until 1960, and that barrels were manufactured here as late as 1980.

Just up Davie Street is, by several residents' accounts and affirmed by city officials, the cornerstone of this neighborhood, namely the 26,000-square-foot Urban Fare grocery/deli/coffee bar. It is like a Whole Foods market in the U.S. Opening only after 2,500 residents were present, the number that Concord Pacific Place believes is needed to make retail successful, the market instantly became the neighborhood social center. A city planner recalled being in the neighborhood at an early stage of the development and seeing no people on the street and thinking to himself the city had made a terrible mistake. When Urban Fare opened, all doubts vanished as the streets here came alive.

The area is really three neighborhoods: Yaletown Edge completed in 2001, Marinaside done in 2002, and Roundhouse, also finished in 2002. Together they contain almost three thousand units.[20] We visited a resident of the first building on Davie. His take on the profile in the neighborhood is that it is occupied primarily by 20-to-30-year-olds, and that a fair number of couples with children are staying. A new school nearby was under construction in May 2003. The nearby developer-supplied day care center has a waiting list. Backing this up is a census finding that there were 835 more children under 15 in downtown in 2001 than in 1996, the largest increase occurring in the census tract that encompasses our interviewee's area (up 580).

In full buildout, Concord Pacific is to contain about 1.9 million square feet of office space, more than half a million square feet of retail, two elementary schools, eight day care centers, two community centers, three marinas, and an $8 million (Cdn.) public art program. While predominately market rate, the project does contain below-market housing; as of December 2002, there were 326 of these units. Their design is such that when asked to pick out a building that contained subsidized units, we were unable to do so.

The retail scene will obviously grow. As of October 2001, there were twenty establishments of various kinds (shops to services), with a Costco suburban-type store slated to be built nearby next to GM Place in 2004. It will contain 147,000 square feet and will have four levels of parking, but it will be within walking distance for False Creek North residents. Restaurants are springing up, joining the older establishments nearby in Yaletown (see later discussion).

What's astonishing is that condominium towers are completely sold before they are built. This is true in nearby neighborhoods as well, such as Yaletown and Downtown South. Here the new towers are lower, and pricing may be less than the waterfront projects. But the signs still say "96 percent sold" while workers scramble over the facade-less superstructure. In other cities this might be wishful thinking or developer hyperbole, but in today's Vancouver it's reality.

Concord Pacific Place skillfully uses its marketing center to, as one spokesperson put it, "sell the dream" or "offer a lifestyle." When we visited in spring 2003, it was selling "The Max," two towers not to be completed until June 2005. Over two years out, six of the ten basic unit types were sold out. This particular project is clearly aimed at the youth market: The models in the slick video appeared to be 20-somethings. The sizes of the units are totally appropriate for this market. Studios are as small as 446 square feet, while the largest unit of two bedrooms with den is only 878 square feet. One-bedroom lofts are also offered. Prices ranged from $168,400 to the $260,000s (Cdn.).

"Club Maxim" will have a pool, concierge, exercise, and yoga rooms, social room with kitchen, meeting room, worship space, and courtyard.

The age profile for downtown as a whole (including the West End) shows the 25-to-29 and 30-to-34 groups the two largest, and along with the 35-to-39 bracket, enjoying the largest increases from 1996 to 2001.[21]

We interviewed another component of the Intown Living phenomenon of downtown Vancouver, the empty-nester moving in from the suburbs after the children have left. Our interviewee had a classic profile: A large house with three empty bedrooms and about five thousand square feet was traded for a 2,300-square-foot, two-level townhome overlooking False Creek. Taxes are lower. The commute and sitting in traffic at a tunnel are gone, the man's wife can travel to work by one of the small ferries on False Creek, they see more of their neighbors by virtue of spending less time in a car, they feel like they are in a village with dog-walkers, nearby shops, and doctors' offices and the like, and the best thing is the people who stream by their window/porch on the walkway. Other than a few "crazies" after a hockey game, the experience of living beside a public walkway is altogether positive, our resident reported.

The design here puts green space and a small level change between their home and the walkway, and shrubs surround the patio, providing a feeling of separation. But neighbors can be called to as they bike, run, or rollerblade by. And a kayak can be taken to a nearby ramp. Biggest complaint: Not enough space in the garage for a proper handyman's shop.

A representative of Concord Pacific Place gave this breakdown of what they were building: About 20 percent is high-end, aimed at people in their fifties and sixties and offering units with three bedrooms and 2,000 to 2,800 square feet. In the middle market is 35 to 40 percent of their condominiums, built for young professionals and couples, including some with children. The units range from 1,500 to 2,000 square feet. The smaller units, another 35 to 40 percent of the total, are 600 to 1,000 square feet and are attractive to investors for rental purposes or to people who might buy something for one of their children. The gay population is large in all the neighborhoods. Always the company will try to have available units in the 1,100-to-1,200-square-foot range.

One interesting sidelight of how a project such as Concord Place evolves came from another interviewee. In the first buildings, the standard was two parking spaces per unit. That is down to one now as the developer saw that people were dropping one car if they had two, or getting by with none and using the garage for storage.

Here is perhaps the most striking figure about the resurgence of a downtown residential population in Vancouver: More people walk to work than drive. The 1996 census found that 39 percent of the downtown workforce walked, 38 percent drove, and 18 percent used transit.

At the symbolic and physical heart of the Concord Place project is a wonderful multipurpose community complex, namely the Roundhouse. It was built by the developer for the Vancouver Parks Board and is at once both a symbolic link to the industrial past of the area and a community arts and recreation center with an amazing array of programs.

The historic buildings are from the Canadian Pacific Railway's maintenance complex and engine turntable, dating to 1889. It was restored for Expo but now has a major new addition and a glassed pavilion where a locomotive is displayed. Bordered by three streets at the very center of this developing neighborhood (it's near the Urban Fare market), it has different components: there's the "neighborhood yard," a "heritage yard" inside the old turntable with its curved facade intact, and then a "street yard" which features old gantry cranes.

There is nearly 50,000 square feet of space available for the multitude of programs here. The mission of the facility was carved out during a retreat in 1996 with an advisory committee, neighborhood representatives, the park board staff, artists, and heritage supporters. The overall mission, the group determined, is to "celebrate diversity . . . of people, values, ideas and activities." The Roundhouse is seen at once as a project, an oasis, and a connection. It calls itself a community center for the people of the area and also a center providing community arts opportunities citywide. The spring-summer 2003 catalogue of programs runs sixty-four pages.

The programs range from arts and crafts to woodworking and include programs for seniors ("Crop 'Til You Drop—Scrapbook Workshop") as well as youth (fitness and martial arts, for instance). There's a University of British Columbia Multimedia Lab here as well. That the Roundhouse is a significant new presence in Vancouver can be gathered from the fact that new Mayor Larry Campbell and ten city councilors took their oaths of office here in December 2002.[22]

Still within Concord Place, let us describe in a little detail one of the projects that typify what's going on here. The Crestmark is a twenty-two-story tower that sits atop a six-story podium that terraces down to four-story townhomes that front the waterfront walkway. It is sited at the traffic circle at the foot of Davie described previously. There's also a ten-story terraced section, stepping down to six stories along the main street here, Marinaside Crescent. Its mass is thus broken up, the tower placed away from the street and walkway. Some of the architecture is nautically inspired.

The townhomes along a park are clearly defined as private places by being raised three feet and set back about twelve feet. Four-story homes line the waterfront walkway, helping create a sense of openness and again, are raised and separated. There's a secondary walkway that meanders between the public trail and the townhomes, with terraces and hedges for separation. There's a semipublic garden space in the middle that has a water feature. At the Davie Street triangle, the building has a rounded corner.

The urban design here reflects neighborliness, enhancement of the public realm, accessibility, and views. At the same time it provides security and privacy.[23]

Still in Concord Pacific Place is the next neighborhood, under construction in spring 2003, the Beach Crescent project, whose principal design feature will be a curved crescent of townhomes at its center. It is sited between two of the area's principal waterfront parks, named for David Lam and George Wainborn, and it was presold.

Leaving Concord Pacific Place but still in an area near the False Creek North neighborhood, in fact due east of it, is still another significant residential project, Citygate, created by Bosa Developments. It, too, fronts on False Creek, located at the easternmost portion at the site of a concrete plant that existed through the 1980s; its southern portion was an industrial area until becoming part of the Expo '86 site.

It contains housing (including nonmarket units) for a resident population of two thousand, plus offices, a Skytrain station, retail space along Main Street, which runs along the back side of the project, and child care facilities. The project has four towers on a platform and several mid-rise buildings. There is also a new park and an upgraded existing park.

Concord Pacific Place is not the entire story at False Creek North. Two parcels to the east of its development, labeled future Creekside development, are projected to contain another 1,100 residential units. They are near the Plaza of Nations left from Expo days.

With this growth and the presence of a sizable number of young professionals come companies that are relocating into or near the downtown, including high-tech firms and a communications company that we heard about.

COAL HARBOUR

We turn now to the north side of downtown and Coal Harbour, former Canadian Pacific Railway lands, 105 acres including water areas. We start with the city's planning principles for the area, which are not mere rhetoric, but here have truly helped drive the project's design and siting. They are:

• Maintain a sense of a diverse urban waterfront, meaning, among other things, retaining the working waterfront elements still present here. Public spaces should be at the water's edge, boat mooring should be enhanced, and views should capitalize on the adjacent working harbor.

- Build on the setting, including taking into account the sun and shadowing, maintaining visual, physical, and functional links between the land and the water, exploiting nearby attractions within walking distance, and respecting views and links to nearby Stanley Park and Canada Harbour Place.

- Integrate with the city, meaning extending the street grid to the project, extending the pattern of nearby areas, having a continuous waterfront walkway linking to downtown and Stanley Park, and linking to downtown via a public open space system.

- Use streets as an organizing device; lots and blocks are to be formed by streets, buildings should orient to streets and have hospitable streetscapes, and pedestrian circulation should be at ground level.

- Create distinct and lively public places, including the streets, parks, plazas, and walkways, including using the site's elevation change to create an identity, reducing the impact of traffic, consciously designing spaces, and subdividing long streets or large spaces into comfortable subareas.

- Create neighborhoods with distinct identities and defined edges, a diversity of people, having well-defined public and private spaces and including community facilities and neighborhood gathering spots.

- Plan for all age groups and incomes, aiming for a robust neighborhood that includes facilities for children as well as seniors and provides for security without sanitizing the spaces.

The plan called for a predominately residential complex containing a total of 2,367 units, nearly all condominiums, with just 270 apartment rentals. A community center and school are called for, as is a hotel, some office and retail, and a section of live/work space. Attention to street-end vistas and larger view sheds is included. The plan sites the buildings to be allowed and gives each its height limit. These range from 330 feet on the eastern, downtown edge to just over 200 feet on the western side.

The generous, handsome Harbour Green Park and beautifully detailed, wide walkway are the centerpieces of this project. From its midpoint, a graceful plaza takes a visitor down to the water's edge, the residential towers behind. The walkway has a handsome railing, artful paving, marks out a bike route along the pedestrian way and connects at several junctures back to the city's street grid. There is a circular lookout space where the walkway makes a turn. Anchoring the walkway are two active marinas, which along with the commercial harbor here, make for a lively waterfront scene, punctuated by an occasional seaplane. Even the marina seawall exhibits a quality of design, as does the street furniture patterned on that found in nearby Stanley Park, a Vancouver fixture since 1888 with its own 6.5-mile waterside trail.

Coal Harbour is like Concord Pacific Place in that it is a complex of residential towers on the waterfront with generous park space, walkway, and civic facilities, but smaller. It is to have eighteen new towers in the Marathon portion when done, plus preexisting taller structures (versus sixty-one in the Concord project). In total, including the adjacent Bayshore Gardens project begun in 1991, there will be 3,100 units of housing on Coal Harbour, plus office towers and a major hotel, looking to a resident population of 5,400 persons, with 600 nonmarket housing units included plus 800 units designed for families. Hence the plan's call for an elementary school and day care centers.

Condominiums here also presell. An ad in the *Vancouver Sun* on May 10, 2003, pictured the twin towers Callisto and Carina, "now selling for completion in summer, 2004." Each was thirty-five stories; the Carina was said to have four units left, Callisto fourteen. Suites with two bedrooms plus den, about 1,700 square feet, sold from $1,195,000 (Cdn.). Five townhomes remained, $580,000 to $825,000 (Cdn.). The ad sells "panoramic vistas of water, mountains and sky," noting that "nothing can ever obscure your stunning view."

The profile is different at Coal Harbour from Concord Pacific Place, according to an architect we interviewed who is active here. Individual units are larger, catering to an older, more affluent clientele. At the same time, because of city policy, a diversity of population is built in with the subsidized and family housing requirements.

One flaw here as of 2003 was the small amount of retail. Planners had thought the shops on nearby Robson Street would fill this need, but they are tourist-oriented and just far enough away (six or so blocks) so as not to work. A solution being worked on is to allow projects along a key interior street (Thurlow) to be allowed greater density in exchange for putting shops in. It's not that there are none, for a cafe exists on the walkway, but so does a jade shop, which is not a neighborhood-centering kind of place.

Helping to make this precinct attractive, besides the park and walkway, is the generous space between towers and the presence of gardens throughout. One critique we would make is that it is not apparent, despite the city's policy in this regard, which are private gardens (Vancouver has a number of these) and which are publicly accessible spaces. There is an ambiguity to some of the entrance points. One was labeled "no outlet," which seemed to suggest visitors weren't welcome.

Here is what one of the components of Coal Harbour is like. The Cascina and Denia Towers are two towers, twenty-three and nineteen stories, with thirty-six townhomes joining them and with a water garden in the center and a waterwall at one entrance. The facade is broken by small porches, and the dominant material is glass, as views everywhere from the towers would be splendid. There are a total of 201 units.

Helping in this precinct is a mix of styles and heights. Along the waterfront walkway, for instance, are three-level townhomes, bright white in color with tinted glass, behind which rises a twelve-story project, behind which is a thirty-two-story tower, largely white in color and again with tinted windows. The general feeling conveyed is again one of lightness and airiness.

A list of what is being extracted from Marathon Developments in its part of Coal Harbour includes parks, community centers, school, social housing, shoreline walkway, child care facilities, library (here it's a payment-in-lieu of the facility) and public art ($1 per leasable square foot), police boat moorage, and a contribution toward saltwater pump stations.

The adjoining project, Bayshore Gardens, is anchored by a Westin Hotel, whose 250 rooms were to be doubled. It had a relatively small residential population of 330 as of 1997.

The pace continues, with the planning department estimating that since the 2001 census there have been ten new apartment towers occupied with an average of 1.5 persons per unit, adding another 3,250 people to downtown between 2001 and 2003, with thousands more to come.

OTHER NEIGHBORHOODS

There are still three more residential neighborhoods on the peninsula to mention, which lie next to the False Creek North complex. They are Yaletown that we describe later, Downtown South, a newly rezoned section with an estimated eight thousand residents in 2003 (which had been its projected total not to be achieved until 2011),[24] and Granville Slopes between Burrard and Granville Bridge, one of the earliest project areas. A signature project in the latter area is 888 Beach Avenue completed in 1993, which has towers of thirty-one and eighteen stories rising above streetside townhomes of from three to seven stories. At street level are curving facades, bay windows and balconies, and light colors, all serving to make pedestrians comfortable and masking the towers behind and above. This is the treatment now being extended around Vancouver's waterfront as it was seen to work well here.

Thus far we have dealt entirely with new construction. The interesting thing about it is that the city and its developers have succeeded in keeping these new precincts from feeling sterile. There's not much patina of age in these areas, to be sure, but since there's been a full decade now of development, plantings, for instance, have grown and help make these new sections feel "lived in." The presence of children's play areas also contributes to the neighborhood feeling, plus active retail spaces and restaurant/ cafe scenes.

One person we interviewed related a telling experience. After having worked on the Concord Pacific project for some years, he anchored his boat and spent a night at a marina on False Creek. He awoke in the morning to the sight of people in robes, some with children in tow, headed for the Starbucks coffee shop. He was somewhat astonished by this parade and went to the shop, although he was not a coffee drinker. And there it hit him, the people had made this *their* neighborhood and were completely comfortable in it despite its newness.

In the early 1980s, Yaletown, a deserted warehouse section, largely built between 1909 and 1913, was discovered by urban professionals. Yaletown was named for a Canadian Pacific Railway yard in the town of Yale, where many workers were before coming to the False Creek yards. Some brought their houses with them. Renovations began, and office spaces, upscale restaurants, and trendy clubs appeared as they have in similar areas of the other cities. Zoning was changed to encourage conversions and the construction of compatible new buildings. There are least nine restaurants in the section.

It carries the label "trendy" and is home to furniture and decorating shops, described as expensive.[25] What makes it interesting is its contrast with the new residential towers next to it.

Yaletown possesses a bit of cachet and helps the next-door Concord Pacific Place project lure its thousands of new residents. "Yaletown" is used by some as the geographic description for the new project area.

What has occurred in Vancouver over the last twenty years is nothing short of dramatic. Dozens of high-rise residential towers have transformed the skyline, bringing about a marked increase in the intown population who enjoy a very urbane lifestyle in a city where over half of the people do NOT drive to work!

Findings

City life, almost because it has not changed much, has more and more
become a mockery of the American dream. The norm of middle-class
aspiration is suburbia, and as our middle class has expanded the
distance between city and the consensus of the good life has grown.
—*William Whyte,* The Anti-City

In this chapter we recap some of the common issues and themes that
we discovered in our eight case cities, backed up by the outside research
we undertook.

YOUNG ADULTS—PLUS

We begin with our major finding about who it was in 2003 fueling
Intown Living. The literature told us we were going to find aging baby
boomers leaving the subdivisions with their traffic woes to downsize into
an urban apartment to enjoy the offerings of the city. Our files are full of
stories with headlines like "Urban Ikes: A new generation of retirees heads
for the cities," from *Preservation* magazine May/June 2000,[1] and, "Boomers
Edging Back to Urban Areas," from *Realty Times.*[2]

What our on-the-ground research has established pretty conclusively,
backed by 2000 census data, is that what's going on today is not a "back-
to-the-city" movement by aging baby boomers, but rather a "forget about
it" movement driven principally by people under 40 for whom the suburbs
hold no appeal. We report Intown Living census tracts where consistently

the largest age group is between 25 and 34. In Central Midtown Atlanta, two-thirds of the population is between the ages of 20 and 39; in downtown Vancouver, the two largest population groups are between 25 and 34 and they, together with the 35-to-39 bracket, are the fastest growing in an expanding downtown; in Uptown Dallas, its two principal census tracts have median ages of 30 and 31, respectively.

The second large population for whom subdivisions hold little attraction is the gay population of every age. All eight of our Intown Living case neighborhoods have a large gay contingent, whose presence was remarked on by many we interviewed, some of them gay themselves. A third market is with divorcees, who may have to move into smaller quarters and for whom an urban neighborhood with a nightlife offers a chance to meet new people. Another market slice is subdivision residents or out-of-town visitors desiring a weekend/second place in or near downtown. This latter phenomenon is big enough to have long-time residents of New Orleans' French Quarter worried because it reduces the number of year-round people and makes it seem all the more a tourist zone. Some people apparently spend only an occasional weekend there in their condominium or apartment. We encountered this phenomenon in Memphis, another major party city, and in Dallas and Houston, where many of the residents were said to have country homes.

THE BOOMERS

Our further finding is that the baby boomers, those born between 1946 and 1964, aren't attracted to Intown Living by and large at present; it is still a little edgy for them. Too many homeless panhandlers for people used to a plain vanilla population. When they downsize, as some are beginning to do, we sense the majority will stay in subdivisions or, perhaps, move to a near-urban setting like Houston's Galleria, into an older, established suburb, or into new retirement havens, but not so much into the center city. Some of the more adventurous will move intown, and we have examples in some of our cases, but we sense many more will flock to the burgeoning counties of Arizona and Nevada, or still to Florida, full, we expect, of "snowbird" retirees. As intown areas become more established in the future, safer and culturally more inviting, perhaps a larger percentage of this huge group—75 million in number—will make the move.

A survey for the National Association of Home Builders Seniors Housing Council backs up this analysis. Margaret Wylde surveyed 55-year-olds who had bought a house in the past two years or were planning to in the next two. Their locational preference? Evenly split between rural, outlying suburban, and close-in suburban, most preferring a single-family, detached house, with half wanting a two-car garage and 24 percent seeking three car spaces! Only 7 percent would settle for a one-car garage. This sample group is clearly not thinking of moving into the city.[3]

Further, many of this group will simply stay put. An article in a *New York Times* magazine special section on suburbs captured this. It was entitled "We Stayed for the Kids . . . . and Stayed and Stayed: The Pleasure of Tending an Empty Nest." The author relates that his idea of a perfect Saturday is to crank up his various gasoline-powered yard tools—mower, blower, edger, whacker, and saw—and then sit on his back deck and oversee his kingdom.[4]

HISTORIC PRESERVATION

The preservation movement is a major force in all of our case cities. The Intown Living story is very much about restoring major portions of the historic fabric in areas such as the Pearl District in Portland, the Warehouse and Lafayette Square areas in New Orleans, the Mill District and North Loop in Minneapolis, Downtown and State-Thomas in Dallas, Downtown and South Main in Memphis, Downtown and NoHo in Houston, Yaletown in Vancouver, and Midtown and Fairlie-Poplar in Atlanta. A large stock of old buildings has been brought back to life in our cities, and the promotional literature for the resulting new apartments and condos all tout the unique architectural features and historic atmosphere.

New Orleans embodies the force that the preservation movement represents. There the Preservation Resource Center, in what might be termed a preemptive strike, issued a report before the 1984 World's Fair was too far along in planning that detailed the historic nature of the riverfront area the fair was about to take over. By calling attention to the historic character of what could have been taken as a cluster of vacant, useless warehouses, the district of that name was spared and today has a colorful mixture of shops, galleries, museums, residences, hotels, and bars/restaurants.

Likewise, the Minneapolis Riverfront Development Coordination Board in 1980 published a fulsome book, *Saint Anthony Falls Rediscovered*, documenting the historic structures along the riverfront. It was designed to help inform public policy decisions and articulates something that all of our cities seem to have taken to heart to one degree or another:

Historical resources are irreplaceable . . . historical resources can be preserved by "recycling" and can be put to new uses. It is hoped that this study will encourage the proper recognition of Minneapolis's historical resources and the preservation of the buildings that were instrumental in the city's growth and development.[5]

It succeeded in large measure.

In Vancouver, where new construction is the emphasis, its old character-filled warehouse section, Yaletown, was discovered by artists in the early 1980s. Today it flourishes with high-end furniture shops and trendy restaurants and offers a contrast to next-door apartment towers. In Houston and Dallas, activists were for years engaged in valiant efforts to try to save their downtown heritage buildings. It is a tribute to these determined individuals that there is growing appreciation for preservation in those cities today.

Preservation is an instinct even in Atlanta, where new is the watchword. Sections of older homes in Midtown are being carefully and lovingly restored in an area blessed with a canopy of large trees.

HISTORIC PRESERVATION TAX CREDITS

We cannot overestimate the importance of the historic preservation tax credits. You instinctively appreciate it, but we were impressed at how many people we visited cited how critical the 20 percent historic preservation tax credit was to making the renovation of older structures feasible financially. A tally by the National Park Service found that since 1976 there were 27,000 properties rehabilitated using the tax credits, with a private investment of over $18 billion.[6] Even though restricted to income-generating commercial projects and thus not available for a condominium conversion, only apartments, the tax credit still is a potent factor as developers pencil out what will make a project work in an older building. To get 20 percent off reconstruction costs and fees, the building must be on the National Register of Historic Places or be in a historic district.

More states are providing historic tax credits as well, which when combined with federal tax relief can create a major incentive. In our case cities, scores of class B office buildings have been saved and converted thanks in large part to the preservation credit.

FINANCIAL INCENTIVES

The array of financial incentives available for developers was key to making Intown Living happen in all of our cities. Basically it's because the cost of downtown land is historically high (driven up by the potential, whether real or not, for commercial development), and there can be complicated negotiations and sometimes costly infrastructure repairs. Thus land in downtown Atlanta is three times as expensive as in nearby Midtown. To overcome this we have very interventionist agencies like the Minneapolis Community Development Agency, the Portland Development Commission, and the Midtown Redevelopment Authority in Houston which function as old-time urban redevelopment agencies—only considerably more enlightened today. They, as we discuss, negotiate agreements with private developers and basically assist in making projects happen. This can be a low-interest loan to help build an underground parking garage (Portland), a package of incentives and grants to underwrite a hotel project (Minneapolis), street, sidewalk, and streetlights (Houston), or tax breaks (Memphis).

Persons interested in this subject will want to contact the Downtown Improvement District in Dallas for descriptions of the Intown Living incentives there. They include tax increment financing, conventional city financing, Section 108 funds, bonds, tax abatements (as much as 100 percent for five years), and development cost reductions.[7]

Another type of agency playing a major role is the "business improvement district" (BID) type of organization such as the Downtown Development District in New Orleans, the Portland Business Alliance, and Midtown Alliance, in Atlanta. They, too, offer incentives, as in New Orleans, for help with facade improvements in a new initiative. They are better known for their visible presence in downtowns as well as their promotional campaigns. In Dallas they have uniformed "ambassadors," who help with visitor information, but whose most important function is to add to a feeling of security. They are on cooperative terms with the police, who look to them to keep an alert eye out. They have in common that a special tax on businesses funds their activities.

In some cases, it's a mixture, as the Midtown Redevelopment Authority in Houston puts a uniformed presence into the neighborhood as well as financing physical improvements. Likewise, the Dallas BID does physical improvements as well as working on cleanups.

In any case, it's not until you start digging around in downtowns and nearby neighborhoods that the influence of city agencies with a mission (and money) and their colleagues in the business communities who organize into quasi-public agencies becomes clear. Not everyone is pleased with BIDs, arguing that they privatize public functions.[8] In today's economy these arguments seem pale when compared to providing a means to get necessary services performed (and not incidentally, creating some jobs) that municipal budgets can't cover.

NEAR-DOWNTOWN NEIGHBORHOODS

As mentioned in the preface, where we describe how we settled on the book's title, it was near-downtown neighborhoods that were the most energetic in 2003 in our case cities. The Midtowns of Atlanta and Houston, Uptown Dallas, Mill Quarter in Minneapolis, and the waterfront in Vancouver. Even in Memphis, where the Intown Living movement started downtown, it has now spread outward to adjoining neighborhoods.

Underlying this is land cost. Downtown land is priced for commercial development, often putting it out of reach for residential projects that are harder to accomplish and don't produce the quick revenues of office buildings, for instance. Subsidies of varied sorts would seem to be the answer until an economic decline sets in that lowers land values.

A sidelight of this is that some of these near-downtown areas were once the elite neighborhoods of their cities and then went into serious decline. Midtown Houston is a case in point where, today, if you look hard enough, an old mansion that was typical of the area in the early years of the twentieth century still remains, albeit forlorn. Other areas that have had the cycle of once being posh, then declining and now making a comeback are Midtown Atlanta, Elliot Park in Minneapolis, and Lafayette Square in New Orleans.

CIVIC LEADERSHIP

It's a cliché that leadership is critical to a city's fortunes. The most dramatic instance of a leadership change that we report on is from Portland, Oregon, where in the early 1970s a total change of direction was taken by the young, new city administration of Mayor Neil Goldschmidt. With his selection came a reform-minded city council with an average age fully fifteen years younger than previously. Bringing life back to a dormant downtown by encouraging Intown Living was a top planning priority of the new team. Bold civic leadership is also evident in Vancouver, where it was decided to rezone in one stroke eight million square feet of commercial space for residential, bringing about a fundamental shift in the character of this city where, as we report, Intown Living is flourishing.

It's a fact of life for today's cities that they are in strong competition with each other. This point was articulated by Peter Hall at the conclusion of chapter 2. Our most telling example: Boeing Company decided to move its headquarters from Seattle. Three cities competed, Chicago, Dallas, and Denver. The winner was Chicago, in a major blow to the ego of Dallas, whose leadership had to come to grips with the fact that its downtown, for all their collective effort, had been found wanting.

Leadership frequently comes out of the private sector. In Atlanta's Midtown, for instance, the business leaders there have put together the Midtown Alliance, with a staff of thirteen and an annual budget of over $3 million raised from its members. This group is powering the change of this neighborhood into a hip—by Atlanta standards—mid-city section that will help attract and keep a bright young population. Business leaders elsewhere, as in Houston, realize that they too have to transform the downtowns from sterile office zones with their "trophy towers," as one interviewee termed them, into more energetic places with a residential population to help bring them to life.

DEVELOPMENT COMMUNITY READY

As mentioned in chapter 1, we were taken as a whole with the intelligence and vision exhibited by the representatives of the private development community whom we interviewed. Without their leadership it's hard to see how a number of the areas we visited would be prospering now. As a group they seem to enjoy risk-taking, they are proud of their work and they want to be part of the next big thing. We found the development community poised to make Intown Living happen, as many were busy doing. Further, we found support for this finding in the literature.

We cite here a report from the Urban Land Institute, the development industry's educational and research arm, entitled "Urban Infill Housing: Myth and Fact." It says developers should look favorably at the opportunity to build housing in cities.[9]

First the report notes the expansion of urban housing activity, namely that city housing permits from 1999 to 2000 were up 35 percent from the average level from 1990 to 1998, and that this new housing was finding eager buyers. "The realization seems to be growing that cities need good housing to become the vibrant centers of cultural and social life that they once were, and thus public and political support for urban infill housing is on the rise," the report says. After reciting the litany of reasons why Intown Living makes sense (makes better use of land, reuses existing property, uses existing infrastructure, causes less environmental damage, supports transit), the report goes on to say that developers see it making sense for them. Some reported their most successful projects in the 1990s were urban infill undertakings, often high-profile and bringing prestige to the company.

"Infill development is seen as part of the solution—not part of the problem—which is why political support for such projects is increasing in strength," the report states. It is more challenging than subdivision work because of one or more of the following factors: social problems in distressed neighborhoods, land assemblage difficulties, financing complexities, regulations, contamination, infrastructure problems, neighborhood opposition, and stringent historic preservation requirements. The report addresses these issues and a number of myths that have grown up in the development industry about infill housing and attempts to calmly set them to rest.

On the land assembly issue, the report notes that many city governments offer developers assistance with the acquisition and assembly of land and that creative options exist. Help can and does include land grants, low-cost leases, and low-interest loans. Redevelopment agencies (think Portland, Oregon and Houston here) acquire acreage and package it for resale. Financial help is offered, such as Memphis's 3 percent loans to help fix older buildings. About permitting difficulties, the ULI report says many cities have streamlined their processes and work cooperatively with development interests, as we found in a number of our examples.

Backing up the suggestion that political support is building for Intown Living is an analysis of what Smart Growth really means, by Anthony Downs of The Brookings Institution. In looking at the policies he identifies that come under the heading of Smart Growth, Downs found that redeveloping inner-core areas and encouraging development on infill sites won wide support from the basic advocacy groups involved in the Smart Growth effort, including some that are at odds with each other. Each interest group favors making cities attractive to middle- and upper-income households, as well as improving conditions for existing low-income people. The objective is "crucial" to inner-city advocates and supported "somewhat less avidly" by the other constituencies, but supported nonetheless, which suggests a political consensus for our Intown Living objective at the local level. Redeveloping cities ranks with preserving open space and developing a stronger sense of community as worthy objectives for the major constituent groups involved in Smart Growth.[10]

As recounted in our introductory chapters, American cities have a history of bad decision-making by the business/political leadership about how to build a city, including the huge misjudgment of bringing interstate expressways into and through cities, often severing communities from their waterfronts (Boston, Cincinnati, Hartford, Louisville, Philadelphia, Portland, and San Francisco [almost]). They have also embraced devastating urban renewal clearance programs. We cite the huge clearance program in Minneapolis where the vacant blocks remain today.

Examples of bad city-making decisions continue today, as in Philadelphia, where a failed waterfront thirty years in the making is still being marketed to developers without a plan, on a political timetable, and without tackling the section's principal problem: severance from a lively center city by an interstate highway. It's not just leadership that is needed, but leadership savvy as to how cities work.

GALVANIZING EVENTS

We were struck by how important a particular building, structure, or artifact—usually historic—can be to a city's psyche, both in a positive and a negative sense.

The restoration of the statue Pegasus to the top of the Magnolia Hotel at midnight January 1, 2000 in Dallas is perhaps the most "Oh, wow" act of symbolism we encountered. This red, fifteen-ton, winged-horse neon sculpture for years had been Dallas's iconic signature. After Dallas had its economy shaken by the savings-and-loan debacle, the repositioning of Pegasus was a signal of real hope for the city. Lighting the major bridge in downtown Memphis in 1986 was cited by a developer there as a turn-around event, an emblem of the city pulling together and coming back.

In Minneapolis, it was the restoration of the Stone Arch Bridge over the Mississippi that people there saw as the catalytic event, signaling that the riverfront there was ready to come to life again after a fitful start in the 1980s. The pedestrian bridge crosses the Mississippi just below St. Anthony Falls in a graceful curve, in front of the historic Mill District that was undergoing a dramatic transformation in 2003, including a large residential component.

Likewise, the reopening of the Peabody Hotel in downtown Memphis and the rehabilitation of the Rice Hotel in downtown Houston, the latter into apartments, were powerful events. Both hotels had functioned as important social centers of their respective cities and had many accumulated memories for older residents. The Peabody today has a major social scene with a huge active central lobby bar area, Thursday night sunset parties on its roof, and major private parties.

The tear-down of the Portland Hotel in the center of that city, the Metropolitan Building in Minneapolis, and the destruction of fine old Victorian homes on the eastern side of Dallas along Swiss Avenue created the historic preservation movements in those three cities, so aroused did citizens become.

Fairs, expos, and community events can be equally powerful change agents. In Atlanta, New Orleans, and Vancouver, hosting a major international event proved a critical, catalytic event that helped transform those cities. The boost in civic pride, the media coverage, not to mention the infrastructure put in place, cannot be underestimated. This occurred in Atlanta, where people still talk about the Olympics like it happened a month ago (it was in 1996). It clearly was a morale-booster for a city with a bit of an inferiority complex, and it left a legacy of structures and parks. The World's Fair in New Orleans went bankrupt, but it left facilities for reuse, such as the core of its convention center, and it spurred the gradual rediscovery of the warehouse area. And Vancouver's Expo '86 gave that city a big uplift, proving to itself it was a major-league North American city. Its importance to our story is that Expo assembled the land that was home to thirty-seven residential towers in 2003, with more to come.

But short of world events, there are the local celebrations. The institution of "Memphis in May" was mentioned as being hugely important. Atlanta's Gay Pride weekend and Dogwood Festival are big occasions. New Orleans has Mardis Gras, continuous parades and celebrations, and, most notably in our book, the Jazz and Heritage Festival in the spring. Dallas attempts a Mardis Gras of its own. Houston hosts a huge rodeo, and there's the In the Heart of the Beast May Day Parade in Minneapolis, said to be the largest and funkiest celebration in the Midwest and a first sign of spring there. Portland stages numerous riverfront celebrations in Tom McCall Park and celebrates the Portland Rose Festival here. All are community builders of one sort or another.

THE ARTS

Another powerful force in our cities is the arts. The presence of galleries nurtures local talents and contributes to a social scene. Public art programs help distinguish and animate a city's parks, walkways, plazas, and all the surprising places it can be discovered—like leaf imprints on the sidewalks in Yaletown in Vancouver.

We acknowledge and pay tribute to the gallery owners and artists who frequently pioneer the comeback of vacant, often richly textured areas—blessed as they are at first with low rents. Examples include the South Main area in Memphis, the Pearl District in Portland, Oregon, Routh Street in Dallas's Uptown, and the Crescent section in Midtown Atlanta. They are the pioneers in these sections and contribute significantly to their present character. The worry, of course, is that with discovery and a developing residential population followed by added commercial, rents will rise beyond the capacity of many low-budget galleries, forcing them into the next new "in" section.

From the new Guthrie Riverfront theater in Minneapolis to the blues scene on Beale Street in Memphis to the D-Day Museum in New Orleans, a common thread in each city was investment in cultural facilities of all kinds by government, nonprofit arts organizations, and private investors. In Memphis we quote a major business leader saying the arts are as important to a city as sports complexes, in what must be a radical notion for some.

TRANSPORTATION

Striking in all the cases was the care and feeding of the automobile and how it was handled, well or not, plus the positive impact of new rail systems.

Traffic calming or the lack thereof was a large factor in our cities. In Atlanta and Minneapolis, the combination of wide streets and/or fast traffic make the pedestrian very uncomfortable. Where cities have one-way pairs of streets, the traffic is faster still. In downtown Houston, to see several lanes with hundreds of cars—lights all synchronized to enable them to speed along unimpeded—is mind-boggling. Houston is making heroic efforts, however, with its Cotswold streetscape plan to put the car in its place and make the area pedestrian-friendly. Calmed traffic (or a relative lack of it, remarkably, in downtown Portland) helps the pedestrian in Memphis, Vancouver, and New Orleans. Street width is important: Portland's narrow streets and short blocks are fundamental to its walkability. Minneapolis's wide streets and large blocks have the opposite effect. The city with the least intrusion of the expressway is Vancouver, and it benefits from this mightily. It's hard to tame the car in North America, but for the sake of our cities, it has to be done.

The amount of territory given to surface parking in our cities, garages as well as on-street parking, is appalling. In Atlanta, Houston, Dallas, and Minneapolis it was particularly dominant, ugly, and deadening. Jane Holz Kay, in describing our "hard-topped nation," says that from 30 to 50 percent of our cities are given over to the car. And parking lots are money-makers. She bemoans "when flattening for parking is more profitable than restoration . . . every building, however historic or attractive, becomes a lure for developers to demolish it for its highest and best use. Too often, that means its potential as a parking lot."[11]

We went by a fairly small surface lot on the edge of downtown Houston where our host told us thousands of dollars were generated every month from just a half-interest in the lot. Figure: $10 a day per car, 40 cars, 20 working days per month equals $8,000, with minor expenses and some taxes. A mixed-use project in Minneapolis works for the developer because it will contain monthly rental parking at its core. At least the garage will be hidden in the middle of a block, surrounded by other uses. Meantime, the policy in Vancouver is to put parking underneath residential buildings there, notwithstanding the higher expense. The result is clearly worth it. We feel this should be the standard everywhere possible, recognizing that it requires subsidy (as in Portland's Brewery Blocks project).

Good public transit, especially trolleys, streetcars, and trains, play—or are about to play—a key role in our case cities. The surveys show, as we cite, that people like trains but are wary of buses. The marketing and customer service director for the transit agency in Memphis was quoted as saying that he thought "people perceive some fear of waiting in a bus stop."[12] Streetcars play an important role in transportation around downtowns, in bringing color to city streets, and in reinforcing a sense of urbanity.

The Uptown area of Dallas would be a less attractive place without its McKinney Avenue historic trolleys (whose tracks help slow traffic). A planned extension to a downtown loop will enhance its practicality. The ridership on Dallas's DART rail network has exceeded projections, and far-flung suburbs push to get their lines laid. Portland's new, narrow Czech-built streetcar is a boon to the Pearl District that it traverses and from whose edge trips to downtown are fare-free. The Memphis Main Street and Riverfront Trolleys add a great deal of ambiance to the areas they serve. MARTA in Atlanta's Midtown area enables people to move easily around certain sections of the city and metro area. Houston's Main Street light rail should transform the center city, which now has only a system of free-wheeled trolleys that transport people around downtown.

DIFFERING REVITALIZATION APPROACHES

We agree completely with authors Roberta Brandes Gratz and Norman Mintz that "a collection of visitor attractions does not add up to a city." They make the distinction between cities that are *rebuilt* and those that instead are *reborn*. The ones rebuilt have done so according to a series of expensive "Project Plans." The result is a collection of tourist attractions connected by an auto-based network versus an organic approach that acknowledges the complexity and richness of cities and the creativity of citizens.[13]

We illustrate the push-pull of these two approaches as they were being played out in downtown Houston, where on the one hand there is a cluster of new, varied attractions and, on the other side of downtown, the more organic approach, evolving from what's present to a more secure and varied future. A resident there likened it to a struggle between those seeing Houston as Santa Barbara and those seeing it as Las Vegas, with the latter usually winning. In fairness, much of Houston was leveled between urban renewal and tear-downs for speculative offices, many of which never materialized, so building isolated attractions would have a certain logic, as in filling in the blank spaces.

By the same token, we also report the positive impact of the minor league baseball stadium in Memphis, an excellent piece of urban design, fitting what could have been a deadly presence instead into a facility with good street presence and limited parking. What's often so discouraging about sports stadiums is that they are surrounded by macadam, empty most of the time. Likewise, the Mill City Museum in Minneapolis fits seamlessly into its setting and enhances the public realm along the riverfront in a major way.

Today's mistakes, when they are made, fall more in the category of grabbing at straws, any straw, that might attract visitors without fully considering what is good in the long run for the creation of an intown community. Or, not stopping to think that it's attractions for the local citizens that are wanted, and the tourists will go there if they are authentic, safe, and fun—or quirky.

PANHANDLING AND THE HOMELESS

The importance of this issue and its impact on the overall ambiance of the downtown was critical to the city leaders in all of our cases to one degree or another. We were surprised at how large an issue it was.

We note for the record that many who panhandle are not homeless and that not all homeless people panhandle. In the public mind the two are often linked, however, and they create discomfort in most middle-class people, especially suburbanites who are not used to people sitting on the sidewalk with empty cups, or loitering around libraries and parks.

We think this issue looms as important as it does because otherwise crime overall in cities is dramatically down—the one underlying factor without which little Intown Living would take place. The general appearance of panhandling and homelessness are reminders of social ills—a situation out of control—with maybe a hint of danger, and it makes people edgy. A downtown leader in Minneapolis we quote notes that it's the "nuisance crimes," as he put it, that scare people and that should, but often don't, command police attention.

We recall a letter to the editor in a June 2003 *Atlanta Journal-Constitution* in which a woman wrote of visiting relatives at the downtown Four Seasons Hotel and walking with them two blocks to a restaurant for dinner. Along the way were four panhandlers that the letter writer was clearly not accustomed to. They took a cab back to the hotel ($9) and resolved never to come to downtown Atlanta again until the panhandling problem was solved.

The related issues of shelters, soup kitchens, and feeding stations were of major concern to the Warehouse Area Business Association in New Orleans because these facilities were a presence in their area.

There's a White House Interagency Council on Homelessness and $35 million spent by several agencies to deal with this problem. The International Downtown Association (IDA) sees the situation as "growing and seemingly more intractable."[14] That organization's hope is that just as ten years ago when urban crime was thwarting redevelopment, a concerted federal/local effort and new approaches can help reduce the problem, particularly the undesirable behaviors associated with homelessness. IDA puts the national homeless population at 2.5 million, with increases as much as 25 percent in Kansas City and 20 percent or more in Chicago, Denver, and New Orleans. The organization further reports that children are the fastest-growing part of the homeless population, 40 percent being under 18 years old. What's happening now, they report, is that low-income housing is in short supply, jobs are scarce, and the working poor have trouble making ends meet.[15]

We mention the issue in most of our case cities, including the insight that the skywalk system in Minneapolis and the tunnels in Dallas and Houston, being privately owned, are at root, efforts to provide "comfortable" suburban-style environments for people to move around and thus avoid panhandlers.

COMMUNITY AMENITIES AND AMBIANCE

Retail

Many we talked with reflected that their intown neighborhood has a real sense of community about it, that it in fact works much like a small town. Many features are within walking distance, and the sidewalks and walkways promote friendliness.

Critical to this is the presence of retail and service clusters in general, and a grocery store in particular. We relate how two new developments didn't really click in the sense of making people feel they were in a real place until grocery stores opened and became the de facto community center. This was the experience we discuss in Vancouver and Memphis. The coming of an upscale Whole Foods store to Midtown Atlanta in 2003 was seen as a real coming of age for the area. Likewise, landing a grocery in Midtown Houston marked a certain verification of that area as up-and-coming. The absence of a grocery in Minneapolis's growing North Loop area (there was, however, a good-sized deli in 2003) was cited by a number as a negative, an indication of how new the settlement there still is.

What's also desired in a residential area, especially with a young population, are neighborhood restaurants that are reasonably priced with innovative kitchens, seen as important to cement a sense of place and functioning as social centers—restaurants/cafes that people can and do frequent often, versus the upscale, high-end type of place that is visited just for the special occasion. Apparently, Midtown Atlanta started out with several of the expensive places that closed because the neighborhood couldn't support them. More moderate places have since opened up, plus one extremely trendy and expensive spot, One Midtown Kitchen, totally packed on a June 2003 Saturday night.

Parks

Recreational facilities such as parks and pathways are vital public amenities for intown neighborhoods. One developer in Portland's Pearl District recognized that in that outdoor-minded city, he would have to have parks in order to be able to rent apartments. The Pearl is to have three parks, each a full block in size, as part of the development agreement with the city. The river trail, parkland, and parkway along the Mississippi in Minneapolis is a beautiful, well-loved green space in the heart of the city, which works in conjunction with the residential developments occurring nearby. And Vancouver's often multitiered waterfront trail system, which circles the entire downtown peninsula—all seventeen miles of it—and ties into trails elsewhere, is a magnificent resource well-used by the citizens. In Houston there's a plan, pieces of which have been accomplished, to remake the Buffalo Bayou as it meanders through downtown into a major new green waterfront resource, which would go a long way toward altering that city's image of itself. In Dallas, downtown residents say their biggest need (more than the grocery store or curbing panhandling) is for park space, which the city is currently at work on.

Educational Facilities

Schools are the bellwether for young families. To our surprise, we found more young families in our sample intown neighborhoods than we would have thought, and we heard reports of more moving in. Public schools in Atlanta and Dallas were mentioned as plausible for middle-class parents, while in New Orleans the assumption was that private schooling would be used. Having safe and productive public schools is probably the biggest hurdle for having young families part of the Intown Living story. Without these families, neighborhoods can indeed flourish, but they lose something by not having young children about.

Universities provide an enriching element in nearly all our cases. In Atlanta, Georgia Tech is making itself a major presence in Midtown with a new campus, while Georgia State University is helping to transform and invigorate its portion of downtown. Likewise, the University of Houston has a downtown campus, and Portland State University is a large presence on the southern side of downtown there. The University of Minnesota is an important player in Minneapolis, where mention was made of a growing Elderhostel market eager for continuing education classes. These institutions, even when they are commuter schools, bring a young population into cities with disposable income and help create markets for bars, clubs, restaurants, and events such as concerts. They add to a place's vitality.

Lofts

The intown housing stock ranged in our cases all the way from high-rise to restored historic single-family homes. "Lofts" were, however, definitely *the* big thing, whether carved out of an old warehouse or completely new. As mentioned in chapter 2, the publicity about SoHo in New York and the imagery in movies, TV, and print media has had a far-reaching—not to say unbelievable—impact. Whether an old conversion or new construction, there was a common feel among them: Exposed beams and duct work, walls of brick or concrete, a basic unfinished look, open-living floor plans with one room melding into the other, where the bedrooms might be the only separate room or a half flight up, lots of windows, and in the newer buildings floor-to-ceiling windows. Decors ran from traditional English country to very sleek contemporary. One common marketing theme was the view—of the downtown skyscrapers or the river, as the case may be. We did see some fantastic views in all of the cities we visited.

DEVELOPMENT INTERESTS

We found that the development community, which apparently had been led to believe along with us that the baby boomers were coming and built accordingly, were shifting gears in 2003. Finding the "price point," to use a developer phrase, is a key. That's the price level at which the market responds. As we report, a project in Minneapolis that was to have been fifteen units selling at over $400,000 was being reconfigured into thirty units starting at $200,000. That's affordable to the young professional population that we have said is the driving force in today's market. The development community is now alert to this. It was telling, again in Minneapolis, that a developer of historic properties told us she had a supply of $500,000 properties available but had none of what were her "price point" units, $200,000 to $300,000. They had all been sold. A sidelight: We find it interesting that the marketplace generally judges downtown/intown residential units to be extremely valuable, where a unit in the Pearl District of Portland costs more per square foot than the previously most valuable properties in the city. In our suburban nation, the market places high value on Intown Living.

In cities that offer incentives to encourage essentially middle-class residents to locate intown, affordable housing is an issue. As we report, a reaction has set in to the subsidy program in Portland, Oregon. What is happening in a positive way is that developers are mandated, when subsidized in one way or another, to include a fixed percentage of low- or moderate-income units in their projects. And they are doing so successfully in a number of our cases. Vancouver is striking in how the design and appearance of an apartment with lower-income residents is indistinguishable on the outside from market-rate apartments. This leads us to the conclusion that this is a problem that has a partial solution at least in hand.

12

Recommendations

Never mind the rhetoric on sprawl and smart growth—the most important thing we can do for our national quality of life is to resolve to focus on urban revitalization. Not only would this diminish suburban sprawl problems, but, far more importantly, we would once again become a nation of thriving cities. The good news is that "urban revitalization" is not that difficult. Programs have been in place for the past few decades that have in fact stopped the urban exodus (some say hemorrhaging) since World War II. Urban centers and neighborhoods, along with small town main streets, are coming alive once again. There is great hope and opportunity if we but make some resolution to build on these programs.
> —*Patricia Gay, Preservation Resource Center, New Orleans*

We began quoting Patricia Gay in our Introduction, and we end with her declaration here. We admire her dedicated work in the trenches over the years and her clear-headed insistence that cities can and should be resettled with a sizable number of middle-class residents and that anti-sprawl action demands it.

Winding up our Intown Living project, fresh from having witnessed new residential neighborhoods being born or carved out of older districts, seeing downtown leadership at work revitalizing and beautifying their cities, appreciating newly alive artistic and cultural scenes, we come away with a measure of hope for a new chapter in the history of urban America. A small but significant number of young adults have adopted a new idea of where and how they want to live, work, and play. They are choosing the city. They are enlivening entire neighborhoods in and near downtowns. They make Intown Living fun (and safe) for all ages. In choosing the city, they have begun to dream something different than the traditional "American Dream." It's a prime task of current civic leadership to make this different dream flourish.

We put forward here some suggestions about how Intown Living can be advanced, drawing from what we observed in our case cities plus looking at case examples in the literature.

MAKE INTOWN LIVING A PRIORITY

While relatively obvious, making city living an explicit priority for the local government, the business community, the arts community, and residents is an important first step.

Emphasis on housing was a key feature in case study cities coming from different sources. The local government urban housing policies and strategies in Vancouver, Portland, and Minneapolis were articulate and very strong. In Houston, Dallas, and Memphis the downtown development organizations stressed the importance of housing, and in New Orleans a combination of business organizations and the preservation community pushed for housing. As is stated in an outline of how Denver has accomplished Intown Living, "The city's goal of investment-quality downtown residential neighborhoods, and the logical ripple-effect of downtown investment, must be clearly articulated to the general public. Otherwise, criticism for directing so many resources downtown at the expense of the rest of the city will inevitably rise."[1] We note in our cases that a number of cities made major public commitments to increasing intown housing—and it happened.

PROVIDE INCENTIVES

Enlist the private development sector in building and rehabilitating intown housing with such incentives as are needed. We think the Center City Commission (CCC) in Memphis does as well as anyone in spelling out clearly what incentives it offers, and why. Commission literature says that it "realizes that downtown development can be costly and complex to achieve. The CCC attempts to mitigate the costs by offering a range of financial incentives, including tax freezes, development loans, broker bonuses and other forms of assistance." The specifics are discussed in the Memphis chapter. The Center City Commission here acts as an expediter for private developers dealing with local governments, a necessary step, we think, to overcome the inherent difficulties of working in cities.

The development community responds to incentives, as one major player in Vancouver candidly told us. Put enough in place and they will do what's sought. In the past, most incentives underwrote subdivisions (cheap land, publicly supported infrastructure, personal income tax deductions for both mortgage interest and local taxes, and usually a favorable political climate). There's a strong indication that the development community is ready for what it terms "infill housing" in urban areas, that it sees the opportunity, and with sufficient help, it will do it—in fact, is doing it as we found in our case cities. See Findings for a discussion of how the development community is poised to act.

This is potentially exciting, for it offers hope that the toehold of Intown Living, as you might term what we report on from our cities, can in fact be extended and expanded. No great national mandate is needed. In fact, many past sweeping federal initiatives have done more harm than good. John Norquist, writing as mayor of Milwaukee in *The Wealth of Cities*, has a telling chapter entitled: "How the Government Killed Affordable Housing."

TAP EXISTING FEDERAL PROGRAMS

Before dismissing the federal government, however, we would observe that there are myriad federal programs on the books now for cities to take advantage of. *The Catalog of Federal Domestic Assistance* is still a telephone-book-sized document listing 1,568 programs currently, 227 of which specifically are classified as "urban." One example: the Environmental Protection Agency's "brownfields" initiative that helps cities clean up abandoned industrial sites, making them available for housing, parks, or other uses. The program spent $335 million between 1997 and 2000.[2] The job of cities is to know about this sort of funding and the multiple other programs in housing, community investment, pollution control, transportation enhancements (like bike trails and transit), and boating facilities, to mention just a few areas. They should use the staff of their congressional delegations to help them maneuver through the system; they are paid, usually well, to do just this. Cities should also be vigilant about lobbying for the continuance/expansion of programs that support Intown Living and city issues in general.

Today's reality, and tomorrow's even more so, is that suburban/subdivision voters dominate Congress, so cities have their job cut out. As the population continues to spread to the Sunbelt and subdivision-style cities, the less likely is national or congressional attention to focus on cities or even inner-ring suburbs. Our Intown Living movement could be a healthy countertrend if allowed to expand.

John Norquist argues that cities have natural advantages as centers of commerce, and rather than wring their collective hands about the lousy deal they have gotten from the federal government (this is a paraphrase), they should set about putting their houses in order and moving ahead. He writes:

The good news is that despite misguided experts and counterproductive Federal policies, some cities have survived, rebounded, even thrived. They have done so by making themselves as livable and affordable as possible while working to reverse the Federal policies that damage them, by creating the conditions in which large numbers of people can conveniently go about their business, by taking the simple but important steps of fighting crime, suppressing fire, protecting public health, creating educational opportunities, inspecting buildings, picking up trash, removing sewage and delivering clean water. Cities that have done these things well have generated opportunities for market activity and widespread prosperity.[3]

ASSURING AFFORDABILITY

To have vital, diverse cities we need to assure a mix of housing types and price tags. Diversity is one of the hallmarks of a healthy community. At a pragmatic level, we need to assure housing for the workforce near and amid the market-rate housing attracting a young, affluent population. This means providing ways for developers to continue to make money at lower price thresholds, which will entail providing incentives as we have described, perhaps lowering parking requirements or otherwise insuring housing units at prices people with modest incomes can afford. We look to Vancouver and Portland especially for lessons here.

ENCOURAGE BANKING REFORM

Lending for real estate development is very rigid and favors subdivision-style projects. The industry regards big-box retail and strip malls as low risk. Apartments over retail or infill projects in cities are not understood, and banks virtually bar such work from conventional lending, which pushes up costs. A developer doing infill work in Dallas is quoted identifying the roadblocks he faced from local banks (he was working in the Uptown neighborhood, incidentally): "They say land costs are too high. They don't like city lots because they don't meet HUD standards. They want you to gate your development, which is bad planning. If you gate, the public sector—which these projects need—won't participate."[4]

EXPAND HISTORIC PRESERVATION TAX CREDITS

The key role that historic preservation played in our Intown Living story was evident in all cases, assisted in a big way by the tax credits available for registered properties. At the national level it should be strengthened and restored to individual undertakings that meet the requirements (on the

National Register or in a historic district). Until this fine day occurs (down the road given current record-setting debt), states and localities can adopt the same credit as it applies to their taxes. As of 2002, twenty-one states had some form of historic tax credit with more thinking about it.[5] Pennsylvania, for instance, was looking into allowing a 20 percent state income tax credit to someone buying and restoring a historic property for home use for a minimum of five years. And the state sales tax was to be waived on building materials.[6]

The power of the tax incentive can be seen from its early days. Rehabilitation investment started at a level of $140 million in the beginning, in 1978, expanding to $2.4 billion in 1985 after use of the credit was enlarged in 1981.[7]

REFORM ZONING

Look at local zoning codes with an eye to how they can be streamlined and made to encourage rather than hinder Intown Living projects. A key reform will be to move away from suburban-level densities that many cities still have in their codes. To build a population base that will support lively commerce and transit, densities need to be increased. Codes in many places effectively have to be urbanized. And by zoning large areas for housing, land costs can be lowered, making city land more competitive with land in outlying areas. Whether property owners have to be compensated when land zoned commercial is changed to housing is a question; you have to ask if it isn't selling, perhaps it's overvalued in the first place.

Again using Denver as an example, its downtown code was established in 1956 and emphasized commercial development, setting up roadblocks for residential growth. The city modified its zoning in the 1990s to include incentives to encourage housing, so that only by including housing in a project would maximum density be allowed, for instance. They have also adopted design guidelines and provide for variances to overcome building and fire codes of an earlier time.[8]

In our Houston example, a building setback requirement was dropped in favor of having buildings come to the sidewalk, a more urban standard. Likewise, codes should encourage commerce on the street and not allow blank, opaque streetfronts. Andres Duany, Elizabeth Plater-Zyberk, and Jeff Speck argue that most city zoning codes focus on numbers and ratios rather than on physical form, that is, what buildings will look like. They would base city codes on a building's volume, articulation, and relationship to the street—its building type. They would legislate height by numbers of floors and forget the traditional Floor Area Ratio (FAR) standard that governs lot coverage. The emphasis would be on what is wanted rather than the opposite, a prescriptive rather than proscriptive approach. A related question is whether a city wants to enact a design code.[9]

Another area to look at is the parking requirement. Developers in a number of our case examples (Minneapolis, Portland, Vancouver for instance) are reducing the amount of parking in their buildings as they discover their young target market requires less garage space. One building in downtown Portland, as we report, has bike spaces only. A developer in Minneapolis is thinking about reducing parking in a project and encouraging the shared car approach. In some cities there is a "flexi car" program where, for a small one-time fee, you register when and for how long you want to use a car and it's provided. It is offered in San Francisco and Washington, D.C., among other cities.

A real estate developer in Berkeley, California, Patrick Kennedy, writing in *UrbanEcologist,* says, "Most cities have ordinances that thwart the very kinds of developments they desire. In my experience, there are three particular areas of local zoning law that are most often used by city staff, opposition groups, and others to kill worthy projects." He cites density, parking, and open space requirements as potential hindrances.[10]

ENCOURAGE REHABILITATIONS

Here, too, standards of an earlier time intended for new construction can put up stumbling blocks to the desired objective of adding housing in and near downtowns. New Jersey is a leader here, adopting in 1997 a Rehabilitation Code that since has been adopted by others, such as Maryland and Wilmington, Delaware. The code puts rehabilitation on a par with new construction in the regulatory realm. The problem is that most existing codes set standards for safety and space that older buildings can't meet. Examples include requiring halls to be 48 inches wide where an old building has 38-inch corridors, or calling for stair widths of 36 inches in an old house where they are 24 inches. Since going into effect, the new code has resulted in a boom in rehabilitation projects in New Jersey, pushing spending for such projects in the state's largest cities up 60 percent in the first year it was in effect.[11]

TAKE STEPS TO TAME TRAFFIC

As many have written, we've spent the last fifty years giving over not only our countryside but our cities as well to the car, where they can take up half the available square footage. To make cities livable and walkable means reversing this and placing the pedestrian's interests ahead of or at least on a par with the motorist's, radical as this notion is.

It can be done in many ways: rerouting through traffic and truck routes away from the center city, reducing lanes (by providing angle parking as in the Cotswold plan for Houston or just adding parking altogether), placing plantings in the middle of streets, installing streetcars, lowering speed limits, putting in rumble strips, stenciling in bike lanes, and dropping one-way pairings. Several cities have boldly torn down or removed highways, most notably Boston and Portland, Oregon.

REDUCE CRIME AND CIVIC DISORDER

As Daniel Kemmis, onetime mayor of Missoula, Montana, writes in *The Good City and the Good Life,* ". . . the steady rise in violence, so often perpetrated by teenagers or young adults, has contributed more than any other single factor to the flight of the affluent and the middle classes from central cities."[12]

Reduction of crime is the single change from the late 1980s and early 1990s that has made the biggest difference in cities. It makes Intown Living possible. With the prosperity of the 1990s and stepped-up policing, most famously in New York City under Mayor Rudy Guiliani's first police chief, William Bratton, city crimes have fallen sharply. The overall number of serious crimes is down in the United States 22 percent since 1991, but because of population growth during the period, the crime rate was off 30.1 percent. The murder rate, for instance, in 2000 was the lowest since 1967, and down 43 percent from 1991.[13] In the nation's largest cities, the drop in crime has been even more dramatic—down by 59.4 percent since the peak year of 1991.[14]

We would add that police and their Business Improvement District allies must tend to the so-called small stuff, the graffiti, the trash, broken bottles, abandoned cars, aggressive panhandling, and other signs of disorder. This is the "broken window" approach to policing. On assignment in Paterson, New Jersey, we saw firsthand the tendency of a police department, no doubt for budget reasons, to concentrate on the large crime issues, drugs and gangs for instance, at the expense of graffiti and other visible signs of breakdown in public order.

EXPLORE SMART GROWTH REFORMS

Cities should look into some of the programs under the Smart Growth movement as they might relate to Intown Living. Bruce Katz of the Brookings Institution identifies five reforms, all beginning at the state government level, as constituting the Smart Growth movement. They are: metropolitan gover-nance, growth management, land use reforms/land acquisition, control over infrastructure spending, and tax sharing.

Examples of the first reform, leading to regional governmental approaches, are most prominent in Portland, Oregon, and Minneapolis. As we report, there is the Greater Portland Metropolitan Service District over-seeing such activities as the regional land planning and transportation. In the Minneapolis area, regional functions such as sewage treatment and transportation are under a Metropolitan Council. Whether such initiatives could help other cities, and would be politically feasible, can be looked into, as well as whether and how they might assist an Intown Living effort.

A number of states have adopted comprehensive planning reforms, with Oregon enacting the earliest and most comprehensive as we discuss in our Portland chapter. These efforts, also in Tennessee, require counties to adopt land use plans that designate growth boundaries of cities and establish rural preservation areas. Counties not complying lose out on state funds. Areas planning collaboratively receive priority in state spending.

There are a number of states with one version or another of open-space land acquisition programs. Where this happens, it too seals off land areas from potential development and helps to refocus on cities or older suburbs.

Another reform enacted in a number of states, with Maryland and New Jersey leading the way, restricts infrastructure spending to designated areas. State road, sewer, and school funds, for instance, are steered away from areas outside what are called in Maryland "priority funding areas." Such policy also helps the refocus on cities, as do programs that direct state infrastructure spending on older communities.

Tax sharing such as is practiced in the Twin Cities area of Minnesota is probably a stretch for most areas. It has 40 percent of the incremental rise in property tax revenues from commercial and industrial development placed in a regional pool, which is then redistributed to communities in inverse proportion to net commercial tax capacity.[15]

Cities interested in promoting Intown Living should promote adoption or expansion of these initiatives, which make sense from a residential perspective.

Gazetteer

Here we summarize articles that describe the Intown Living phenomenon in various cities in North America beyond our eight case examples. They were selected for a range of city size and geography and to illustrate some of the different types of housing as well as examples of the creative financing taking place. In each item, the primary sources are listed.

BIRMINGHAM, ALABAMA

In this suburban-style city, where wooded suburbs lie just minutes from downtown, there wouldn't seem to be much prospect for intown residential projects. Yet in 1998, there were already fourteen buildings with apartments and six more projects under way, creating a total of 236 center city residences.

Initially the units were rental apartments, but as the market became established, ownership increased to where fully 45 percent were acquired and mostly owner-occupied. Live/work space was involved for some, such as in an old furniture warehouse where studios as well as living space housed a photographer, a film editor, and an advertising firm.

Developers then began tackling some of the taller old office building stock in the downtown, such as the John Hand Building, a twenty-one-story former bank. It, together with three others at the corner of First Avenue North and 21st Street, were the city's first skyscrapers. It was bought at auction in 1997 for $1.45 million. Above new space for the

Bank of Birmingham were to be offices on floors four to seven, while floors eight to nineteen were to be condominiums and the top two floors, an athletic club. The conversion was to cost $10 million.

Another conversion taking place was in the Watts Building, bought for just $327,000 in 1995. With the help of a low-interest loan from the city, renovation was under way in 1998 for a combination of offices and rental apartments ranging in size from 880 square feet to penthouses with 2,540 square feet and renting for $2,300.[1]

BRIDGEPORT, CONNECTICUT

An innovative nonprofit agency based in Minneapolis, which creates live/work space for artists, was set to tackle the conversion of Read's department store here in 2001. Artspace Inc. owns and operates twelve such artists' buildings, generally historic conversions, offering below-market space for artists (see Hartford on page 244).

Funding had been lined up to create sixty-four housing units, at a cost of $11.5 million, including a low-interest loan for $2.74 million and low-income and historic tax credits of $8 million. Foundations and local businesses contributed another $540,000. The city acquired the building by eminent domain, along with other parcels, and was to transfer it to Artspace for $1, obviously a key to making the numbers work.

The facade was to be retained, while a large gallery space was to be located on the first floor. The Read conversion was to team with the renovation of a nearby rundown hotel and arcade to form the nucleus of a cluster of shops, restaurants, and offices.

Within the Read, one-bedroom units will be 1,100 square feet in size, the two-bedrooms units will have 1,300 square feet, and the three-bedrooms units will have 1,600 square feet. The rents, which are pegged to the artists' income, will range from a low of $260 a month up to $820.

Helping to set the stage for the Read project has been a succession of new projects in downtown Bridgeport over the years, including a community college relocating to downtown in 1997, the opening of a minor league ballpark (for the Bridgeport Bluefish) in the next year, and the presence of the Polka Dot Playhouse, relocated into a remodeled bank building. An ice hockey rink was nearly completed in 2001 also.[2]

CAMDEN, NEW JERSEY

This city, New Jersey's poorest, has all the urban ills of our time—poverty, crime, homelessness, abandoned buildings, political corruption (three mayors indicted in ten years)—you name it and Camden probably has it.

Into this picture in August 2003, the first middle-class residents on the Delaware River began settling into the 341-unit Victor, an apartment carved from the old RCA Nipper Building. Rents range from as low as $775 for a studio and $975 to $1,400 for one-bedroom units, up to $2,100 for two bedrooms. Seventy-five units were leased in summer 2003, although the conversion was not to be done until February 2004.

Developer Carl Dranoff, a veteran of downtown conversions across the river in Philadelphia, hopes his seventy-second project will be a catalyst for the city. He took over the building in 1999 after it stood vacant for eleven years, a six-story hulk recalling the city's glory days as a manufacturing center. It is a National Register building, making historic preservation tax credits a part of the equation, dictating that the residential be rental for the prescribed five years, after which it could turn condominium.

Financing for the $58 million project was complicated, arranged by Fleet Bank. The bank and two others provided $30 million, the casino authority committed $9 million for environmental cleanup, among other things, $8 million in cut-rate funding came from the port authority, and another $11 million came from Dranoff and a New York investment firm.

The first residents will have no retail or restaurants next door, although a nearby aquarium expansion promises same. Due in November 2003 were an in-house grocery, dry cleaner, and other services.

There is transportation of varied sorts across and up the river, but venturing into Camden itself is a bit dicey. One middle-aged resident allowed as to how she would not be walking around the streets, and she would drive a carefully chosen route to her work.

Features at the Victor are to include a lobby of slate, an atrium courtyard in the center, twenty-four-hour concierge, conference rooms, a theater, and a fitness center in the building's tower, from which are commanding views.

The building was named, incidentally, for the RCA logo of Nipper the dog listening to the Victrola (a record-player, for those under a certain age), depicted in stained-glass windows in the tower's top.

The State of New Jersey has pledged to pump $175 million into beleaguered Camden over three years. If the Victor succeeds, don't be surprised if in ten years you are reading stories about the comeback of Camden.[3]

CHARLOTTE, NORTH CAROLINA

A survey in 2002 found twenty residential projects in the downtown here, ranging in size from a condominium with fifteen units to an apartment project with 450. The spurt in downtown residential here was said to have been especially strong in the late 1990s, cooling off a bit but continuing in the early 2000s.

The buyers and renters are described as young professionals, first-time buyers as well as empty nesters. A restaurant, nightlife, and museum scene in the downtown contributed to building the population to 7,390 in 2002, up from 5,523 seven years earlier. Charlotte Center City Partners was predicting the total would reach 8,600 as this was written in 2003. Parks are also part of the equation.

Looming ahead, Johnson & Wales University is to open a Gateway Village campus in fall 2004, stimulating demand for student and faculty housing. Additional parks are planned in two downtown wards, and publicly owned land along the north-south spine street, Tryon, is to have shops and offices with residential above. A grocery store was to have opened in summer 2003 in a retail area, and there's a downtown arena in the works as well.

Observers trace the residential growth to 1994 when a developer, Jim Gross, bought the venerable Ivey's department store and converted it to condominiums. Bank of America, with headquarters here, then followed with two condominiums of its own. Prices were such that developers were saying they couldn't find land where affordable housing would work. Bank of America Community Development then bought some land and made it available at a bargain price to make housing projects feasible for entry-level buyers and working-class families.[4]

CHICAGO, ILLINOIS

It's not just housing that is being built in and near downtown Chicago, but it is high-end properties that are being offered. Two venerable hotels, the Blackstone on South Michigan Avenue with views of the lake and the Ambassador West on the north shore, are being converted to luxury condominiums.

Two new projects are also being developed along Lake Shore Drive, at 65 East Goethe where units sold for $3 million to $5 million, and 840 Lake Shore Drive, seventy-three units, with prices from $1.5 million to $9 million.

"This is Brave New World territory for Chicago," a downtown Realtor was quoted. Where three years ago there were twenty-five residences selling for above $2 million, in 2001 the number grew to forty-five. And in 2002, fourteen such properties were under contract and another 121 were on the market.

The buyers are said to be both empty nesters and young couples already downtown trading up. One broker said their statistics put it that one in every four buyers was moving in from the suburbs.

In 2002 the renovation of the Blackstone Hotel, built in 1908, was under way at an estimated cost of $120 million and whose condominiums were to sell for $3.4 million to $8.5 million. And at the Ambassador West, 25 percent of the converted condominiums sold at prices from $1.2 million to $2.5 million before construction began.

In the Lincoln Park neighborhood, north of the Gold Coast along Lake Michigan, another phenomenon was occurring: the construction of new mansions. In the last half of the 1990s, dozens of palatial residences were built, containing 6,000 square feet and more, where there had been hardly any construction of this type in the center city for years. The purchasers are said to be couples and families in their thirties and early forties who made money in the boom economy of the time.[5]

CLEVELAND, OHIO

It's been fifty years since this industrial city has had the fastest-growing anything, but now its downtown is among the leaders in population growth. While the city overall had another population decline from 1990 to 2000, 27,000 in number and 5.3 in percentage terms, over 3,000 moved into the core.

The census found a downtown population of 8,105, up 51 percent from the 5,367 of ten years earlier. Further, there's growth on the city's east side, propelled by the Cleveland Clinic and University Hospitals there. The West Side also has census tracts reflecting an influx of new, young residents and empty nesters.

To insure that the trend continues, Mark Rosentraub, a dean at Cleveland State University, recommends that the city become more "developer-friendly," not necessarily offering incentives, but insuring that its permitting and policies don't deflect new housing to other areas. Further, he writes, there's no need for concern about displacement. Cleveland once had more than 900,000 living there, while now it is down to just over 500,000, meaning there's space for growth. Rosentraub acknowledges that gaining several thousand new residents in the downtown does not mean the city has turned the corner and will start growing. Rather, he sees it as an opportunity to build on.[6]

Meanwhile, Cleveland's historic Warehouse District is a classic story of urban regeneration. The area had steadily declined, and city efforts to pump new life into it had not succeeded as of 1990. Two lawyers turned developers, John Carney and Bob Rains, formed Landmark Management Ltd., to redevelop the underused buildings located just feet from Public Square in the heart of the city.

Their first project was tackling the City Mission, converting a homeless shelter to market-rate housing. A decade later, the firm has developed fifteen buildings into 540 market-rate apartments, a 180-room hotel, parking, and first-floor retail. The district as a whole enjoyed a resurgence during the 1990s and in 2001 had over 1,000 apartments, white table-cloth restaurants and trendy bars making it a major entertainment district. Total investment in the area is $133 million.

Helping the conversions were historic preservation tax credits as the district was on the National Register of Historic Places. Significant city help was forthcoming, using an array of federal programs such as an urban development action grant (UDAG), community development block grant, and Section 108 loans as well as its own Neighborhood Development Fund. A consortium of local companies called the Cleveland Development Fund, set up to spur local development, also played a role with gap funding.

A survey in 1995 found that the Warehouse District was 60 percent male, median age 35, making $75,000 a year, and most were college graduates.[7]

DENVER, COLORADO

The story of the revival of the Lower Downtown neighborhood here— LoDo—can be traced to the mid-1980s when the bottom fell out of the oil market and downtown suffered. The upside was that real estate values dropped, too, making possible the acquisition of warehouses and other properties downtown on the cheap, setting up their eventual conversion.

The process started in the late 1980s and proceeded, with many a political battle, recalls former Mayor Federico Pena, until the area became the site of the Coors Field baseball stadium in 1995, firmly establishing its prominence.

The population downtown is put at 4,230, up 51 percent from 1990, but still too small in the view of some to sustain varied retail. Too many sports bars is how one resident sees it. The population that is here is said to be young, late twenties and thirties, with the money necessary to buy what may well be their first home. Their social life takes place in LoDo as well.

The area also has offices and small businesses, which is characteristic of downtown in general.[8]

HARTFORD, CONNECTICUT

The goal here is to add 1,000 units of market-rate housing in the downtown, to combine with other initiatives such as redevelopment of the riverfront, to breathe new life into a city deserted by the middle class where private developers have not invested since the 1980s. This is part of an initiative of Gov. Rowland called the Six Pillars Revitalization Plan for Hartford, the state capitol.

One project, restoring the Goodwin mansion located near the University of Connecticut campus in the well-to-do West End, was moving toward completion in early 2003. Another ambitious undertaking was planned for the old Colt Armory factory complex along the river and was under way in 2003.

The Goodwin is to have seven high-end flats in the mansion and fifty-six new townhomes on the estate, each with three bedrooms in what is the first new upper-end residential development in downtown Hartford in twenty years. There will be ten acres of unspoiled meadows and wetlands surrounding the project.

The former Colt Armory complex, twelve buildings beside the Connecticut River, dates to the 1850s and is part of a historic district. It was bought for $5.7 million in early 2003 by a residential developer. The buildings contain 700,000 square feet of space, and they were partially occupied by a variety of tenants at the time of the sale, including artists and small manufacturers. The plan is to invest $110 million in a conversion of most of the buildings into a residential complex that will contain three hundred apartments, 650 to 1,400 square feet in size, plus a number of somewhat larger lofts. Office, retail, and restaurants were to be included. The Colt project was pegged to a long-delayed mixed-use project nearby, Adriaen's Landing, to consist of residences, retail, a hotel and entertainment venues now under way.

Meanwhile, Artspace Inc. of Minneapolis (see Bridgeport) converted an abandoned 1910 building into forty-three artists' live/work apartments. The 84,000-square-foot building cost $6.5 million to renovate, and it opened successfully in 1998 fully rented and as a for-profit enterprise. Rents are charged at what percentage of the city's median income the artist earns.[9]

MIAMI, FLORIDA

Lofts are said to be hip and funky, and no matter that most of them are new construction, they are booming in South Florida.

A few are, in fact, in former industrial buildings, such as the Terminal Loft, where artists live and work, and the Parc, a twenty-eight-unit condominium in the performing arts district. Lofts are being built meanwhile in Miami Beach, Fort Lauderdale, Kendall, and elsewhere as well as downtown Miami. For instance, a five-story building with 111 units, the Meridian, was planned for Miami Beach and would be that section's largest.

Most of what is being offered features luxury amenities along with the open-space, high-ceiling look. Prices start at the mid-$100,000 range and reach $2.5 million. On Biscayne Boulevard in Miami are various twenty-six-story and thirty-nine-story buildings being marketed as lofts.

A project along the Miami River called Neo Lofts, the project of a 28-year-old developer named Lissette Calderon, sold most of its 199 units in a few months. The buyers were mostly young professionals, including artists, lawyers, hairdressers, and models. Says Calderon: "It takes a certain person to love a loft. Lofts are hip and funky. But they are also functional."[10]

PHILADELPHIA, PENNSYLVANIA

Center City Philadelphia is an anomaly. It is growing as the city overall gradually declines. It is overwhelmingly white in a city increasingly Hispanic and black. It is a middle-class stronghold while fully 70 percent of the population of the region lives in the suburbs and beyond, a larger portion than ever, the 2000 census found.

"Downtown rentals are going through the roof," read a story in *The Philadelphia Inquirer* in August 2001. "Moving to Philadelphia? Good luck. Occupancy is 95 percent," it added. By section, the occupancy rates recorded in the census ranged from 86 percent in Chinatown to 97 percent in the newly hot Northern Liberties section.

The two Center City census tracts had nearly 50,000 residents in 2000, up 4,241 from 1990, growing by 10 percent or so while the city as a whole lost 68,000 people or 4 percent. The striking thing about Center City is its composition: Center City East is 75 percent white, 12 percent Asian, and 9 percent black. Its counterpart on the west is 82 percent white, 8 percent Asian, and 7 percent black. This in a city that as a whole is 45 percent white, 43 percent black.

Beyond the population numbers are real estate prices, which the Center City District and Central Philadelphia Development Corporation say increased overall by 16 percent in the second half of the 1990s. Analysis by zip code had increases in Center City of variously 56 to 81 percent between 1995 and 2000.

And the beat goes on. A story in *The Philadelphia Inquirer* of June 2003 tells us that "Center City apartments are still in high demand." Pushed by a ten-year tax abatement program enacted in 1997, numerous old industrial and office buildings downtown have been converted to apartments. The estimate is that since 1997, as many as five thousand new apartments have come on the market in Center City, according to the Center City District, an economic development agency. Occupancy remains at 95 percent.

Northern Liberties was a perennially dilapidated neighborhood to the north of Center City that became so hot it was pricing people out of the market, into the next neighborhood, Fishtown. Recalled one resident who got in early, in 1986, "It was a ghost town." Now rents start at $750 a month for one-bedroom apartments. The boom in the area is said to have started around 1999, and it was 25-year-olds who began the move into the area. Part of the appeal was a popular club, the 700 Club, and Ortleib's Jazzhouse.[11]

PITTSBURGH, PENNSYLVANIA

The largest housing project since World War II was taking shape on an old industrial dump beside the Monongahela River on the affluent eastern side of the city in the early 2000s. Summerset is to be a self-contained residential community with 713 single-family homes, townhomes, and apartments. The project's price tag is $243 million and involves clearing a slag dump left from the days when Pittsburgh's blast furnaces manufactured steel along the river.

While under site preparation, the project had already attracted a waiting list of five hundred, the developer, Rubinoff Co., reported. One of the attractions besides the river views is nearby Frick Park, one of the city's oldest attractions. The cleanup includes tackling a polluted stream that runs though the property. The watershed improvements will add 130 acres to the park.

The offerings were to feature houses with two to five bedrooms, ranging in price from $180,000 to $375,000. Each home is to have a two-car garage. The project is to be built in three phases over an estimated ten years, with construction beginning in winter 2002, after tons of dirt were dumped on the site. The first phase was to cost $42 million.[12]

RICHMOND, VIRGINIA

About 1,200 apartments had come on the market in downtown Richmond between 1995 and 1999, city officials and private developers say. They anticipated the trend would continue in the years ahead. Renovated spaces were renting in the $800 to $1,200 range by and large, although some one-bedroom flats could be obtained for $500.

The market: Young people (twenties to forties), graduate students, medical students, interns, and residents from the Medical College of Virginia, generally from outside the city. One apartment survey determined that 85 percent come from outside Richmond, with half working downtown and the other half reverse commuting.

One developer, aided by tax abatement benefits and Virginia Housing Development Authority tax credits, was putting together a different type of project in an old Richmond Dairy building. Most units were to be affordable, in the $425 to $625 range, appealing to entry-level workers, working students, the elderly, and support workers at nearby facilities.

There's an arts scene along Broad Street, with apartments over galleries and a theater. Otherwise, the downtown was said to be having trouble filling up office space, with retail also lagging, although interest on the part of delis, shops, and small restaurants was picking up in 2000.[13]

SEATTLE, WASHINGTON

Close to the center of downtown Seattle with its concentration of office towers is a wildly successful apartment project, Harbor Steps. Begun in the mid-1990s when there was thought to be little demand for downtown housing, this project was renting out twenty-five-story towers in just months. In all, Harbor Steps was to have four towers containing 730 apartments plus office and retail space overlooking steps leading to the famed Pike Place market and the waterfront.

The first twenty-five-story towers moved so fast despite high rents that the schedule of the next two towers, seventeen stories each, was speeded up. Hard-hat tours were being given in spring 2000 to prospective renters, with opening set for later that year. Rents have jumped since the first apartments were leased in 1994, studios going from $683 to $955 in 1998 and to $1,100 by 2000. Comparable increases have been experienced across the board, with two-bedroom units, for instance, going from $1,437 up to $2,680 just six years later. Harbor Steps was said to be 98 percent occupied at the end of the decade in its first towers, which contain 454 apartments.

Stimson Bullitt, the chairman of Harbor Properties, began assembling the land for Harbor Steps in the 1970s, when the area consisted of run-down bars, flophouses, and the like. The property was cheap, but Bullitt thought that since it was in the center of the city, "the area had a good future." He relates that he couldn't get construction loans at first, that bankers just "rolled their eyeballs toward the ceiling." After the first building did so well, further financing was easier.

Another developer, Continental-Bentall, was building a comparable product in 2000, Westlake Tower, with 366 apartments. And there were also low-rise buildings felt to be ripe for redevelopment. The firm is a subsidiary of the Bentall Corporation of Vancouver, British Columbia.[14]

ST. LOUIS, MISSOURI

A dozen or so former office buildings and warehouses along and near Washington Avenue have been or are in the process of being converted to apartments as well as condominiums. The street once housed the headquarters of the city's apparel and footwear companies, who began to leave ten to fifteen years ago. The departures drove down real estate prices to a level where residential conversions became feasible, especially when backed by federal and state historic tax credits amounting to a combined 45 percent of development costs. As of 2001, 280 lofts had been put on the market and another 1,800 were under construction or planned.

This work marks the first real residential population in the center city for St. Louis, which even in the 1950s did not have many people living in the city. This made the first condominium project in the area somewhat of a risk. But the 10th Street Lofts just off Washington, offering thirty-one for-sale units, had an open house in September 1999. Two thousand people showed up. Fifteen units were sold in one day, and the rest were purchased within six weeks.

This led to another, larger condominium project, Terra Cotta Lofts, in the General American Life Insurance Building, which was to provide ninety-eight units in the $120,000 to $175,000 range. As of mid-2001, twenty-five were sold and the first move-in set for early 2002. The city, meanwhile, seeing this spurt of investment, was to contribute $17.5 million in streetscape improvements, which will, among other things, double the width of the sidewalks along Washington.

Historic Restoration Inc. of New Orleans bought the block-long Merchandise Market Building, which it was to convert to 219 rental apartments. The firm previously invested $250 million to renovate two long-vacant hotels at the eastern edge of the redeveloping Washington Avenue area, to become Marriott Renaissance hotels near the city's convention center.[15]

WASHINGTON, D.C.

The area east of DuPont Circle to Logan Circle is an example of explosive middle-class gentrification. The census numbers 1990 to 2000 begin to tell the story, but inasmuch as data was collected in April 2000, it is out of date by three years as this is written, in a most dynamic marketplace.

First, the numbers from the seven census tracts that run from DuPont Circle east to 11th Street Northwest and between Florida Avenue on the north and Massachusetts Avenue Northwest along the southern boundary. The total population grew by just 522 in ten years, but the composition changed dramatically. The white population was up by 2,498, and correspondingly, the black population was down by 3,985 (of a total of 27,949). And this includes two tracts where the white population is still relatively small, namely the two easternmost areas.

Overwhelmingly, the census reported, this was a young population. The 25-to-34-year-old age group is generally twice as large as any other bracket in the largely white districts. For instance, 1,491 aged 25 to 34 versus 692 people aged 35 to 44 in a sample tract. Per-capita incomes are well above the city average of $28,659. Three of the tracts have per-capita incomes above $50,000.

A Fannie Mae study in 2002 entitled "Housing in the Nation's Capital" described the Logan area as a "booming home ownership market, up 33 percent from 1990-to-2000."[16] Average home sale prices went from $98,500 in 1994 to $144,200 in 2002, up 46 percent, and the median income of homebuyers was $80,000.

Further, in the downtown area south of Massachusetts Avenue we have a transformation described as "truly remarkable because of its speed and scope," in the phrase of *Washington Post* urban columnist Roger Lewis. "Eastern downtown intermingles places to live, shop, dine, engage in cultural pursuits, and, last but not least, play and be entertained. A vibrant, pedestrian-oriented neighborhood is taking shape in which one could reside comfortably without owning an automobile," he wrote further. The housing being built is encouraged by significant incentives from the city, according to the Downtown DC Business Improvement District.[17]

Notes

PREFACE

1. Myron Orfield, *Metro Politics,* Washington, D.C., Brookings Institution Press, 1997.
2. *The New York Times Almanac,* 2003, p. 263.

CHAPTER 1: INTRODUCTION

1. Patricia Gay, *Preservation in Print,* Sept. 1995, New Orleans: Preservation Resource Center.
2. Richard Moe, "Civil Codes," *Preservation,* The National Trust for Historic Preservation, Washington, D.C., Sept./Oct. 2000.
3. Steve Belmont, *Cities in Full: Recognizing and Realizing the Great Potential of Urban America* (Chicago: Planners Press, American Planning Association, 2002), pp. 213, 451.
4. Real Estate Research Corp., "The Costs of Sprawl," Washington, D.C.: U.S. Government Printing Office, 1974.
5. Robert Putnam, *Bowling Alone: The Collapse and Revival of American Community* (New York: Simon and Schuster, 2000), p. 27.
6. Quoted in *Downtown Inc.: How America Rebuilds Cities* by Bernard Freiden and Lynne Sagalyn (Cambridge, Mass.: MIT Press, 1989), p. 208.
7. Roberta Brandes Gratz with Norman Mintz, *Cities Back From the Edge: New Life for Downtown* (New York: Preservation Press/John Wiley & Sons Inc., 1998), pp. 302, 316.

8. David Brooks, *BOBOS** (**Being Bourgeois Bohemians*) *in Paradise: The New Upper Class and How They Got That Way* (New York: Simon and Schuster, 2002), p. 104.

9. Jane Jacobs, *The Death and Life of Great American Cities* (New York: Vintage Books, 1963) pp. 29–30.

10. Jane Jacobs, ibid. pp. 50–54.

11. Allan B. Jacobs, *Great Streets* (Cambridge, Mass.: MIT Press, 1993).

12. Steve Belmont, op. cit., p. 10.

13. Quoted in Roberta Brandes Gratz with Norman Mintz, op. cit., p. 329.

14. Ibid., p. 343.

15. Steve Belmont, op. cit., p. 238.

16. Richard Moe and Carter Wilkie, *Changing Places: Rebuilding Community in the Age of Sprawl* (New York: Henry Holt & Co., 1997), p. 83.

17. Roberta Brandes Gratz, op. cit., p. 107.

CHAPTER 2: BACKGROUND

1. Good summaries about what happened to American cities can be found in, among other works: John Gunther, *Direction of Cities* (New York: Penguin Group, 1996); Robert M. Fogelson, *DOWNTOWN: Its Rise and Fall, 1880–1950* (New Haven, Conn.; Yale University Press, 2001); John Norquist, *The Wealth of Cities: Revitalizing the Centers of American Life* (Reading, Mass.: Addison-Wesley, 1998); Witold Rybczynski, *City Life: Urban Expectations in a New World* (New York: Scribner, 1995), and Robert Fishman, *Bourgeois Utopias: The Rise and Fall of Suburbia* (New York: Basic Books Inc., 1987). To our minds, these works contain the classic telling of the how and why of true suburbs and their deterioration into today's cul-de-sacs. There's also *Suburban Nation: The Rise of Sprawl and the Decline of the American Dream* by Andres Duany, Elizabeth Plater-Zyberk, and Jeff Speck (New York: North Point Press, 2000), which has a brilliant analysis of recent urban history, but a limited solution, namely building better-designed subdivisions that mimic aspects of cities. If we have to have subdivisions, and we do, let them be better. But it still means new development outside core cities, towns, and traditional suburbs.

2. Bruce Katz, "Smart Growth: The Future of the American Metropolis?", Centre for Analysis of Social Exclusion, London School of Economics, UK, July 2002, p. 4.

3. James Howard Kunstler, *The Geography of Nowhere: The Rise and Decline of America's Man-Made Landscape* (New York: Simon & Schuster, 1993), p. 10.

4. Peter Blake, *God's Own Junkyard* (New York: Holt, Rinehart and Winston, 1964).

5. Haya El Nasser and Paul Overberg, "Towns in the Suburbs Spurt to Big-City Status," *USA Today,* Nov. 20, 1997, p. 5A.

6. Robert Fishman, *Bourgeois Utopias* (New York: Basic Books, 1987).

7. Robert Lang and Patrick Simmons, "Boomburgs: The Emergence of Large, Fast-Growing Suburban Cities in the United States," FannieMae Foundation Census Note 06, June 2001.

8. Timothy Egan, "Urban Sprawl Strains Western States," *The New York Times,* Dec. 29, 1996, p. 1.

9. The Brookings Institution, summary, "Growth in the Heartland," Dec. 9, 2002.

10. Stephen A. Holmes, "Leaving the Suburbs for Rural Areas—Hint of Racial Tension Behind a Widespread White Movement," *The New York Times*, Oct. 19, 1997, p. 34.

11. Bruce Katz, op. cit., p. 27.

12. William L. Hamilton, "The New Mall Lineup Includes Housing," *The Minneapolis Star-Tribune*, March 2, 2002, p. H7.

13. Arnold Berke, "The Bishop in the City," *Preservation*, March/April 1997, p. 53.

14. Jonathan Salant, "A Workweek Idling in Traffic," *The Philadelphia Inquirer*, May 2001, p. A20.

15. Jere Downs, "Area Ranks Eighth in Costs of Travel," *The Philadelphia Inquirer*, Dec. 11, 2000, p. B12.

16. Jane Holtz Kay, *Asphalt Nation: How the Automobile Took Over America and How We Can Take It Back*. (New York: Crown Publishers, 1997), p. 20.

17. Katherine Shaver, "The Road Too Much Travelled," *The Washington Post*, Jan. 27, 2003.

18. Katherine Shaver, "In the Car for Life," *The Washington Post*, April 20, 2003, p. C 1.

19. Patricia Leigh Brown, "In 'the Other California,' A Land Rush Continues—Commuters Go East for Cheaper Housing," *The New York Times*, Dec. 27, 2000, p. A10.

20. Lyndsey Layton, "Mass Transit Rules the Roads," *The Washington Post*, April 17, 2001, p. 1.

21. "Relationship between Urban Sprawl and Physical Activity, Obesity, and Morbidity," *American Journal of Health Promotion*; *Measuring the Health Effects of Sprawl* (Surface Transportation and Policy Project and Smart Growth America).

22. Lori Montgomery, "Suburbia's Road to Weight Gain," *The Washington Post*, Jan. 21, 2001, p. C 1.

23. Laura Pappano, *The Connection Gap: Why Americans Feel So Alone*. (New Brunswick, N.J.: Rutgers University Press: 2001), p. 75.

24. Jane Brody column, "Suburbs Breed Sedentary Lifestyle," *The Houston Chronicle*, Oct. 22, 2000.

25. Martha T. Moore, "Walk/Can't Walk—The Way Cities and Suburbs are Developed Could Be Bad for Your Health," *USA Today*, April 23, 2003, p. 1.

26. Ibid.

27. Center for Science in the Public Interest, *Nutrition Action*, Jan./Feb. 2001.

28. Abby Ellin, "Shed Some Pounds (and Get a Bonus)," *The New York Times*, Aug. 10, 2003, p. 12.

29. William L. Hamilton, "How Suburban Design Is Failing Teen-Agers," *The New York Times*, May 6, 1999, pp. 1, 4.

30. Sara Rimer, "An Aging Nation Ill-Equipped for Hanging Up the Car Keys," *The New York Times*, Dec. 15, 1997, p. 1.

31. Carey Goldberg, "Real-Space Meetings Fill In the Cyberspace Gaps," *The New York Times*, Feb. 25, 1997, p. A12.

32. Sith Schiesel, "The PC Generation, Back to the Board," *The New York Times*, April 10, 2003.

33. Robert Putnam, *Bowling Alone: The Collapse and Revival of American Community,* (New York: Simon & Schuster, 2000).

34. Neal Pierce column, "Committed Foundations: Smart Growth's Ace in the Hole," Retrieved from the World Wide Web on Dec. 29, 2002.

35. Andrew Jacobs, "McGreevey, Environmental Soldier, Enlists in the 'War on Sprawl,'" *The New York Times,* Jan. 2, 2003, p. B5.

36. Steve Adubato, "On 'Smart Growth,' Public Not Too Bright," *The Press of Atlantic City* (N.J.), June 1, 2003, F 5.

37. Lori Montgomery, "Maryland Land-Use Weapon Backfires," *The Washington Post,* May 14, 2000, pp. C 1, 5.

38. Peter Whoriskey, "Density Limits Only Add To Sprawl," *The Washington Post,* March 9, 2003, p. 1.

39. Richard A. Oppel, Jr., "Efforts to Restrict Sprawl Find New Resistance From Advocates for Affordable Housing," *The New York Times,* Dec. 26, 2000, p. A 18.

40. Neal Peirce column, "Smart Growth in the Crosshairs," March 23, 2003, http://www.npeirce@citistates.com.

41. Robert Fishman, "The American Metropolis at Century's End: Past and Future Influences," FannieMae Foundation, *Housing Facts & Findings,* May 14, 2000.

42. Robert Sharoff, "Putting That 'Great' Back in State Street," *The New York Times,* May 14, 2001, p. 31.

43. Amy Waldman, "In Harlem's Ravaged Heart, Revival" *The New York Times,* Feb. 18, p. 1, and Janny Scott, "White Flight, This Time Toward Harlem," *The New York Times,* Feb. 25, 2001, p. 19.

44. William L. Hamilton, "A Dot on a Map Connected By People," *The New York Times,* April 15, 1999, D 1.

45. Louis Jacobson, "Internet Business Boosts Cincinnati's Over-the-Rhine," *Planning,* August, 2000.

46. Joel Kotkin, "A Suburb Sees the Future In Its Old Downtown," *The New York Times,* Aug. 22, 1999, p. 6.

47. Andrew Jacobs, "Vibrant Area of Newark Suffers With Success," *The New York Times,* March 10, 2000, p. 1; Andrew Jacobs, "A Newly Cool Newark Says, 'C'mon Over!'" *The New York Times,* Nov. 24, 2000, p. B1; and Brent Staples, "No Longer the City That Fear Built, Newark Puts Its Fiery Riot Behind It," *The New York Times,* Nov. 21, 2002.

48. Ehrenkrantz Eckstut & Kuhn Architects, "Revitalizing Downtown Indianapolis," *Urban Solutions.* Issue 1. Newsletter published by Ehrenkrantz Eckstut & Kuhn.

49. Andrew Stone, "Community Is Reborn by Going Back to Its Roots," *USA Today,* Feb. 27, 1996, p. 4A.

50. Jacqueline L. Urgo, "Mill Town Recasts Itself," *The Philadelphia Inquirer,* Nov. 13, 2002, p. 1.

51. Robert L. Simison, "Detroit's Economic Revival May Stick—Mayor's Improved City Services Are Seen as Sustaining Boom," *The Wall Street Journal,* Jan. 10, 2003.

52. Mark Gordon, "Jacksonville Beach Is Drawing a New Crowd," *Florida Times-Union,* May 20, 2002.

53. Alan Berube and Benjamin Forman, "Living on the Edge: Decentralization Within Cities in the 1990's," The Brookings Institution, Center on Urban and Metropolitan Policy, October, 2002.

54. Paul Jargowsky, University of Texas at Dallas, "Stunning Progress, Hidden Problems: The Dramatic Decline of Concentrated Poverty in the 1990's," The Brookings Institution, May, 2003.

55. Joel Kotkin, "A Bit of a Chill For Hot Times In the Big City," The Washington Post, March 24, 2002, B-1.

56. Richard Florida, The Rise of the Creative Class and How It's Transforming Work, Leisure, Community and Everyday Life (New York: Basic Books, 2002), pp. 44–56.

57. Neal Peirce column, "Gays and Off-Beat Culture: Signal a City's Ready to Grow?," Retrieved from the World Wide Web on July 9, 2002.

58. Florida, op. cit., p. 217.

59. Oldenberg, Ray, The Great Good Place (New York: Marlowe & Company 1989, 1997).

60. Florida, op. cit., pp. 223–34, 246–47.

61. Bill Bishop and Richard Florida, "O, Give Me a Home Where the Like-Minded Roam," The Washington Post, March 23, 2003, p. B5.

62. Range Stacey, "Hip Cool Cities," Lansing (Mich.) State Journal, March 25, 2003.

63. Jim Carrier, "Party Animals Breathe Life Into a Long-Gone Area," The New York Times, Dec. 18, 1998, p. A26.

64. Mary Beth Marklein, "Come for a Diploma, Stay for Life," USA Today, April 23, 2003, p. 1.

65. "The New Spatial Order? Technology and Urban Development," Lincoln Institute of Land Policy, Cambridge, Mass., Nov. 9, 2000, pp. 4–34.

66. Evan Halper, "A Bohemian Rhapsody? 'Creative Class' of Artists Could Be Key to Cities' Economic Development," The Los Angeles Times, Sept. 14, 2002.

67. Steven Lagerfeld, "Where the Nerds Are," Preservation, Jan./Feb. 2001, p. 72.

68. Halper, op. cit.

69. Peter Hall, "Cycles of Creativity," Urban Age, Fall 1999, p. 13.

CHAPTER 3: ATLANTA

1. James Howard Kunstler, The City in Mind (New York: The Free Press, 2001), p. 63.

2. Joseph Skibell, "One Street at a Time," The New York Times, Retrieved from the World Wide Web on March 3, 2002, Travel Section.

3. Walter Woods, "Susan M. Mandheim," Business to Business, March 2001.

4. Midtown Neighbors' Association, e-mail March 10, 2003.

5. Tony Wilbert, "Venerable Law Firm Negotiates to Move," Atlanta Journal-Constitution, Jan. 21, 2003, p. D1.

6. Atlanta Journal-Constitution Ultimate Metro Atlanta Guide Book, 2001–2.

7. Fred Willard, Down on Ponce (Atlanta: Longstreet Press, 1997).

8. Atlanta Business Chronicle, Midtown Market Report, Oct. 25–31, 2002.

9. Walter Woods, "Wayne Clough's Vision: How He Brought Georgia Tech Back to Midtown," *Business to Business,* March 2001.

10. William Herbig, Trupti Kalbag, Amy Gore and Gaoxiang Luo, "Midtown Population and Housing, A Demographic Analysis of Midtown from 1990 to 2002," January 2002. Georgia Tech, graduate student paper.

11. David Pendred, "Intown Area's Pulse Strong," *Atlanta Journal Constitution,* Jan. 27, 2003.

12. *Worth* magazine online, May 2000.

13. Pendred, op. cit.

14. Ibid.

15. "Your Opinion Counts: Announcing Blueprint Midtown II," *Midtown Journal, Special Issue,* Summer 2003.

16. "Restaurants," *Atlanta,* October 2002, p. 304.

17. *Atlanta Journal-Constitution,* April 25, 2002.

18. "Downtown Dilemma: Liberals vs. the Homeless," *Creative Loafing,* January 23–29, 2002, p. 15.

19. Melissa Turner, "Making a University Connection," *Atlanta Journal-Constitution,* January 18, 1999, p F1, 2002, p. C9.

20. Michael Brick, "From an Old Mill Site to a New Urban Complex," *The New York Times,* Dec. 18, 2002, p. C9.

21. Robert Bullard, Glenn S. Johnson and Angel O. Torres, editors, *Sprawl City: Race, Politics and Planning in Atlanta.* (Washington, D.C.: Island Press, 2000), p. 8.

22. Editorial, "Zoning Groups Can Plan Interference," *Atlanta Journal-Constitution,* Aug. 17, 2003.

23. *The New York Times,* March 5, 2000.

24. Robert Bullard, Glenn S. Johnson and Angel O. Torres, op. cit.

25. *Atlanta Journal-Constitution,* June 29, 1999.

26. *Atlanta Journal-Constitution,* Dec. 9, 2002.

CHAPTER 4: DALLAS

1. Quoted in Daniel Kemmis, *The Good City and the Good Life: Renewing a Sense of Community* (Boston: Houghton Mifflin Company, 1995) p. 61.

2. Darwin Payne, *BIG D: Triumphs and Troubles* (Dallas: Three Forks Press, 2000).

3. Downtown Development District Market Data.

4. Huntley Paton, "Downtown Dallas' Awful Truth," *Dallas Business Journal,* March 16, 2001.

5. Jim Henderson, "Big D means Downtown," *Houston Chronicle,* Aug. 8, 1999, p. 1.

6. Preservation Dallas Web page, 2000.

7. DART Web page, Annual Report, 2001.

8. Downtown Improvement District "market data."

9. Payne, op. cit., pp. 496.

10. David Dillon, "Urban Salvage," *Dallas Morning News,* March 18, 1998.

11. Henderson, *Houston Chronicle,* op. cit.

12. Gail Thomas, *Pegasus* (Dallas: The Dallas Institute Publications, 1993), p. 1.

13. Ibid.

14. Downtown Improvement District, 2002 Annual Report.

15. *Dallas Morning News* editorial, Feb. 14, 2002.

16. *Dallas Morning News*, June 11, 2001.

17. Lisa Tanner, "Downtown Promoters Pushing City for More," *Dallas Business Journal*, April 19, 2002.

18. Henderson, *Houston Chronicle*, op. cit.

19. Amanda Bishop, "A 24-Hour Downtown?" *Dallas Business Journal*, May 7, 1999.

20. Huntley Patton, "Downtown Dallas Is Coming Back," *Dallas Business Journal*, Oct. 9, 1998.

21. David Dillon, "Shock of the NEW—The Downtown-Housing Boom has Forged Winners and Losers," *Dallas Morning News*, Jan. 14, 2001.

22. William McDonnell, *Dallas Rediscovered: A Photographic Chronicle of Urban Expansion 1870–1925*, (Dallas: Dallas Historical Society).

23. Mary Ann Esquinel and Jack Booth," Running Out of Time—State-Thomas Area Swallowed by Development" *Dallas Times-Herald*, June 29, 1986.

24. *Dallas Times-Herald*, Sept. 27, 1977.

25. Darwin Payne, op. cit.

26. "History of MATA'S Cars," no date.

27. Uptown Dallas Association, Inc.

28. "Next Great Neighborhoods," *Travel + Leisure*, June 2003, p. 68.

29. Uptown Dallas Association, Inc., "Update," Spring 2002, vol. 3, no. 1, p. 4.

30. Stephen Kinzer, "Dallas Has Its Cool Club Scene,"*The New York Times*, April 8, 2001, p. 8.

31. Steve Brown, "West End Awakening," Business section, *Dallas Morning News*, Feb. 28, 2003, p. 1, 10.

CHAPTER 5: HOUSTON

1. Ralph Bivens, "Retailers Build Like Mad," *Houston Chronicle*, Feb. 22, 2003, p. 1.

2. David Kaplan, "The Inner Loop: Clashing Visions of Urban Living," *Houston Chronicle*, April 8, 2001.

3. Ralph Bivens, *Houston Chronicle*, Feb. 22, 2003, op. cit.

4. Ralph Bivens, "Houston Neighborhood to Boast 'Main Street'-Style Retail Center," *Houston Chronicle*, March 27, 2002.

5. Kim Canon, "Spring Branch's Appeal on the Upswing," *Houston Chronicle*, October 11, 2001.

6. Mike Snyder, "'Smart Growth' Re-examines Sprawl," *Houston Chronicle*, March 19, 2000, op. cit.

7. Ken Hoffman, "Traffic Mess Can Drive You Insane," *Houston Chronicle*, Feb. 18, 2003, p. 1.

8. Ken Hoffman, "Embattled Road Warriors Weigh In on Traffic Woes," *Houston Chronicle*, Feb. 23, 2003.

9. Blueprint Houston Web site (www.blueprinthouston.org).

10. Mike Snyder, *Houston Chronicle*, March 19, 2000, op. cit.

11. Stephen L. Klineberg, Houston Area Survey (1982–2002), Rice University.

12. Allan Turner, "Preserving Historic Treasures—Tide Changing in Favor of Saving Landmarks," *Houston Chronicle,* July 16, 2000.

13. *The Great Houston Source Book,* Greater Houston Convention and Visitors Bureau, 2003.

14. Houston Downtown Management District, map "Above and Below Downtown," no date.

15. *Houston Post,* Nov. 11, 1984.

16. *Houston Chronicle,* Aug. 9, 1992.

17. Downtown Houston Management District, "Downtown Fact Sheet," no date.

18. Thompson Design Group Inc./EcoPLAN, *Buffalo Bayou and Beyond: Visions, Strategies, Actions for the 21st Century.* Note: The Waterfront Center in the persons of Ann Breen and Dick Rigby took part in the early stages of the plan development and previously did work for the Buffalo Bayou Partnership.

19. Debra Beachy, "New Roles for Historic Buildings," *The New York Times,* Mar. 15, 1998, Real Estate, p. 40.

20. John Williams, "Living Downtown—It May Not Be for Everyone, but a Lot of Weary Suburbanites Are Ready to Trade a Long Commute for a Short Stroll to Work and Urban Ambiance," *Houston Chronicle,* Oct. 12, 1997.

21. Houston Downtown Management District, *Downtown Fact Sheet, 2002.*

22. *Wall Street Journal,* March 29, 2000.

23. Ralph Bivens, "Something Is Cooking on Main," *Houston Chronicle,* Aug. 2, 2000.

24. Marty Racine, "Bayou City Bohemia," *Houston Chronicle,* Dec. 3, 1999.

25. Clifford Pugh, et al., "Destination: Downtown After Dark," *Houston Chronicle,* Jan. 28, 1999.

26. Dina Cappiello, "Allison's Floods Could Have Been Worse," *Houston Chronicle,* Feb. 23, 2003.

27. John Williams, "Downtown's Viability Draws Mixed Reviews," *Houston Chronicle,* Oct. 13, 1996.

28. Allan Turner, "High on Downtown—Number of Residents Expected to Triple by 2010," *Houston Chronicle,* Oct. 22, 2000.

29. Greg Hassell, "Downtown Downer/Construction Threatens Restaurants, Diners," *Houston Chronicle,* Jan. 6, 2002.

30. *Houston Chronicle,* Jan. 6, 2002.

31. Downtown Houston Management District Fact Sheet, Jan. 22, 2003.

32. "Main Street Houston: The New Economic Corridor," pamphlet, Urban Land Institute Houston District Council, no date.

33. Roberta Brandes Gratz with Norman Mintz, *Cities Back from the Edge: New Life for Downtown* (New York: Preservation Press/John Wiley & Sons, 1998), p. 2.

34. "Colorado: Aquarium Changes Hands," *New York Times,* March 6, 2003.

35. Mike Snyder, "New Concept Promoted for City Planning," *Houston Chronicle,* Feb. 21, 2003.

36. Midtown Redevelopment Authority, *Fact Sheet,* Jan. 22, 2003.

37. Ralph Bivens, "Changing the Face of a Community," *Houston Chronicle,* March 27, 1999.

38. Madeline McDermott Ham, "Midtown Dwellers Drawn to Urban Life," *Houston Chronicle,* Jan. 14, 2001.

39. Lisa Zapalac, "Downtown Real Estate Market Forges Growth for 2003," *Houston Chronicle,* Feb. 16, 2003, pp. 2, 26.

40. *Greater Houston Source Book,* Greater Houston Convention and Visitors Bureau, 2003.

41. K. Pica Kahn, "Light Rail Aims Tracks at Area Traffic Problems," *Houston Chronicle,* Feb. 23, 2003, p. 2.

42. Jimmy Myatt, "Renters, Owners Address Issues," *Houston Chronicle,* Feb. 11, 2003.

43. David Kaplan, *Houston Chronicle,* April 8, 2001, op. cit.

44. Market Research Summary Report, "Housing Potential in Downtown Houston," March 1999, CDS Market Research, Houston.

CHAPTER 6: MEMPHIS

1. Center City Commission (CCC), "History of Memphis," 2001.

2. "Everybody's Gift—A Conversation with CCC president Jeff Sanford," *Definitely Downtown,* special publication of CCC and *Memphis,* 2002, p. 5.

3. Deborah M. Clubb, "Orpheum Rescue Raised Curtain on Long-Run Downtown Revival," *The Commercial Appeal,* Jan. 1, 2002.

4. David Royer, "Downtown Attracting Restaurants but Larger Retail Remains the Same," *Memphis Business Journal,* July 18–24, 2003, p. 5.

5. Perre Mayners, *Past Times Stories of Early Memphis* (Memphis: Parkway Press, 1994).

6. *Daily News,* July 7, 2003.

7. Royer, op. cit.

8. Stephanie Myers, "Memphis Economics Loses Ground to Like-Sized Cities," *The Commercial Appeal,* May 25, 2003.

9. *The Commercial Appeal,* July 3, 2003.

10. CCC, "Downtown Development Projects," May 22, 2003.

11. Catherine Elliott, "World Class Logistics and Life Sciences," *Memphis,* December 2002/January 2003, special section.

12. CCC, "Downtown Development Projects," op. cit.

13. CCC, "Downtown Development Projects," op. cit.

14. Christopher Bland, "Big Donors Step to the Plate for the Arts," *The Commercial Appeal,* July 18, 2003, pp. 1, A-9.

15. CCC, "History of Memphis," op. cit.

16. CCC, "Residential Occupancy Report," June 12, 2003.

17. "Condos Moving Quickly in Downtown Memphis," *Memphis Business Journal,* July 22, 2002, via Smart Growth News.

18. CCC, "Downtown Development Projects," op. cit.

19. CCC, "Residential Occupancy Report," op. cit.

20. Wayne Risher, "Elvis Lauderdale Unit Set Apart as Renovation Starts," *The Commercial Appeal,* Nov. 21, 2002.

21. "Uptown Memphis Overview," The Uptown Partnership, November 2002.

22. "Phrases Commonly Said by South Bluffs Leasing Staff," Henry Turley Co. pamphlet.

23. Karen Finucan, "Central Station, Memphis," *Planning*, March 2001, pp. 8–9.

24. Lieff Benderly, "Heartbreak Motel," *Preservation*, Jan./Feb. 2003, pp. 34–38.

25. *Memphis* magazine, op. cit.

26. *Daily News*, June 20, 2003.

27. *Daily News*, June 17, 2003.

CHAPTER 7: MINNEAPOLIS

1. Holly Day and Sherman Wick, *Insiders' Guide to the Twin Cities* (Guilford, Conn.: Globe Pequot Press, 2002), pp. 35–36.

2. Ellen Nigon, "Planning a Better Downtown," *Skyway NEWS*, March 4–10, 2002.

3. According to an article by Judith Martin and Paula Pentel of the University of Minnesota in the *American Planning Association Journal*, Autumn 2002.

4. "Metro Center, 1985, Study for Development of Program and Proprieties for Expanded Job and Investment Opportunity in Central Minneapolis," March 1970.

5. Minneapolis Community Development Agency (MCDA), "Riverfront Revival: Collaboration and Change Along the Mississippi Riverfront in Minneapolis," Jan. 2003.

6. MCDA, "Riverfront Revival," ibid.

7. Joseph Hart, *Down and Out: The Life and Death of Minneapolis Skid Row* (Minneapolis: University of Minneapolis Press: 2002).

8. Marjorie Pearson for the Minnesota Historic Preservation Commission, "Downtown Minneapolis: An Historic Context," August 2000.

9. Calvin Schmid, "Social Saga of Two Cities: An Ecological and Statistical Study of Social Trends in Minneapolis and St. Paul," Minneapolis Council of Social Agencies, 1937.

10. Connie Nelson, "Loft Living," *Minneapolis Star-Tribune*, Feb. 17, 2000, p. 6.

11. MCDA, "Riverfront Revival," op. cit.

12. Bette Hammel, "The New Downtown Guthrie Design: Echoes of the Mills or Legoland Revisited," *Skyway NEWS*, Feb. 18–24, 2002, pp. 1, 12.

13. Minneapolis Community Development Agency, "Riverfront Revival," op. cit.

14. Ibid.

15. Minneapolis Planning Department and Minneapolis Downtown Council, "Minneapolis Downtown 2010," November 1996.

16. *Insiders' Guide to the Twin Cities*, op. cit., p. 166.

17. Minneapolis Community Development Agency, "Riverfront Revival," op. cit.

18. Adam Platt, ed., "Great Places to Call Home," *Mpls/St. Paul*, July 2001, p. 80.

19. Jim Buchta, "Gay Sway: Twin Cities 'Creative Class' May Boost Economy," *Minneapolis Star-Tribune*, June 23, 2000.

20. Minneapolis Community Development Agency, "Riverfront Revival," op. cit.

21. Linda Mack, "A New Neighborhood Blooms Along the Riverfront," *Minneapolis Star-Tribune*, May 1, 2000.

22. Ellen Nigon, "Will Future North Loop Condo Owners Share Cars?" *Skyway NEWS*, May 26–June 1, 2003, p. 1.

23. "Hot Dish—Downtown's Complete Restaurant Listings," *Skyway NEWS*, July 14–20, 2002, p. 20.

24. Minneapolis Community Development Agency, "Riverfront Revival," op. cit.

25. Ibid.

26. Bob Gilbert, "Art, Sports, Religion, Green Space and Good Food: A Walk Around Loring Park," *Skyway NEWS*, May 17–25, 2003.

27. Figures from Citizens for a Loring Park Community Web site. For what's it worth, census tract 52 covering much of the area south of 12th Street South had 4,721 persons, the 25-to-34 age group again predominate at 23.5 percent of the total, with the next age bracket the 35-to-44-year-old, 14 percent. Nonfamily households constitute 80 percent of this census tract, with 71 percent single and 77 percent renters. Part of Loring Park is in another census tract along with another neighborhood, Stevens Square; together they have 3,851 people.

28. Report to City Planning Commission and City Council, "Central Community Analysis and Action Recommendations," Spring 1965.

29. *Mpls/St. Paul*, July 2003, p. 179.

30. David Brauer, "Survey Says: Most City Residents Feel Downtown is Safe and Clean," *Skyway NEWS*, March 4–10, 2002.

31. "Crime in Downtown Minneapolis, July 1–7, 2003," *Skyway NEWS*, July 14–20, 2003, p. 4.

32. Mike Mosedale, "Bum-B-Gone™," *City Pages*, July 16, 2003, p. 12.

33. *Minneapolis Star-Tribune*, Feb. 11, 2003.

34. "Loft Living in the Twin Cities," *Minneapolis Star-Tribune*, Feb. 9, 2003.

35. Ellen Nigon, "Why Young Homeowners Choose Downtown," *Skyway NEWS*, May 19–25, 2003.

36. Rachel E. Stassen-Berger, "Downtowns Are on the Upswing—More and More People Choosing to Call Downtown Minneapolis and St. Paul Home According to the 2000 Census," *St. Paul Pioneer-Press*, April 3, 2002.

37. Sam Grabarsky, "How Many People Live in Downtown Minneapolis," *Skyway NEWS*, Jan. 29, 2001.

CHAPTER 8: NEW ORLEANS

1. "Historic Neighborhoods of New Orleans," Preservation Resource Center of New Orleans (PRC).

2. Michael Giusti, "Canal Street Corridor's Upper Floors Hold Puzzling Potential," *New Orleans City Business*, March 2003.

3. Clayton Elliott Jr. et al., *New Orleans Historic Warehouse District: An Analysis of Revitalization* (Cambridge, Mass.: Harvard Business School), 1982.

4. Warehouse Area Business Alliance, "Study of Neighborhood Pathway Development and Neighborhood Identity for the Warehouse Area. Part One," July 2001.

5. *ACCESS New Orleans* guidebook, 1996, Harper Perennial, p. 70.

6. James Amdal, "The Historic Warehouse District: A Personal Perspective," *Preservation in Print*, June 18, 1997, p. 18.

7. "A Vision for the City," *entree*, 1999, special issue, p. 20.

8. *Historic Warehouse District Study*, Caplinger Planners for Preservation Resource Center, 1982.

9. Bruce Eggler, "The Award Goes to . . . ," *New Orleans Times-Picayune*, Jan. 19, 2002, p. 1.

10. For a first-person account, read *The Second Battle of New Orleans* by Bill Borah and Richard Baumbach.

11. *New Orleans Times-Picayune*, Nov. 6, 1984.

12. Neil Irwin and Dana Hedgpeth, "D.C. Places a Bet on Long-Term Economic Benefits," see chart "Big, But Far from the Biggest," Tradeshow Week, *The Washington Post*, March 31, 2003, p. 10

13. *New Orleans Historic Warehouse District*, op. cit.

14. Evan Soule, "Federal Fibre Mills Celebrates Centennial," *Preservation in Print*, Sept. 2003, p. 17.

15. "Here Goes the Neighborhood," *entree*, op. cit., p. 5.

16. Downtown Development District, "Acres of Diamonds."

17. Keith Brannon, "In the Shadow of the CBD, Everything Old is New Again," *New Orleans City Business*, March 2003, p. 13.

18. *WHERE New Orleans*, Where International, March 2003, (hotel guide), pp. A24–25.

19. MetroVision, *Perspectives 2002* (economic development factbook), p. 33.

20. Economics Research Association, *Downtown Development District Database, New Orleans, LA*, August 2000. Project Number: 13632, p. 33.

21. Ibid.

22. Ibid.

23. Sonya Stinson, "An Awakening in Lee Circle," *New Orleans City Business*, Jan. 31, 2000, p. 1.

24. Ibid.

25. Greg Thomas, "Saulet Developers Are Ready for Their Payday," *New Orleans Times-Picayune*, March 25, 2003 MONEY section, pp. l, 9.

26. Felicity St. Redevelopment Project Inc. brochure.

27. Lil LeGardeur, "SAVED: AAHP Celebrates the Sale of Kid Ory's Jackson Avenue Home," *Preservation in Print*, August 2000.

28. *New Orleans Times-Picayune*, March 30, 2003.

29. Coleman Walker, "French Quarter's Residential Base Holding On," *New Orleans Times-Picayune*, July 4, 2001, p. A 11.

30. Greg Thomas, "French Quarter Conversions Popular," *New Orleans Times-Picayune*, April 12, 2003.

31. Fred Koenig, "The Global Evolution of the Warehouse District, *entree*, op. cit., p. 7.

CHAPTER 9: PORTLAND, OREGON

1. Gordon DeMarco, *Short History of Portland* (San Francisco: Lexikos, 1990) and Carl Abbott, *Greater Portland: Urban Life and Landscape in the Pacific Northwest* (Philadelphia: University of Pennsylvania Press, 2001).

2. Carl Abbott, op. cit.

3. Linda Harris, "How Portland, Ore., Turned Its Parking Problems," *Philadelphia Inquirer,* March 30, 2002.

4. Gordon DeMarco, op. cit.

5. Richard Moe and Carter Wilkie, *Changing Places: Rebuilding Community in the Age of Sprawl* (New York: Henry Holt and Co., 1997), p. 213.

6. Carl Abbott, op. cit.

7. "The Portland Region: How Are We Doing? Highlights of the Region's Land Use and Transportation Performance Measures," *Metro,* March 2003.

8. Portland Development Commission (PDC) and Portland Business Alliance (PBA), "Greater Downtown Portland Housing Report 2002," prepared by Cogan, Owens Cogan LLC.

9. PBA, "Fall Downtown Portland Residential Occupancy Report," Oct. 20, 2002.

10. Peter Sleeth, "District of Portland, Ore., Hot with Construction of Apartments and Condominiums," *The Oregonian,* Jan. 24, 2003.

11. "Pearl District Arts Festival," *Willamette Weekly,* Oct. 1–7, 1987.

12. Marshall Wells Lofts brochure.

13. *The Oregonian,* Jan. 24, 2003.

14. PBA, "2003 Central City Development and Redevelopment Projects," Jan. 3, 2003.

15. Peter Sleeth, "Despite Slow Economy, Development Project in Portland, Ore., Attracts Renters," *The Oregonian,* Aug. 26, 2002.

16. Susan Hauser, "Housing Replacing an Oregon Railyard," *The New York Times,* Jan. 13, 2002, p. 14.

17. PDC, "River District Housing Implementation Strategy, Annual Report, Fall 2002."

18. Dylan Rivera, "Port of Portland, Ore., Votes to Sell Riverfront Land for Development," *The Oregonian,* Aug. 3, 2000.

19. Bill Coutant, "Portland's Downtown Streetcar Line Could Have National Impact," *The Oregonian,* June 16, 1999.

20. Bill Stewart, "Portland, Ore., Streetcar Surpasses Expectations in Its First Year," *The Oregonian,* Nov. 28, 2001.

21. PBA, "Fall Downtown Portland Residential Occupancy Report," Oct. 20, 2002.

22. PDC, "River District Housing Implementation Strategy," op. cit., p. 4.

23. Pearl District Development Plan Steering Committee, "Pearl District Development Plan: A Future Vision for a Neighborhood in Transition," Oct. 2001.

24. PDC, "Fall Downtown Portland Residential Occupancy Report," op. cit.

25. Scott Learn, "Perks in the Pearl," *The Oregonian,* June 27, 2003.

26. Andy Dworkin, "Potential Renters Explore Many Apartments in Downtown Portland, Ore.," *The Oregonian,* May 20, 2002.

27. Connie Potter, "Mosaic—Colorful, Eyecatching Project Offers Something Different Downtown," *The Oregonian New Home Monthly,* May 13, 2003, p. 3.

28. PBA, "2003 Central City Development and Redevelopment Projects," Jan. 3, 2003.

29. Ann Breen and Dick Rigby, *WATERFRONTS: Cities Reclaim Their Edge* (New York: McGraw-Hill, 1994), pp. 134–37.

30. City of Portland, Bureau of Planning "North Macadam Concept," April 24, 2002.

31. "L.A. Firm Wins Competition for Portland Aerial Tram," *Architectural Record,* May 2003.

32. "South Waterfront District Agreement Taking Shape," *Daily Journal of Commerce (Portland Ore.),* June 13, 2003.

33. "Advisory Panel Split in Backing S. Waterfront," *The Oregonian,* June 25, 2003.

34. PBA, "2003 Central City Development and Redevelopment Projects," Jan. 2, 2003.

35. Gordan Oliver, "New Projects Promise to Give Portland, Ore.'s Lloyd District Domestic Appeal," *The Oregonian,* Aug. 12, 2002.

36. Carl Abbott, op. cit.

37. "State Land Commission OKs Urban Expansion," *The Oregonian,* June 10, 2003.

38. Carl Abbott, op. cit.

39. Metro, "The Nature of 2040: The Region's 50-year Plan for Managing Growth."

40. Carl Abbott, op. cit.

41. Ibid.

CHAPTER 10: VANCOUVER

1. Vancouver City Planning Commission, "Goals for Vancouver," Feb. 1980.

2. Tilman Streif, "Vancouver Rates Highest in International Survey," *Deutsche Press-Agentur,* Dec. 9, 1997.

3. "Canada's Global City (Not Toronto)," *The New York Times,* Nov. 26, 2001.

4. City of Vancouver, "City Facts 2003" update Jan. 2003.

5. Vancouver Planning Department, Census 2001.

6. Vancouver Office of Cultural Affairs, "City of Vancouver Public Art Walk: Downtown Shoreline," Oct. 2002.

7. Dan Rowe, "'Culture Capital' Title Means Big Money for Vancouver," *Vancouver Sun,* May 9, 2003, p. 1, A5.

8. Howard Schneider, "Vancouver's Boom has a Dark Side—New Business Brings Drug Trafficking," *The Washington Post,* April 25, 1997.

9. *Deutsche Press-Agentur,* Dec. 9, 1997.

10. *Vancouver* magazine, Jan./Feb. 2003.

11. Vancouver's Coalition for Crime Prevention and Drug Treatment, www.crimepreventiondrugtreatment.com

12. Don Harrison and Frances Bula, "Too Many Rules, Cops Threaten Addicts' Safe-Injection Centre," *The Gazette, Montreal,* Sept. 14, 2003.

13. Brian Morton, "Drug Dealing Cleanup Going Faster, Police Say," *Vancouver Sun,* April 29, 2003.

14. Mike Howell, "Police Crackdown Having an Effect," *Vancouver Courier,* May 7, 2003, p. 11.

15. David Carrigg, "City's Homeless Head Counter Reports Dramatic Rise in March," *Vancouver Courier,* May 7, 2003, p. 10.

16. *Vancouver, Lonely Planet* (Melbourne: Lonely Planet Publications, April 2002).

17. *Zoning News*, American Planning Association, April, 2002.

18. Karenn Krangle, "Towering Problem May Boost City Design Panel," *Vancouver Sun*, May 9, 2003.

19. Central Area Plan: Goals and Land Use Policy, 1991, Vancouver Planning Department.

20. City of Vancouver Planning Department Information Sheet, "Concord Pacific Place," Dec. 2002.

21. Vancouver Planning Department, Census 2001.

22. Vancouver Economic Development Commission newsletter, Dec. 11, 2002.

23. Vancouver Planning Department, "Vancouver's Urban Design: A Decade of Achievement," Dec. 1999.

24. *Business in Vancouver*, March 11–17, 2003.

25. *Vancouver, Lonely Planet,* op. cit., pp. 90–91.

CHAPTER 11: FINDINGS

1. Ben Brown, "Urban Ikes: A New Generation of Retirees Heads for the Cities," *Preservation*, May/June 2000, p. 14.

2. *Realty Times*, May 17, 1999.

3. Alan Heavens, "Author Evaluates Home-Buying Preferences of Aging Baby-Boomers," *The Philadelphia Inquirer*, April 2, 2003.

4. *The New York Times* magazine, April 9, 2000, pp. 80–81.

5. Minneapolis Riverfront Development Coordination Board, *Saint Anthony Falls Rediscovered* (Minneapolis: Minneapolis Riverfront Development Coordination Board, 1980).

6. Skip Kaltenheuser, "Credit Problems," *Preservation*, May/June 2003, p. 16.

7. Downtown Improvement District, fact sheet, "Intown Living," 1200 Main/ Suite 125, Dallas, TX 75202.

8. Sharon Zukin, *The Culture of Cities* (Cambridge, Mass.: Blackwell Publishers, 1995), Chapter 1.

9. Richard Haughey, "Urban Infill Housing: Myth and Fact," Urban Land Institute, Washington, D.C. 2001.

10. Anthony Downs, The Brookings Institution, Washington, D.C., "What Does 'Smart Growth' Really Mean?" *Planning*, American Planning Association, April 2001.

11. Jane Holz Kay, *Asphalt Nation*, op. cit. p. 64.

12. *Daily News*, June 26, 2003.

13. Roberta Brandes Gratz with Norman Mintz, *Cities Back from the Edge: New Life for Downtowns*, New York: John Wiley & Sons, 1998, pp. 1–5.

14. International Downtown Association (IDA), *Downtown News Briefs*, first quarter 2003.

15. International Downtown Association (IDA), *Downtown News Briefs,* third quarter 2002.

CHAPTER 12: RECOMMENDATIONS

1. Jennifer Moulton, "10 Ways to Promote Downtown Housing," *Denver Rocky Mountain News*, April 2, 2000.

2. Tom Horton, "Brownfields as Fertile Ground for EPA," *LAND & PEOPLE*, Trust for Public Land, spring 2000, p. 36.

3. John Norquist, *The Wealth of Cities: Revitalizing the Centers of American Life* (Reading, Mass.: Addison-Wesley, 1998), p. 22.

4. James S. Russell, "Profound Forces are Reshaping American Cities," *Architectural Record*, March 2000, pp. 76–82, 206–207.

5. www.PATAXCREDIT.COM

6. "Hammer Home a Point. Tax Breaks Can Help Rebuild Communities," *The Philadelphia Inquirer*, March 12, 2001, editorial, p. A10.

7. David Listokin, "Living Cities, Report of the 20th Century Fund Task Force on Urban Preservation Policies, background paper," New York: Priority Press Publications, 1985.

8. Jennifer Moulton, op. cit.

9. Andres Duany, Elizabeth Plater-Zyberk, and Jeff Speck, *Suburban Nation: The Rise of Sprawl and the Decline of the American Dream* (New York: North Point Press, 2000), pp. 176–77.

10. Patrick Kennedy, "An Infill Developer Versus the Forces of No," *UrbanEcologist, the Journal of Urban Ecology*, Number 2, 1995, p. 11.

11. Lori Montgomery, " 'Smart Code' Targets Crumbling Buildings," *The Washington Post*, April 24, 2000, p. B1.

12. Daniel Kemmis, *The Good City and the Good Life: Renewing the Sense of Community* (Boston: Houghton Mifflin Co., 1995), p. 30.

13. *The New York Times Almanac*, 2003, (New York: Penguin Putnam Inc.), p. 303.

14. Pam Belleck, "Blighted Areas Are Revived as Crime Drops," *The New York Times*, May 29, 2000, p. 1.

15. Bruce Katz, "Smart Growth: The Future of the American Metropolis?" Centre for Analysis of Social Exclusion, London School of Economics, July 2002.

CHAPTER 13: GAZETTEER

1. Philip A. Morris, "Downtown Birmingham Offices Become Apartments," *The New York Times*, Dec. 13, 1998.

2. Eleanor Charles, "Housing for Artists—and a Spur for Downtowns," *The New York Times*, Aug. 26, 2001, p. 7.

3. Antoinette Martin, "Upscale Rentals to Open in Downtrodden Camden," *The New York Times*, Feb. 2, 2003, p. 7; Elisa Ung, "Victor's First Tenants Boost an Area that Isn't Conditioned to Move-ins: The Arrival of Riverfront Residents Changes the Equation in Camden," *The Philadelphia Inquirer*, Aug. 30, 2003, p. B 3.

4. Doug Smith, "Uptown Housing: The Appeal of Urban Life Draws Thousands to the Center City Boom," *The Charlotte Observer*, Nov. 10, 2002.

5. Robert Sharoff, "Wave of Ultraluxury Condos in Chicago," *The New York Times*, Feb. 3, 2002, p. 22; Robert Sharoff, "New Gold Coast Near Downtown Chicago," *The New York Times*, July 16, 2000, p. 36.

6. Mark S. Rosentraub, "Cleveland's Fastest-Growing Neighborhood," *The Plain Dealer*, Oct. 21, 2002.

7. Jill M. Walker, "From Abandoned Warehouses to Loft Apartments," *Multifamily Trends*, Fall Meeting Issue, 2001, p. 34.

8. John McMillan, "Central Denver: Regional Advertising Report: The World's Most Central Business District," *Colorado Business Magazine*, Vol. 26, March 1, 1999, pp. 50–51, 53; James Brooke, "Denver Stands Out in Trend Toward Living in Downtown," *The New York Times*, Dec. 29, 1998, p. 1.

9. Eleanor Charles, "After Long Drought, High-End Housing for Hartford," *The New York Times*, Feb. 16, 2003, p. 7; "Housing for Artists and a Spur for Downtowns," *The New York Times*, Aug. 26, 2001, p. 7.

10. Bella Kelly, "Loft Living," *The Miami Herald*, Sept. 15, 2002.

11. Thomas Ginsburg and Marc Schogol, "Growth Remains Strong in Suburbs" *The Philadelphia Inquirer*, March 11, 2001, p. 1; Antonio Gilb, "Downtown Rentals Are Going Through the Roof," *The Philadelphia Inquirer*, Aug. 22, 2001, p. B10; "Paying Big to Live in Prime Areas," *The Philadelphia Inquirer*, May 5, 2002; Linda K. Harris, "Phila.'s Hot Spot: N. Liberties," *The Philadelphia Inquirer*, Aug. 13, 2002; and Henry J. Holcomb, "Center City Apartments Are Still in High Demand," *The Philadelphia Inquirer*, June 26, 2003.

12. Chriss Swaney, "Houses to Replace a Pittsburgh Slag Heap," *The New York Times*, Jan. 28, 2001, p. 32.

13. Rob Walker, "Lofty Expectations: Downtown Apartment Market Flourishes,"*Richmond Times-Dispatch*, Sept. 13, 1999, p. D 18.

14. Harriet King, "High-End Rentals in Downtown Seattle," *The New York Times*, June 18, 2000, p. 26.

15. Robert Sharoff, "In St. Louis, Office Buildings Are Becoming Lofts," *The New York Times*, June 24, 2001, p. 8.

16. Margery Austin Tuner et al., "Housing in the Nation's Capital 2002," FannieMae Foundation and The Urban Institute, Washington, D.C., p. 23.

17. City of Washington Planning Department Web site for census data; Roger Lewis, "Remodeled Buildings, Retail Projects Are Rejuvenating Eastern Sector of Downtown D.C.," *The Washington Post*, Nov. 30, 2002, p. H3.

Selected Bibliography

Abbott, Carl. *Greater Portland: Urban Life and Landscape in the Pacific Northwest.* Philadelphia: University of Pennsylvania Press, 2001.

Barnett, Jonathan. *The Elusive City: Five Centuries of Design, Ambition and Miscalculation.* New York: Harper & Row, 1986.

Belmont, Steve. *Cities in Full: Recognizing and Realizing the Great Potential of Urban America.* Chicago: Planners Press, 2002.

Berman, James, ed., *Saint Anthony Falls Rediscovered.* Minneapolis: Minneapolis Riverfront Development Coordination Board, 1980.

Blake, Peter. *God's Own Junkyard: The Planned Deterioration of America's Landscape.* New York: Holt, Rinehart and Winston, 1964.

Breen, Ann and Rigby, Dick. *The New Waterfront: A Worldwide Urban Success Story.* London, UK: Thames & Hudson Ltd., 1996.

Breen, Ann and Rigby, Dick. *WATERFRONTS: Cities Reclaim Their Edge.* New York: McGraw-Hill, 1994.

Brooks, David. *BOBOS* in Paradise (*Bourgeois Bohemians): The New Upper Class and How They Got There.* New York: Simon & Schuster, 2000.

Bullard, Robert, Glenn S. Johnson and Angel O. Torres. *Sprawl City: Race, Politics and Planning in Atlanta.* Washington, D.C.: Island Press, 2000.

Duany, Andres, Elizabeth Plater-Zyberk and Jeff Speck. *Suburban Nation: The Rise of Sprawl and the Decline of the American Dream.* New York: North Point Press, 2000.

Ehrenhalt, Alan. *The Lost City: The Forgotten Virtues of Community in America.* New York: Basic Books, 1995.

Fishman, Robert. *Bourgeois Utopias: The Rise and Fall of Suburbia.* New York: Basic Books, 1987.

Florida, Richard. *The Rise of the Creative Class and How It's Transforming Work, Leisure, Community and Everyday Life.* New York: Basic Books, 2002.

Fogelson, Robert M. *Downtown: Its Rise and Fall, 1880–1950.* New Haven: Yale University Press, 2001.

Frieden, Bernard J. and Lynne B. Sagalyn. *Downtown, Inc., How America Rebuilds Cities.* Cambridge, Mass.: The MIT Press, 1989.

Gratz, Roberta Brandes. *The Living City.* New York: Simon & Schuster, 1989.

Gratz, Roberta Brandes with Norman Mintz. *Cities Back from the Edge: New Life for Downtowns.* New York: John Wiley & Sons, 1998.

Guinther, John. *Direction of Cities.* New York: Viking Penguin, 1996.

Jackson, Kenneth T. *Crabgrass Frontier: The Suburbanization of the United States.* New York: Oxford University Press, 1985.

Jacobs, Jane. *The Death and Life of Great American Cities.* New York: Vintage Books, 1963.

Kay, Jane Holtz. *Asphalt Nation: How the Automobile Took Over America and How We Can Take It Back.* New York: Crown Publishers, 1997.

Kemmis, Daniel. *The Good City and the Good Life: Renewing the Sense of Community.* New York: Houghton Mifflin Company, 1995.

Kunstler, James Howard. *The City in Mind: Notes on the Urban Condition.* New York: The Free Press, 2001.

Kunstler, James Howard. *The Geography of Nowhere: The Rise and Decline of America's Man-Made Landscape.* New York: Simon & Schuster, 1993.

Listokin, David. *Living Cities: Report of the Twentieth Century Fund Task Force on Urban Preservation Policies Background Paper.* New York: Priority Press Publications, 1985.

Moe, Richard and Carter Wilkie. *Changing Places, Rebuilding Community in the Age of Sprawl.* New York: Henry Holt and Company, 1997.

Norquist, John O. *The Wealth of Cities: Revitalizing the Centers of American Life.* Reading, Mass.: Addison-Wesley, 1998.

Oldenburg, Ray. *The Great Good Place: Cafes, Coffee Shops, Community Centers, Beauty Parlors, General Stores, Bars, Hangouts & How They Get You Through the Day.* New York: Marlowe and Company, 1989, 1997.

Orfield, Myron. *Metropolitics: A Regional Agenda for Community and Stability.* Washington, D.C. and Cambridge, Mass.: The Brookings Institution and The Lincoln Institute of Land Policy, 1997.

Pappano, Laura. *The Connection Gap: Why Americans Feel So Alone.* New Brunswick, N. J.: Rutgers University Press, 2001.

Putnam, Robert D. *Bowling Alone: The Collapse and Revival of American Community.* New York: Simon & Schuster, 2000.

Relph, Edward. *The Modern Urban Landscape.* Baltimore: Johns Hopkins University Press, 1987.

Rudofsky, Bernard. *Streets for People.* New York: Van Nostrand Reinhold Company, 1982 (first published by Doubleday, 1969).

Rybczynski, Witold. *City Life: Urban Expectations in a New World.* New York: Scribner, 1995.

Stilgoe, John R. *Borderland: Origins of the American Suburb, 1820–1939.* New Haven: Yale University Press, 1988.

White, Morton and Lucia White. *The Intellectual Versus the City.* New York: Mentor Book, 1964; also Cambridge, Mass.: Harvard University and MIT Press, 1962.

Whyte, William. *City: Rediscovering the Center.* New York: Doubleday, 1988.

Zukin, Sharon. *The Cultures of Cities.* Cambridge, Mass.: Blackwell Publishers, 1995.

Index

About the Authors

ANN BREEN and DICK RIGBY are founders and co-directors of the Waterfront Center, a nonprofit organization based in Washington, D.C., since 1981. The Center organizes an annual international conference on urban waterfront planning, development, and culture, conducts an international awards program, and does community consulting.